Know
Your New Testament

by

Ralph Earle, M.A., Th.D.

**Professor of New Testament
Nazarene Theological Seminary**

BEACON HILL PRESS OF KANSAS CITY
Kansas City, Missouri

ISBN: 083-410-2137

PRINTED IN THE UNITED STATES OF AMERICA

FOREWORD

This volume, from the gifted pen of Dr. Ralph Earle, Jr., is his second book in the field of New Testament study guidance. His first book, "The Story of the New Testament," is in the nature of a brief introduction to the books of the New Testament—their history, authorship, purpose, and plan. This new volume is a study of the contents of the New Testament, with only such discussion of external questions as seems essential to the author's purpose.

Dr. Earle brings to his task a mind richly furnished in the realm of New Testament scholarship. But his distinctive qualification for the authorship of a book like this is his devotion to Christ. He is a college professor, but is not a mere theorist; for he is also a pastor and preacher who enjoys a most successful ministry. These varied activities have greatly enriched his study of the New Testament and have increased the value of this volume.

It is published as a Christian Service Training textbook. But it is designed for the widest possible use among persons interested in New Testament study. May God grant His blessing as it goes forth on its silent ministry of guidance and help.

J. GLENN GOULD

PREFACE

This book is intended as an aid to the study of the New Testament. The student who wishes to derive the most benefit from it should have his open Bible before him as he reads. One could very profitably spend several months in a continuous study of the New Testament, using this book as a guide through its pages.

All quotations from the New Testament are from the American Standard Edition of the Revised Version, unless otherwise indicated. The student will find it convenient to use this version, which is divided helpfully into paragraphs. An inexpensive cloth bound copy should be secured for study use, even though the King James Version is still retained for devotional and public use.

The student should also possess a copy of the author's shorter work, *The Story of the New Testament* (Nazarene Publishing House, 1941), which treats briefly the matters of general introduction to each book. These two volumes will be found to supplement each other.

The author wishes to express his debt of gratitude to Professor Byron L. Osborne, of Cleveland Bible College, and Professor Merrill C. Tenney, of Gordon College of Theology and Missions, Boston. These two teachers have done much to inspire in the writer a consuming interest in the study of the New Testament which has led him to devote his life to the great task of understanding and expounding its message.

This book is sent forth with the prayer that it may lead many Christians to a more thorough study and greater appreciation of the New Testament Scriptures. May the Holy Spirit, who inspired men of old to write these words, illuminate our minds to understand them and our hearts to receive them.

RALPH EARLE

CONTENTS

INTRODUCTION

The World of the New Testament

The Political World

1. JUDEA

"There was in the days of Herod, king of Judea, a certain priest named Zacharias." Thus begins the life of our Lord, as recorded by Luke.

Two characters are here introduced to us, contemporary but strongly contrasting. Of Zacharias and his wife Elisabeth it is said that they were righteous and blameless. Herod was neither.

Herod the Great—great in political power but not in piety—ruled as king of Judea from 37 B.C. until his death in 4 B.C. By clever diplomacy and military prowess he gained and held this coveted office when the imperial throne itself was a very insecure position.

Herod was an Idumean. His father, Antipater, had played politics with both Pompey and Caesar, but had finally met the same fate as the latter, only a year after that Roman ruler was assassinated. Herod adopted the present day policy of executing his political opponents in large numbers to preserve his throne.

But this barbarous king did not content himself with the massacre of forty-five wealthy Sadducees. He proceeded to murder his brother-in-law, the favorite one of his ten wives, his mother-in-law and three of his own sons. One of the last acts of his reign was the massacre of the innocent babes of Bethlehem, in the vain attempt to destroy the infant King of the Jews, whom he feared as a rival to his throne.

One of the outstanding incidents of Herod's reign was the reconstruction of the Jewish temple on a magnificent scale. Solomon's golden temple had been destroyed in 586 B.C., by

—9—

Nebuchadnezzar's armies. The Jews who returned from their Babylonian captivity under Zerubbabel sought to rebuild the house of God, but they did not have the means with which to restore the beauty of the former edifice. Herod sought to restore the ancient grandeur, and the work continued after his death. In fact, this Temple of Herod was not fully completed until A.D. 64, shortly before its destruction by the Roman armies of Titus in A.D. 70.

Herod did not have any son strong enough to succeed him on the throne. However, one son, Archelaus, was appointed ethnarch of Judea. After ten years of misrule he was banished by the emperor.

The government of Judea from that time until its overthrow by Titus was in the hands of procurators, with the exception of four years (A.D. 41-45) when Agrippa I ruled as king. Three of these procurators are of special interest to us. It was Pontius Pilate (A.D. 26-36) who condemned Jesus to be crucified, and by this miscarriage of justice condemned himself to endless infamy and eternal doom. Felix and Festus both tried the Apostle Paul, but passed no sentence of judgment upon him. The procurators had the power of life and death, as we see in the case of Pilate. Only Roman citizens could appeal from them to the emperor, as Paul did.

The administration of justice in the various small communities of Judea was left largely in the hands of local courts, or sanhedrins. The most notable of these was the great Sanhedrin at Jerusalem, which came to exercise authority over all Judea. It had the right to arrest and try criminals and even to condemn them to punishment. But the death sentence could be executed only by the procurator.

The Sanhedrin was a council of seventy full-blooded Hebrews. It was composed of chief priests, elders and scribes (Acts 4:5). Both Pharisees and Sadducees, the conservatives and liberals of that day were represented in this august assembly (Acts 23:6).

2. SAMARIA

The name Samaria is given to the district lying between Judea on the south and Galilee on the north. In the time of Christ it was inhabited by a mixed race of Jews and Gentiles, the result of the Assyrian policy after the destruction of the city of Samaria in 722 B.C. (2 Kings 17:24). The contempt of the Jews for the Samaritans is reflected in the Gospels. To the Jews the Samaritans were "half-breeds."

This antagonism due to racial differences was increased by religious differences. The Samaritans carried on their worship on Mount Gerizim, using the Pentateuch, or five books of Moses, as their only sacred Scriptures. They worshiped the same God as the Jews, but the latter contended that the Samaritan worship was not pure. The woman at the well of Sychar raised this question with Jesus (John 4:20).

Samaria, although differing from Judea in race and religion, was yet united to it politically. This territory was included in the province of Judea, under the rule of the procurators.

Another small district included in the province of Judea was Idumea, from which Herod the Great came. This was a region lying south of Judea proper. Its inhabitants were supposed to have descended from Esau.

3. GALILEE

The Palestine of the time of Christ, as we look at it on our maps, was divided into three main sections—Judea in the south, Samaria in the center and Galilee in the north. These are the divisions which are indicated clearly in the movements of Jesus, as recorded in the four Gospels.

It was in Galilee that Jesus spent the larger part of His time during His public ministry. Although born in Bethlehem, in Judea, he was brought up in Nazareth, a village of Galilee. Here it was that He taught the multitudes on the shores of the Sea of Galilee. He made His headquarters at Capernaum, on the northwest corner of this lake.

Upon the death of Herod the Great, Galilee was given to his son Herod Antipas, as tetrarch. He ruled from 4 B.C. to A.D. 39. He was thus in power when Jesus toured this region. It was he whom Jesus called "that fox" (Luke 13:32).

Herod Antipas shared his father's zeal for building, constructing the new city of Tiberias on the southwestern shore of the Sea of Galilee, and making it his capital. But he also shared his father's low morals. He had married the daughter of Aretas, king of Arabia. But on a certain visit to Rome he fell in love with his brother's wife, Herodias, and married her. Herodias was an unprincipled woman of scheming cruelty, who obtained the head of John the Baptist to satisfy her revenge against him for denouncing the unholy union But when this Herod, at the instigation of Herodias, sought from the emperor the title of king, he received banishment instead, in A.D. 39.

4. PEREA

United politically with Galilee in the tetrarchy of Herod Antipas was Perea, a region east of the Jordan River, and so now called Trans-Jordan. It was considered by the Jews as being next to Judea in the purity of its Judaism. Galilee, which lay farther distant from Jerusalem and had a large proportion of Gentiles in its population, was looked down upon by the Judean Jews, although not with the same measure of contempt as was accorded Samaria.

It was in Perea that Jesus spent much of His time during the latter part of His ministry, as recorded by Luke. Here He sought solitude, that He might devote more of His attention to instructing His disciples in preparation for their future ministry. Here too, doubtless, He sought to prepare Himself for the terrible ordeals of His trials and crucifixion.

5. THE ROMAN EMPIRE

The establishment of the Roman empire was one of the greatest political achievements of all history. Other nations had carried out vast military conquests, but it was the glory of the Romans to consolidate and conserve.

The special contribution which Rome furnished for the spread of Christianity consisted of world peace, stable government and good roads. In many ways it was easier for Paul to travel around the Mediterranean world than it would be for a missionary today. He could pass from one territory to another without being stopped at the boundaries by customs officials.

Justice was administered under the imperial government to a remarkable degree. The Romans had a genius for law. This offered a protection for the messengers of Christ, as is evidenced by Paul's experiences at Corinth and at Ephesus.

The splendid Roman roads and bridges which were built to every corner of the vast empire were waiting for the eager

feet of the missionary, to facilitate his travel. How solidly
these roads were constructed is demonstrated by the remains
of them which are still to be seen in Britain and elsewhere.

The Intellectual World

1. ALEXANDER AND THE GREEK EMPIRE

The conquests of Alexander the Great are an amazement
to every student of ancient history. To follow on a map the
line of his battles—succeeding one another so closely in time—
across Asia Minor, down through Palestine into Egypt, and
then eastward to the Tigris-Euphrates valley and on to India
is almost breath-taking. At the age of twenty-three he de-
feated the Persian army of Darius at Issus (333 B.C.). Then,
after conquering Phoenicia, Palestine, Egypt and the Fertile
Crescent, he delivered a smashing blow to Darius only two
years later at Arbella (331 B.C.); and the Greek empire
succeeded the Persian, as that had succeeded the Babylonian
two hundred years earlier. But he who had conquered a world
failed to conquer himself, and Alexander died at the early age
of thirty-three (323 B.C.), probably as the result of a drunken
debauch.

At his death there was no one strong enough to succeed
Alexander as the sole ruler of this new empire. Four of his
leading generals each took a section of the vast territory.
Palestine was alternately under the rule of the Ptolemies of
Egypt and the Seleucids of Syria, called in Daniel "the king
of the south" and "the king of the north." Finally, after some
eighty years of Maccabean independence, Pompey entered
Jerusalem in 63 B.C., and Palestine passed under the dominion
of Rome.

2. THE SPREAD OF GREEK LANGUAGE AND LEARNING

The political results of Alexander's conquests were in-
significant and shortlived as compared with those of Caesar
and the other Roman generals. But the cultural and intellectual consequences were far-reaching and permanent.

In the first place, the Greek language became the common
medium of communication throughout the territories which
composed the Roman empire. In Egypt, Palestine, Syria,
Babylonia, Asia Minor, Macedonia, Greece and Italy the same
language could be heard in the marts of trade and ports of
commerce.

All this was of the utmost significance for the early spread of Christianity. The heralds of the new faith could proclaim the glad tidings of salvation everywhere throughout the empire in the common Greek tongue. Language barriers as well as political boundaries had been swept away by Greece and Rome in preparation for the spread of the first great world religion. Truly, "in due time" Christ came.

Not only did the Christian missionary have Roman roads on which to travel, Roman peace to protect him as he traveled and the Greek language in which to preach the gospel, but he also carried with him the sacred Hebrew Scriptures in the new universal language. About two hundred years before Christ the Hebrew Bible—our Old Testament—had been translated into Greek. This translation, known as the Septuagint Version, was made by some seventy Jewish scholars at Alexandria, Egypt. Thus the Christian missionary in the first century was saved, not only the arduous task of learning a new language, but also the still more difficult task of translating the Scriptures into that language.

The conquests of Alexander spread Greek culture and learning, as well as the Greek language, throughout the eastern Mediterranean world. It was thus made easier to explain the truth of Christianity in the common thought-concepts that the Greeks had furnished.

There is a sense in which Socrates, Plato and Aristotle had helped to prepare the way for Christ. They had not only led the people to see the folly of their belief in the many gods of Greece, but they had also pointed the way to a higher conception of the Supreme Being and of the universe. Paul and John used the vocabulary of Greek philosophy and of the mystery religions to portray the wonderful truths concerning Christ and His relation to His universe.

The Epicureans taught that pleasure is the highest good in life. The Stoics held that virtue is the highest good and taught the duty of self-control. Many representatives of the latter school were noble characters. But Paul found them all bankrupt spiritually when he met them at Athens (Acts 17:18). Greek philosophy, like all other merely human thinking, had failed to find ultimate truth. This can be found only in Him who said, "I am the way, the truth, and the life."

The Religious World

1. JEWISH RELIGION

The religious life of the Jews in the time of Christ centered largely in two institutions, the temple and the synagogue. It will be necessary for us to look at each of these briefly.

a. *The Temple at Jerusalem.* The temple was the outgrowth of the tabernacle, the pattern of which had been given to Moses at Sinai. Readers of the Old Testament will recall how King David felt that the ark—symbolical of God's presence in the midst of His people—should have a permanent home. When told by Nathan the prophet that he himself was not to build the house of God, he began preparations for the magnificent building which his son was to erect.

Solomon made the temple a thing of grandeur and beauty, a fit palace for the King of glory. But when Israel forgot her God, He forsook the holy place and allowed the Babylonians to destroy it. As we have already noted, the second temple, built by the remnant that returned from exile, was a poor reproduction of the first. It remained for Herod to give the Jews a sacred place of which they could be proud.

This temple, which stood in Christ's day, was an impressive one both in size and in beauty. An area of some twenty-six acres was surrounded by a great wall and supported by an immense foundation of masonry. As a worshiper entered through one of the massive gates in this wall, he would pass through a series of courts, the inner ones surrounded by the outer ones, and each a few steps higher than the one surrounding it.

The outer court was called the Court of the Gentiles. To proceed any farther the Jewish worshiper must pass through one of the nine gates in the high wall that enclosed the inner sanctuary. He would enter first the Court of the Women. As a male Jew he could pass on into the Court of Israel. If a priest, he could proceed into the Court of the priests, with its altar of burnt offering. Behind the altar was the temple itself, consisting of a vestibule, the holy place and the holy of holies. It is thought that this sanctuary was between one hundred and one hundred and fifty feet in height, with marble walls and a roof covered with gold, "It may well be questioned whether in all the world there was a more strikingly beautiful sacred place."[1]

In this sanctuary the priests ministered daily. Besides the regular morning and evening sacrifices, at nine o'clock and three o'clock, there were many offerings of various kinds brought by individuals. The temple must have been a very busy place at times, but Jesus objected to its becoming a place of business. The mercenary spirit of the Jews defiled the sacred place of worship, so that Jesus took radical steps to cleanse it.

The expenses of the temple were met in part by a tax of a half-shekel, levied upon all male Jews twenty years old or above. These taxes were supplemented by personal gifts, often in large amounts by the wealthy, so that the temple treasury was a storehouse of gold and silver.

b. *The Synagogues.* It seems impossible to say just when or how the institution of the synagogues began. But the reason for the appearance of these places of worship is rather obvious. It was probably during the exile in Babylonia that the Jews, deprived of their sacred temple at Jerusalem, sought for some form of gathering to preserve their religion. Scattered as they now were, they found in the synagogue the answer to their need.

It must be remembered that in the time of Christ not all the Jews were living in Palestine. The ten tribes had been taken captive by the Assyrians and deported to regions east of the Euphrates River. Nebuchadnezzar, the Babylonian king, had carried away into captivity all except the poorest of the inhabitants of Judea. Some of the people in Jeremiah's time fled into Egypt, carrying him with them. In the Persian period only a small remnant of the Jews returned to Palestine, and during the Greek period many of their descendants followed the new routes of trade and located themselves all over the Mediterranean world. Alexandria had a very large Jewish population, and Jewish colonies were to be found in almost every city in the Roman empire.

Wherever ten male Jews were living in a town a synagogue might be formed. These synagogues were very numerous in the first century. Rome had its share. It is said that the

[1] Mathews, Shailer, *New Testament Times in Palestine.* New and Revised edition. (Macmillan, 1933), p. 205.

two leading synagogues in Antioch and Alexandria were among the grandest buildings in those great cities. Jerusalem is claimed by some writers to have had as many as 480 synagogues before its destruction in A.D. 70. James stated that there were synagogues "in every city" throughout the Gentile world (Acts 15:21).

These synagogues were not only places of worship but also centers of instruction. The Jews gave much attention to the religious education of their children. It was in the synagogue school that the young Jewish boy memorized the sacred Scriptures and learned their meaning.[2]

The presence of Jewish synagogues everywhere in the Roman empire facilitated very greatly the early spread of Christianity. Whenever Paul entered a new city his customary procedure was to join the worshipers in the synagogue on the Sabbath day. When given an opportunity to speak he would "expose" Christ in the Scriptures. (He was an expository preacher of the Old Testament.) This gave him a starting point for his evangelization of the city.

Another thing that helped was the fact that many Gentiles had become proselytes to Judaism. Some were merely "God-fearers," who enjoyed the synagogue worship and the spiritual comfort which its prayers brought to them. "They observed the Sabbath and festivals, accepted baptism and observed certain regulations about food."[2] But the regular proselytes submitted to the rite of circumcision, were counted as full members of the Jewish community, and so were supposed to keep the entire Law.

The Jews, by planting synagogues throughout the Gentile world and teaching the heathen about the one true God, had done much to prepare the way for the coming of Christ. In fact, Angus declares that "the dispersion" (Diaspora) of the Jews among the nations was probably the largest single factor in the preparation for Christianity.[3]

2. GENTILE RELIGION

Religiously, the world of the first century was waiting for the coming of the "Desire of all nations." Both Greek and Roman religions were largely bankrupt. Socrates and other philosophers had taught the Greeks to laugh at their weak

[2] Angus, S., *The Environment of Early Christianity* (Scribners, 1917), p. 158.
[3] *Ibid.*, p. 143.

and wicked gods. The Romans, with the Greeks, had succumbed to an attitude of pessimism in religion.

The Romans emphasized practical piety and the Greeks philosophical speculation, but the masses of people wanted something personal in their religion. This desire was answered by the Roman emperors in seeking to have themselves deified. But they could hardly pass for gods in the eyes of the people. More and more, thinking individuals turned within themselves, seeking to find an inward peace and satisfaction which they could not experience in the outward religious ceremonies of their day.

This desire for individual religious experience explains the rapid growth in popularity of the mystery religions which spread throughout the empire in this period. Here the individual was initiated into a new circle of those who sought preparation for the next life. The cry for a religion of redemption, a means of salvation, was to be met in the second century by the ceremony called the Taurobolium.

This rite of the mystery religions was a very significant one. The worshiper knelt beneath a platform on which a bull was slain. As the warm blood of the bull ran down upon him, the initiate was supposed to be cleansed from sin and born again for eternity.

But the cry for redemption, to which this answer was offered, had been felt for a long time. It is well expressed in the words of Seneca: "Where shall He be found whom we have been seeking for so many centuries?" That cry could be answered only by Christ. In Him the world at last found its Savior.

I. THE MESSIAH-KING

The Gospel of Matthew

Introduction

It is altogether fitting that our study of the New Testament should begin with the Gospel According to Matthew. It is true that the Gospels were not the first books of the New Testament to be written, but they stand logically at the beginning of our New Testament because they give us the historical foundations of our Christian faith in the life, ministry and death of Jesus Christ.

It is the consensus of scholarly opinion that Matthew's Gospel was not written the earliest of the four. That place is given to the Gospel According to Mark. But Matthew has furnished us with an invaluable link between the Old and New Testaments. His opening words carry us back into the pages of the older revelation, from which he quotes frequently throughout his Gospel, and his purpose is to present Jesus as the Christ, the fulfillment of the Messianic predictions of the Old Testament.

Concerning the author very little is known. All three Synoptics record the call of Matthew, and all three state that he was "sitting at the receipt of custom," or, as the Revised Version has it, "sitting at the place of toll." He was thus in the employ of the Roman government, working either in the custom house at Capernaum or at the toll gate on the great road which ran through that city (Matthew 9:9; Mark 2:13, 14; Luke 5:27, 28).

Mark refers to this new disciple of Jesus as "Levi the son of Alphaeus." Luke designates him as "a publican, named Levi." But the author of the first Gospel simply mentions himself as "a man, named Matthew." His self-effacing humility is shown by the fact that in the list of the twelve apostles he alone of the three Synoptics adds the opprobrious title, "the publican" (10:3).

Matthew, then, belonged to a class of men who were heartily despised by the Jews. The publicans were given the task of collecting taxes for the Roman government. They were thus a symbol of foreign oppression. The Jews, always very tenacious of national freedom, hated them and took delight in classifying them with sinners.

About Matthew's later life we know nothing with certainty. The traditions about his missionary labors do not appear to be very trustworthy.

There seems to have been universal agreement in the church of the second and third centuries as to the Matthean authorship of our first Gospel.[1] This view has been sharply opposed in recent years, on the grounds of internal evidence. But it is not our purpose in this study to enter into the discussion of critical problems.

We have no definite data by means of which to establish the date of writing of Matthew's Gospel. It would appear, however, that all three of the Synoptics were written before the destruction of Jerusalem, in A.D. 70. Conservative scholars generally place the date of Matthew close to A.D. 60. It was evidently written to Christian Jews to confirm them in their new-found faith in Christ, by proving the messiahship of Jesus.

With just these few words of introduction we shall turn now to our study of the Gospel itself. We shall notice, in turn, the preparation, the preaching, and the passion of the Messiah.

The Preparation of the Messiah

1. THE GENEALOGY OF JESUS (chapter 1)

The opening words of Matthew's Gospel are very striking: "The book of the generation of Jesus Christ, the son of David, the Son of Abraham." This was evidently intended by the author to be the title of the book.

The term "Christ" is from the Greek *Christos*, which is the equivalent of the Hebrew word "Messiah." Both mean "the anointed one." The name Jesus means "Savior." The word "generation" is a translation of the Greek *genesis*. So we might render this first verse of Matthew's Gospel, "The book

[1] For citations of early Christian traditions, see the author's *The Story of the New Testament* (Nazarene Publishing House, 1941), p. 30.

of the genesis of Jesus the Messiah, the son of David, the son of Abraham." In other words, it is the record of the beginning of the work of the Messiah, the King of the Jews. Just as the Book of Genesis in the Old Testament records the beginnings of creation, so Matthew tells us of the beginning of the new creation through Jesus Christ. This verse thus forms an introduction, not only to the genealogy of Jesus recorded in the first chapter of Matthew, but also to the entire Gospel, and, more than that, to the whole of the New Testament.

Matthew begins with a genealogy. That is perfectly natural, for the Jews attached a great deal of value to their genealogical records. One has only to think of the long lists of generations in Genesis and in First Chronicles to realize that. In fact, the Book of Ezra describes the sad plight of some Levites who were put out of the priesthood because of the loss of these records. Jesus must present His genealogy first of all, if He is to be accepted by the Jews as their Messiah.

Then, again, it is very important for a claimant to the throne that he be able to produce the evidence of his royal descent. If Jesus was to be regarded as the King of the Jews it was necessary to demonstrate the fact that He was the son of David.

In the first two chapters of Matthew we find three names applied to this Person who was to appear. In 1:21 we are told that an angel said to Joseph, "Thou shalt call his name Jesus; for it is he that shall save his people from their sins." In 1:23, "They shall call his name Immanuel, which is, being interpreted, God with us." And in 2:4 we read that Herod asked the wise men "where the Christ should be born." As we meditate on the significance of these names for us, we feel like joining in singing, "Wonderful the names He bears."

2. THE BIRTH AND CHILDHOOD OF JESUS (chapter 2)

The most definite brief statement of the virgin birth of Jesus is given in 1:20, "That which is conceived in her is of the Holy Spirit." The account indicates clearly that Mary was unmarried at the time. We must either accept the miraculous birth of Christ or reject the validity of this Gospel record.

The account of the birth and babyhood of Jesus as given by Matthew is from the standpoint of Joseph. It is he who received the announcement from the angel and who was further instructed in his care of the young Child and His mother.

Most of the infancy narratives recorded by Matthew are peculiar to his Gospel. Only here do we find the annunciation to Joseph, the visit of the wise men, the flight into Egypt, the slaughter of the innocents, the return to Nazareth. Matthew and Luke are the only two who have included infancy narratives, and they differ completely in their selection. As we shall see later, this is due to the fact that Luke writes the story from the point of view of Mary, the mother of Jesus.

The coming of the Magi from the east to Jerusalem with the question on their lips, "Where is he that is born King of the Jews?" indicates that others besides the Israelites were looking for a Messiah to come. Christ came to answer the longing cry of hearts the world over for a Savior and Lord, one who could cleanse the heart and rule the life.

3. THE PREACHING OF JOHN THE BAPTIST (3:1-12)

While Jesus himself was preparing for His public ministry, the people were being prepared for His coming by John the Baptist. This Elijah of the New Testament appeared suddenly out of the wilderness with his stern call to repentance. The thunders of Sinai were in his voice. With piercing eye and pointing finger he denounced the sins of the people and demanded that they turn from their evil ways. A startling revival was held on the banks of the Jordan, as John baptized those who confessed their sins.

4. THE BAPTISM OF JESUS (3:13-17)

Among those who came one day to be baptized was Jesus, the cousin of John the Baptist. In spite of John's protests Jesus insisted on submitting to the rite. As He came up out of the water the Holy Spirit descended upon Him as a dove, and a voice from heaven said, "This is my beloved Son, in whom I am well pleased."

This is the first clear presentation of the Trinity to be found in the Bible. The doctrine of a triune Godhead is nowhere stated definitely in the Old Testament.[2] But here we

[2] See Dr. H. Orton Wiley's discussion of this point in his *Christian Theology* (Nazarene Publishing House, 1940). Vol. I, pp. 398-403.

find all three Persons of the Godhead participating at the baptism of Jesus.

5. THE TEMPTATION OF JESUS (4:1-11)

The public inauguration of Jesus at His baptism was followed by His private preparation in the wilderness. Here for forty days He engaged in an artillery duel with the enemy of mankind. Finally, sword in hand, "The sword of the Spirit which is the Word of God," He closed in on the devil and put him utterly to rout.

The devil first approached Jesus from the side of physical desire. Jesus was hungry. Satan tried to stab Him in the stomach, but he failed. Christ was feasting His soul in fellowship with the Father.

Next the devil tried to persuade Jesus to jump down from the pinnacle of the temple. If He would do something spectacular, He would have the world at His feet. But Jesus came to be a Savior, not a circus performer. He rejected the temptation to sensationalism. Even though Satan quoted fragments of Scripture, as many of his followers have since done, Jesus came back at him again with a clear command from God's Word.

In his third assault the devil offered to show Jesus an easy way to the throne. It was unnecessary for Him to suffer and to die. If He would only worship Satan, He could have all the kingdoms of the earth. But Jesus knew full well that for Him to submit to Satan would have wrecked the universe which He had created. Asserting that God alone should be worshiped, He drove the devil from the field of battle and resolutely faced the cross.

The Preaching of the Messiah

1. THE BEGINNING OF HIS PUBLIC MINISTRY (4:12-25)

When Jesus heard that John the Baptist had been arrested by Herod He left Judea for Galilee. Saying farewell to His home at Nazareth, He chose Capernaum as the center for His preaching tours in Galilee. This place, situated at the northwest corner of the Sea of Galilee, was the home city of Peter, and Jesus made His headquarters at Peter's house.

Jesus began His preaching with the same text which John the Baptist had used, "Repent ye; for the kingdom of heaven

—23—

is at hand." This phrase, "The kingdom of the heavens" (lit.), is very prominent in Matthew's Gospel, occurring some thirty-two times. We have already noted that Jesus is presented by Matthew as King, so "kingdom," which occurs some fifty-two times in this Gospel, is central to the whole purpose and theme of Matthew. The above phrase refers to the rule or reign of God. Jesus was offering the Jews God's kingdom, if they would accept His rulership of their lives.

The first disciples whom Jesus called to follow Him were four fishermen, whom He found on the shores of Galilee. They left their fishing to become fishers of men.

In 4:23 we have a summary description of the great Galilean ministry of Jesus, "And Jesus went about in all Galilee, teaching in their synagogues, and preaching the gospel of the kingdom, and healing all manner of disease and all manner of sickness among the people."[3] His ministry consisted of teaching, preaching and healing.

As in the case of John the Baptist, Jesus met with early popularity. We read in 4:25, "and there followed him great multitudes from Galilee and Decapolis and Jerusalem and Judea and from beyond the Jordan." All Palestine—except Samaria—as well as Trans-Jordan, turned out to hear this new preacher.

2. THE SERMON ON THE MOUNT (chapters 5-7)

The Sermon on the Mount has well been called the Constitution of the Kingdom of Heaven. The Beatitudes give us the qualifications for entrance into the kingdom. The follower of Christ must first of all confess his spiritual poverty and mourn over his sins. He must be humble and must truly hunger and thirst after righteousness. He must be merciful, remembering his own failings. Then he must be pure in heart, a peacemaker, and one who is steadfast under persecution.

The nature of the Christian is stated in 5:13-16. Inwardly, he acts as salt, to season and preserve. Outwardly, he shines as a light, to guide and guard.

The seventeenth verse of this fifth chapter, in conjunction with the twentieth, introduces us to the rest of the chapter. Jesus declared, "Think not that I came to destroy the law or the prophets: I came not to destroy, but to fulfill." His teach-

[3] This statement is repeated in 9:35.

ing was a reinterpretation of the law. He did not seek to abolish righteousness, but to give it a higher meaning.

The key verse of the Sermon on the Mount is found in 5:20, "For I say unto you, that except your righteousness shall exceed the righteousness of the scribes and Pharisees, ye shall in no wise enter into the kingdom of heaven." The righteousness of the scribes and Pharisees was outward, ceremonial, legal, formal. The higher righteousness of the Christian must be inward, ethical, personal, spiritual.

This suggests the theme of this sermon, which might be called "True Righteousness." Jesus here discusses true righteousness as applied to the moral, social, religious and economic life of man.

First, righteousness in the moral realm. The Mosaic law said, "Thou shalt not kill." Jesus said, "Thou shalt not hate." Christ took the old law against murder and gave it a vastly higher meaning by identifying hatred with murder. It is the inner attitude, not the outward act, that counts with God.

This same principle is next applied to adultery. Jesus asserted that a lustful look constitutes adultery. Many men who have prided themselves on their life of outward morality would be arraigned before the bar of their consciences in the light of this truth.

These two topics, murder and adultery, have both moral and social significance. The same is true of the remaining three topics of this chapter, with the emphasis perhaps more on the social.

The Christian's conversation, Jesus taught, should be straightforward and truthful. If so, there will be no need for swearing that one is telling the truth.

Again, Jesus taught that a Christian must not fight back. If compelled to do something, he should do it graciously. While going the second mile, he would have an opportunity for giving an effective testimony.

In this period of war hysteria it is needful to remember Jesus' teaching that hate is never right, not even in time of war. Love is always the Christian attitude. The man who hates his enemies, no matter who they are, is not a Christian.

This section of the sermon ends with the sweeping command, "Ye therefore shall be perfect, as your heavenly Father is perfect" (5:48). From our study of the chapter it is evident that the perfection here enjoined is perfection in love, in inward attitude and motive. Jesus' way of dealing with man is not by outward reformation, but by inward transformation.

The first half of the sixth chapter treats of the righteousness as applied to the religious life. The first verse states the general principle, "Take heed that ye do not your righteousness before men, to be seen of them." This principle is then applied to giving (vs. 2-4), praying (vs. 5-15), and fasting (vs. 16-18). In the activities of each of these three phases of religious life Jesus urged sincerity and simplicity.

To these two emphases—sincerity and simplicity—a third one, singleness, is added in the next paragraph (vs. 22-24). These three were paramount with Jesus and should be pre-eminent in the life of the Christian.

With regard to the economic life Jesus taught that the essential thing is to maintain the supremacy of the spiritual over the material. The latter has its place, but first things should be kept first. The one who consistently seeks first God's kingdom will experience God's care of his needs.

In the first paragraph of the seventh chapter Jesus denounces the attitude of carping criticism. Instead of using the magnifying glass on others we should use the looking glass on ourselves. Judging others produces church quarrels; judging ourselves produces church revivals.

Jesus ended this discourse by asserting, "Not every one that saith unto me, Lord, Lord, shall enter into the kingdom of heaven; but he that doeth the will of my Father who is in heaven." And then He emphasized this statement and illustrated the entire sermon by describing the two houses, one built on the rock, and the other built on the sand. The one who hears the sayings of Jesus and does them is like a wise man who gives attention to the foundation of his house, so that it weathers the storms and floods. The one who hears but does not obey is like a foolish man who builds without a foundation, and so finds his life ending in wreckage and ruin.

3. THE MIRACLES OF THE MESSIAH (chapters 8, 9)

Jesus preached by action as well as by word. His miracles were intended to reveal His character and to emphasize and illustrate His messages, as well as to alleviate the sufferings of humanity.

Chapters eight and nine of Matthew record a number of miracles performed by Jesus in His early Galilean ministry. He cleansed a leper, healed the centurion's servant of paralysis, freed Peter's mother-in-law of her fever, stilled the storm on Galilee, cast a legion of demons out of the Gadarene demoniac, healed the paralytic, cured the woman who touched His garment, raised the daughter of Jairus, restored sight to two blind men and cast the demon out of the dumb demoniac.

Here are ten representative miracles of Jesus recorded in the short space of two chapters. We can take time for a discussion of only three of them.

The healing of the centurion's servant is a demonstration of the power of the King's command. The centurion cited the example of his own authority over his soldiers and suggested that Jesus assert His authority as King of creation. Jesus marveled at such faith, especially since it was exhibited by a Gentile. Contrasted with this is the only other instance where it is recorded that Jesus marveled, and that was at the unbelief of His own townspeople (Mark 6:6).

The other two miracles may be treated together. The healing of the woman with an issue of blood is sandwiched into the account of the raising of Jairus' daughter. While Jesus was on His way to the synagogue ruler's house the needy woman pressed up close behind Him and touched His garment. Jesus stopped for a testimony meeting, to strengthen her faith by public confession, and then went on with Jairus.

The significant thing about these two miracles is that they illustrate two phases of salvation. In one sense, our salvation depends on our own action in coming to Jesus for forgiveness and cleansing. But, from another point of view, the one who is "dead in trespasses and sins" is just as helpless as was the daughter of Jairus. Our salvation depends on the love and power of God, but it also depends on the attitude of our own will.

Inserted in the narrative of these various miracles are two brief sections of teachings. In 8:18-22 there is a paragraph on the cost of discipleship. Jesus declared that if a person would follow Him he must be willing to forsake everything.

In 9:14-17 Jesus answered the question of John the Baptist's disciples about fasting by teaching that the new wine of the Christian gospel must not be put into the old wineskins of Judaistic legalism. It was to be put into the new wineskins of the Christian Church and individual Christian lives.

4. THE MISSION OF THE TWELVE (chapter 10)

The preaching tours of Jesus throughout Galilee were now to be supplemented by the work of His twelve chosen apostles. Jesus sent them forth to seek "the lost sheep of the house of Israel." It was their task to offer the kingdom to Israel. Their text was brief, "The kingdom of heaven is at hand" (v. 7). They were to perform miracles of healing such as they had seen Jesus doing.

The Master commanded them not to take with them any luggage or money, for Oriental hospitality would wait on their needs. They were "poor preachers," like the Lollards of England in Wycliffe's day who prepared the way for the Protestant Reformation in that land.

Jesus warned these messengers of His that they would meet opposition and even persecution. It is evident that these predictions relate more fully to their preaching after Pentecost than to this brief tour at this time.

5. JESUS AND JOHN (chapter 11)

John the Baptist was still confined in prison at Machaerus, Herod's citadel east of the Dead Sea. Here he had been held since his arrest some months before. It would seem that he shared the common Jewish belief that the Messiah would set up an earthly kingdom. When this did not materialize, John began to wonder if Jesus really was the Messiah, so he sent some of his disciples to ask Jesus.

In answer to their question, "Art thou he that cometh?" Jesus instructed John's disciples to report to their master the things which they saw Him do and heard Him say. His miracles and messages constituted sufficient demonstration of His Messiahship.

Then Jesus turned to the crowd that stood around Him. After paying high tribute to the character of John the Baptist, the last and greatest of the prophets, He began to upbraid the people for their unbelief. Poor John, languishing in prison, had some excuse for his doubts. But not they. Having seen His miracles, they stood condemned for not believing in Him.

After denouncing the Galilean cities for their stubborn rejection of Him, Jesus thanked His Father for revealing the truth to the poor and ignorant. Then He uttered that matchless invitation, "Come unto me, all ye that labour and are heavy laden, and I will give you rest. Take my yoke upon you, and learn of me; for I am meek and lowly in heart; and ye shall find rest unto your souls. For my yoke is easy, and my burden is light" (11:28-30).

6. JESUS AND THE PHARISEES (chapter 12)

One of the prominent features of the Synoptic Gospels is the conflict between the Pharisees and Jesus. The main point of issue at this time was the question of keeping the Sabbath. Two instances of this are given in the twelfth chapter.

a. *The Plucking of Grain on the Sabbath* (12:1-8). The Pharisees had already in their hearts accused Jesus of blasphemy for presuming to forgive the sins of the paralytic (1:3). Now they find fault with His disciples for breaking the Sabbath, as they thought. Weary and hungry, the disciples were plucking the grains of wheat or barley—probably the latter at this time of the year—and rubbing the husks off before eating them. In the eyes of the Pharisees, to whom molehills sometimes looked like mountains, this constituted nothing less than harvesting and threshing grain!

But Jesus protected His followers against these unreasonable charges. He reminded the Pharisees that the priests had to work on the Sabbath, but were guiltless. These carping critics had forgotten Hosea's message that God desires mercy on the part of His people, rather than ceremonial sacrifices. They had also failed to recognize Jesus' authority as "lord of the sabbath."

b. *The Healing of the Man with the Withered Hand* (12: 9-14). A fresh encounter between the Pharisees and Jesus took place soon after in the synagogue. Noticing a man there with a withered hand, the fault-finders asked Jesus if it was lawful to heal on the Sabbath day. They were not seeking for information but for accusation.

Jesus, as He frequently did, turned the question on them. He asked them which one of them would leave his valuable sheep in a hole where it had fallen on the Sabbath day. Then He laid down a summary principle regarding all Sabbath observance: "Wherefore it is lawful to do good on the sabbath day." He thereupon suited action to word by healing the man's hand. Instead of worshiping this wonderful Christ, the Pharisees went out in anger to plot His death.

c. *The Blasphemy of the Pharisees* (12:22-37). By this time their hatred of Jesus was getting so hot that they became reckless and unrestrained in their statements about Him. When they heard the multitudes, amazed at His miracles, saying, "Can this be the Son of David?" they could stand it no longer. So they accused Him of casting out demons by the power of the prince of demons.

After showing the absurdity of this idea Jesus uttered a solemn warning against blasphemy. He declared that blasphemy against the Holy Spirit would never be forgiven. The implication is that the Pharisees had been guilty of blaspheming the Holy Spirit by attributing the works of the Spirit to Satan. This is indicated more clearly in Mark's account (Mark 3:30).

d. *The Sign of the Prophet Jonah* (12:38-45). At this juncture some scribes and Pharisees asked for a sign. Jesus offered only one, taken from their Scriptures. Jonah's experience in the sea-monster was a sign of Jesus' death and resurrection.

7. SEVEN PARABLES OF THE KINGDOM (chapter 13)

One outstanding characteristic of Matthew's Gospel is the topical arrangement of the material. In the thirteenth chapter we find a collection of seven parables, each of which (except the first) is introduced by the expression, "The kingdom of heaven is like unto." These are the parables of the sower, the tares, the mustard seed, the leaven, the hidden treasure, the pearl of great price, and the drag-net. The first and third of these are found in all three of the Synoptics. The fourth, about leaven, is in Luke. The other four are found only in Matthew.

The parable of the sower does not require any explanation, as Jesus gave a definite interpretation of it to His disciples. The same is true of the second parable, that of the tares.

Concerning the parables of the mustard seed and the leaven there are differences of opinion. The traditional interpretation refers the first to the rapid spread of the gospel in the world and the second to the leavening of human society by Christianity. Such Bible students as Scofield and Gabelein object to this. For them the mustard tree is a picture of the phenomenal growth of the Catholic Church, with wicked spirits (birds) lodging in the offices (branches) of the ecclesiastical organization. They also contend that leaven is always a symbol of evil in the Scriptures, and should be so interpreted here. This parable, for them, predicts the corruption of the church in the middle ages. The student is free to take his choice of these two interpretations.

The parables of the hidden treasure and the pearl of great price have two possible applications. They may be referred to Christ as paying the supreme price to purchase His Church, or to the individual as giving all in order to receive the kingdom of God in his heart. Probably the latter was intended by Jesus.

The last of the parables, that of the drag-net, is interpreted by Christ as referring to the close of the age ("end of the world"). This parable and that of the tares certainly deny the idea that human society will be fully Christianized in this age. At its close there will still be tares and bad fish.

8. THE PREPARATION OF THE MESSIAH'S MESSENGERS (chapters 14-18)

The great Galilean ministry of Jesus was followed by a period of several months in which the Master gave special attention to training the twelve apostles, that they might carry on the work after His departure. In order to have privacy for this more intimate ministry to His disciples, He withdrew several times from the thronged roads, streets and shores of Galilee. We find Him with His chosen few wending His way northward or eastward to get beyond the reach of the crowd.

a. *The First Withdrawal; Feeding of Five Thousand* (14:13-21). The first withdrawal was across the lake of Galilee to "a desert place apart." Here He tried to find seclusion and rest for Himself and His disciples. But the crowd went hurrying on foot around the end of the lake and was waiting for Him when He disembarked. Having compassion on the people Jesus ministered to them until evening, then gave them their supper and sent them home.

After directing His disciples to row across the lake again, Jesus spent the night in prayer on the mountain. Before daybreak He came to them, walking on the water. Landing in Gennesaret, He ministered there to the sick and suffering.

b. *Controversy over the Washing of Hands* (15:1-20). The Pharisees were still looking for opportunities to quarrel with Jesus. So they asked Him why His disciples transgressed "the tradition of the elders" by neglecting the prescribed ceremony of washing their hands before eating.

In answer to their question Jesus not only asserted that in some of their practices they were transgressing the commandment of God in order to observe the tradition of the elders, but He also made a clear statement as to the difference between their religion and His. They were concerned with outward ceremonialism. Christianity is the religion of an inward transformation. It is not concerned so much with the outward washing of the hands as with the inward cleansing of the heart. Paul had to take the same stand against the Judaizers of his day, and the issue is still a live one today in the Church.

c. *The Second Withdrawal; to Tyre and Sidon* (15:21-28). Following this controversy with the Pharisees Jesus withdrew again, this time into the region of Tyre and Sidon, the coastal cities of Phoenicia. Here He found a Canaanite woman, a Gentile, who had more true faith than all His pharisaical critics. Because of her humble, yet persistent faith, Jesus healed her daughter.

d. *The Third Withdrawal; Feeding of Four Thousand* (15:29-38). This incident was followed by Jesus' third withdrawal. The parallel account in Mark states that Jesus first went northward to Sidon and then eastward and southward into Decapolis, taking care to avoid the territory of Herod Antipas. Here, on a mountain, He found the multitudes flocking around Him again. After ministering to them, He fed the whole crowd of four thousand people.

e. *The Fourth Withdrawal; to Caesarea Philippi* (16:13-20). After another brief skirmish with the Pharisees 16:1-4), Jesus withdrew for the fourth time. On this trip He went straight north to the region of Caesarea Philippi, near the ancient city of Dan. Here Jesus asked His disciples who people thought Him to be. After receiving various answers He asked the more momentous question, "But who say ye that I am?" Peter rallied to the occasion with his affirmation, "Thou art the Christ, the Son of the living God." Jesus declared that Peter had received this information by nothing less than divine revelation.

It has been claimed by some that Jesus said He would build His Church upon Peter. But the Greek word for Peter means little rock, or stone. Jesus declared that He would build His Church upon the great rock ledge, the foundation doctrine of His deity. Peter's confession at Caesarea Philippi was followed by Jesus' disclosure of His coming sufferings, death and resurrection at Jerusalem. This was the first time, but not the last, that He broached this painful subject. From now on (verse 21) it will be always upon His mind and often upon His lips.

f. *The Transfiguration* (17:1-8). A week later Jesus took Peter, James and John with Him up into the mountain of transfiguration—perhaps snow-capped Mount Hermon, which is nearby. Here these disciples had a glimpse of His glory (17:1-8). But Jesus refused to stay in the heavenly atmosphere of that mountain top. Instead, He returned down the hill to meet the waiting multitudes and to minister to their needs.

g. *The Greatest in the Kingdom of Heaven* (18:1-4). We next find Jesus back in Galilee, where for the third time He foretells His death (17:22, 23). But the disciples entered so little into the significance of His words that they were occupied with the question of who would be greatest in the kingdom of heaven. Jesus answered them by placing a child in the midst and saying, "Whosoever therefore shall humble himself as this little child, the same is the greatest in the kingdom of heaven."

h. *A Lesson on Forgiveness* (18:15-35). The remainder of chapter eighteen is taken up with teaching on forgiveness. If our brother sins against us, we are not to tell all the neighbors about it but to talk with him privately. If he will not listen to reason, we should take with us a committee of witnesses. If he will not listen to them, the matter should be reported to the church, as a last resort. If he refuses to listen to the church, he is to be dropped from Christian fellowship. This is Jesus' formula for taking care of trouble in the church.

It might be noted in passing that Matthew is the only Gospel writer who mentions the word "church." It occurs twice here (verse 17) and once in connection with the Great Confession at Caesarea Philippi (16:18). The term "kingdom" holds the place in the Gospels which is held by "church" in the Epistles.

But—returning to the narrative—Peter wanted to know how often he was to forgive his brother. He thought seven times was being generous. But Jesus said "seventy times seven"; in other words, indefinitely.

To illustrate His teaching on forgiveness Jesus told the parable of the unmerciful servant, which is found only in Matthew. When God has forgiven us for the debt of sin which we could never pay, what kind of Christians are we who refuse to forgive our brother for some trifling trespass?

9. The Last Trip to Jerusalem (chapters 19, 20)

The time had now come for Jesus to begin His final journey to Jerusalem. So, "He departed from Galilee, and came into the borders of Judea beyond the Jordan" (19:1)—what was called Perea. Here again He ministered to the multitudes.

a. *The Question of Divorce* (19:3-12). The Pharisees were still following His trail, seeking to trap Him into saying something that would form the basis for an accusation against Him. This time they asked His opinion on the matter of divorce. They hoped He would contradict the Mosaic regulation, so that they could get Him into trouble. In His answer Jesus indicated that divorce was not allowable, except for the one cause of fornication. In this matter He was more strict than Moses. He went back past the bigamous practices of the Old Testament characters and reminded His hearers that God had ordained monogamy in the beginning of human history.

b. *The Rich Young Ruler* (19:16-26). The story of the rich young ruler and Jesus' statement about the difficulty of rich people being saved are found in all three of the Synoptics. Evidently the incident made a strong impression on the disciples. They, as well as Jesus, must have been saddened by the unwillingness of this promising inquirer to forsake all and follow the Master. The story teaches that one cannot be saved by his own goodness, but only by personal surrender to Jesus Christ.

c. *The Parable of the Laborers in the Vineyard* (20:1-16). This parable is recorded only by Matthew. Some today, with the objectors in the story, would question the justice of the householder's action in giving the same pay to those who worked a short time as to those who labored all day long.

That there is a difficulty will be admitted readily. But it will help much to link this parable with the question of Peter in the previous section, "What then shall we have?" (19:27). Jesus told this story as a rebuke to the attitude indicated by that question. We are not to serve God for pay, but out of love. We should not have the attitude of trying to measure our service by the exact reward which we think to get. Nor should we find fault with God for blessing those who may have turned to Him late in life, while we have served Him throughout our days. Our service should be unselfish and generous.

d. *The Selfish Ambition of James and John* (20:17-28). On this last journey, "as Jesus was going up to Jerusalem, he took the twelve disciples apart," and told them for the fourth time what was to befall Him at the end of the trip. But the disciples were still thinking about thrones instead of crosses. The mother of James and John came to Jesus with the ambitious request that her sons might sit on either side of Him in His kingdom. Jesus asked the two disciples if they could share His sufferings, and they thoughtlessly answered, "We are able," just as so many people today sing those words with little appreciation of their deep significance. But the Master took advantage of the situation to warn His disciples against seeking to "lord it over" (lit. Greek) one another. They were to follow His example, "Even as the Son of man came not to be ministered unto, but to minister, and to give his life a ransom for many."

e. *The Healing of Blind Bartimaeus* (20:29-34). This miracle, which took place near Jericho, is recorded in all three of the Synoptics. But whereas Matthew and Mark say that Jesus was leaving Jericho, Luke says that He was approaching the city. This has been seized upon by unfriendly critics as an example of contradictory statements in the different Gospels. Perhaps there were two distinct Jerichos at that time. Jesus was leaving the old Jericho and approaching the new Jericho which Herod had rebuilt. Or Luke's statement may simply mean that the miracle took place "near" Jericho.

10. THE BEGINNING OF PASSION WEEK (chapters 21-23)

a. *The Triumphal Entry* (21:1-9). Jesus' last week of public ministry began with what is usually called "The Triumphal Entry into Jerusalem," recorded in all four Gospels. Jesus rode into the city on a colt, with the crowds blessing Him as the "son of David." But the triumph was short-lived, for the rulers of the city rejected their Messiah. The incident only served to add to the jealousy and hatred of the Pharisees.

b. *The Cleansing of the Temple* (21:12-16). All three Synoptics tell of the cleansing of the temple. John's Gospel describes one which took place at the beginning of Jesus' ministry. It is not difficult to believe that the temple would need cleansing again after an interval of perhaps two or three years.

c. *The Cursing of the Fig Tree* (21:18-22). On Monday morning the fig tree was cursed by Jesus. The purpose was evidently twofold—to give the disciples a lesson on faith, and to illustrate the doom of the Jewish nation.

d. *The Challenge of the Jewish Rulers* (21:23-27). All three Synoptics record the challenging of Jesus' authority by the Sanhedrin. When they asked the source of His authority, He put them in a dilemma by asking them to state the source of John's authority. Their reasoning here shows how utterly unethical they were. They were not concerned at all as to what was true, but only as to what was expedient. When they refused to answer, Jesus refused to reply to their question.

e. *The Parable of the Two Sons* (21:28-32). Matthew alone records how Jesus took advantage of the opportunity to tell these Jewish rulers a parable especially for their benefit. He described two sons, one who promised but failed to keep his promise, and another who rebelled but later obeyed. Lest they should miss the point Jesus told them plainly that the "down-and-outers" were going into the kingdom ahead of them.

f. *The Parable of the Wicked Husbandmen* (21:33-44). To make the iniquity of their treatment of Him still more evident Jesus went on to tell the parable of the wicked husbandmen, recorded in all three Synoptics. Jesus made it rather plain that the Jewish people were the wicked husbandmen, in that they had mistreated and killed the prophets of God and now were about to kill the Son of God. "And when the chief priests and the Pharisees heard his parables, they perceived that he spake of them." But instead of repenting, they tried to arrest Him.

g. *The Parable of the Marriage of the King's Son* (22:1-14). Jesus added a third parable to these, that of the marriage of the king's son. The purpose of this one was also to show that because the Jews had rejected Christ, the Gentiles would be welcomed into the kingdom.

h. *The Question of the Tribute Money* (22:15-22). Chapter 22 records the efforts of the Pharisees and Sadducees to ensnare Jesus in His talk. First the Pharisees sent some of their followers, along with some Herodians, to ask Jesus about tribute to Caesar. If He said "Yes," the crowds would taunt Him with being untrue to the interests of Israel. If He said "No," the Herodian politicians would report Him for disloyalty to the Roman government.

They thought they had Him in a corner. But Jesus was more than a match for their clever contrivings. He asked for a piece of tribute money. When they handed Him a denarius, He asked whose picture and title were on it. The evidence of ownership was there. Jesus' next words perhaps suggest that if they had given God what belonged to Him they would not now be compelled to pay tribute to Caesar.

i. *The Question Concerning the Resurrection* (22:23-33). Next the Sadducees took their turn, with the hypothetical story of the woman with seven successive husbands. Which husband could claim her as wife in the resurrection? These hypocritical Sadducees thus tried to show the ridiculousness of any belief in a resurrection. But Jesus charged them with ignorance of both the Scriptures and the power of God. After

—37—

explaining the future state of the righteous, He reminded them that God said "I am," not "I was," the God of Abraham.

j. *The Greatest Commandment* (22:34-40). When the Pharisees heard that Jesus had silenced the Sadducees, they foolishly decided to try their hand again. This time they asked what was the great commandment of the law. For good measure, Jesus gave them two—love to God and love to man. He then proceeded to ask the Pharisees a question which they could not answer. How was Christ both David's son and David's lord? The conclusion of this day of conflict between Jesus and the Pharisees and Sadducees was that "no one was able to answer him a word, neither durst any man from that day forth ask him any more questions" (v. 46). Jesus had effectively silenced His critics, so that they did not again risk a public debate before the people.

k. *Woes on the Pharisees* (chapter 23). Chapter 23 is taken up largely with Jesus' stern denunciation of the scribes and Pharisees. After His exposure of their hollow hypocrisy—masquerading as pious leaders—He uttered those words of tender pathos, "How often would I have gathered thy children together, even as a hen gathereth her chickens under her wings, and ye would not!"

11. THE OLIVET DISCOURSE (chapters 24, 25)

The disciples were still proud of their beautiful temple, built by Herod. But Jesus predicted its final and complete destruction. The disciples then asked, "When shall these things be? and what shall be the sign of thy coming, and of the end of the world?" (24:3). The remainder of the chapter records Jesus' answer to these questions.

We shall not stop here to analyze this material, which is found in much the same form in Mark 13 and Luke 21. We simply call attention to the fact that whereas the Sermon on the Mount is mainly ethical this Olivet Discourse is eschatological; that is, it deals with future things. It relates to the return of Christ and the end of the age.

The material of chapter 25, however, is peculiar to this Gospel. Here we find the parable of the ten virgins, the parable of the talents and a picture of the judgment at the close of the age. The two parables teach the necessity of both heart experience and active service as a preparation for the coming of Christ. Those whose inward light is dimmed or whose zeal in service is cooled will not be ready for His return.

The Passion of the Messiah

While Jesus had been busy preaching to the multitudes and teaching His disciples the Pharisees and Sadducees had also been busy plotting His death. They decided, because of the crowds that flocked around Him, to wait until after the feast (26:3-5). But Jesus had already predicted that He would be crucified at this Passover season (26:2). And so it was to be.

1. THE ANOINTING AT BETHANY (26:6-13)

Jesus was already entering the shadows of Gethsemane and Calvary. But one more hour of comfort and congeniality was given to Him at a home in Bethany. Here, as He was reclining at the table with His friends, Mary, who had loved to sit at His feet and listen to His words, came in with an alabaster box of ointment, which she poured on His head. The disciples protested at the waste, but Jesus said that this was done in preparation for His burial. Evidently Mary had grasped Jesus' teaching about His death more clearly than anyone else. It is noticeable that she was not among the women who went to the tomb on Easter morning to anoint the body of Jesus.

2. THE BARGAIN OF JUDAS (26:14-16)

Judas, maddened by the display of costly value poured on Jesus, went to the Jewish rulers and bargained to betray the Master to them. They paid him thirty pieces of silver, and he began to watch for an opportunity to deliver Jesus into their hands.

3. THE LAST SUPPER (26:17-30)

On the evening before His crucifixion Jesus ate the Passover meal with His disciples in the upper room. It was a sad occasion, as Jesus predicted His betrayal by one of His own disciples.

The last supper concluded with the institution of the Lord's Supper. Probably Judas had left before this, as indicated by John's Gospel. It should always be remembered that the institution of the Lord's Supper was in the very shadow of the cross.

4. JESUS IN GETHSEMANE (26:36-46)

In the gloom of the garden Jesus poured out His soul in prayer, while the weary disciples slept nearby. Though His humanity shrank from the cup of bitter sorrow which was His to drink, He obediently said, "Thy will be done," and courageously faced the cross.

5. THE ARREST OF JESUS (26:47-56)

One of the saddest scenes in Jesus' life is the picture of Judas, His own disciple, planting the kiss of betrayal on the face of the Master. Even then, Jesus called him "Friend."

Reproving Peter for seeking to defend Him with a sword, Jesus meekly submitted to His captors and was led away to the house of Caiaphas.

6. THE TRIAL BEFORE THE SANHEDRIN (26:57-66)

At the house of the high priest the Sanhedrin had assembled to try Jesus. After it had appeared that the case might be defaulted for lack of consistent witnesses, the high priest commanded Jesus, under oath, to state whether He was the Messiah, the Son of God. When Jesus affirmed that He was, the Sanhedrin condemned Him to be worthy of death because of His blasphemy.

7. THE DENIALS OF PETER (26:69-75)

Poor Peter, who had declared so vehemently his loyalty to Christ, and who had indeed drawn his sword in the garden to protect his Master, was yet no match for the accusations of a maid. After denying three times that he knew Jesus, Peter went out to weep bitter tears of repentance.

8. THE SUICIDE OF JUDAS (27:3-10)

Judas had evidently expected Jesus to escape from His captors, using His miraculous powers. He, Judas, would then have the money, while at the same time Jesus would be safe. When it became evident that Jesus would make no effort to save Himself, Judas returned the money to the chief priests and hanged himself. The priests decided to use the money for purchasing the potter's field. When we recall Jeremiah's experience at the potter's house it suggests that this potter's field, filled with broken and marred pieces of rejected pottery, is a type of a world of wrecked humanity purchased with the price of Jesus' blood.

9. JESUS BEFORE PILATE (27:11-26)

As we have already seen, the Sanhedrin was not permitted by the Roman government to execute the death sentence. So the Jews delivered Jesus to Pilate.

In spite of the fact that Pilate knew that the Jews were moved wholly by envy, overriding his wife's warning he drove on to his own doom. He made a public show of washing his hands of the affair and turned Jesus over to His tormentors.

10. THE CRUCIFIXION (27:33-56).

It is a melancholy scene that greets us as we look at the cross on Golgotha's hill. While brutal soldiers cast lots for His clothes, onlookers wagged their heads contemptuously at Him, and Jewish rulers mocked Him cruelly, Jesus had nothing but words of kindness on His parched lips. It would seem that hate had triumphed in that hour, but actually love had conquered all things. While it appeared that hate had nailed Jesus to the cross, it was love that held Him there while He paid the penalty for the sins of a guilty world.

Finally nature drew a veil of darkness over the sacred scene. Out of that darkness, which had penetrated the soul of Jesus, came the cry, "My God, my God, why hast thou forsaken me?" So mighty was the impression made by His death that the Roman centurion said, "Truly this was God's Son" (literal translation).

11. THE BURIAL (27:57-66)

Joseph of Arimathea, a member of the Sanhedrin who had had no part in the vote of that body against Jesus, begged from Pilate the body of Jesus and laid it in his own new tomb. Some women observed where He was buried and prepared spices for anointing His body. At the earnest request of fearful Pharisees and Sadducees, Pilate dispatched a guard of soldiers to watch the sepulcher.

12. THE RESURRECTION (chapter 28)

Sunday morning found the faithful, devoted women at the tomb. Here they saw angels where they had expected to find the body of their Lord. As they left the sepulcher, Jesus greeted them. Matthew alone records this appearance to the women. Matthew is also the only one who tells us that the Sanhedrin instructed the soldiers to say that Jesus' body was stolen. He is also alone in describing the appearance to the eleven disciples on a mountain in Galilee.

The Gospel of Matthew closes with Jesus' Great Commission to His disciples, "Go ye therefore, and make disciples of all nations . . . and lo, I am with you always, even unto the end of the world."

II. THE SERVANT OF JEHOVAH

The Gospel of Mark

Introduction

Early church tradition is definite in ascribing our Second Gospel to the pen of Mark. It is also unanimous in stating that Mark has given us in his Gospel the preaching of Peter. Not less than six writers of the second and third centuries make definite statements to that effect.

John Mark accompanied Barnabas and Paul on their first missionary journey as far as Perga in Pamphylia. From there he returned home to Jerusalem. When Barnabas wanted to take him along again on their second trip, Paul objected. Since they could not agree on the matter they parted company. Barnabas took Mark with him to Cyprus, while Paul chose a new colleague for his second journey (Acts 15:37-40).

Years later, however, when Paul was in prison at Rome, he thought better of young Mark. Writing to Philemon (v. 24) and to the Colossians (4:10, 11), he calls Mark his fellow laborer. And in his last epistle, the second to Timothy, he says, "Take Mark, and bring him with thee: for he is useful to me for ministering" (4:11).

Evidently he was useful to Peter also. Not only does Peter call him "my son" in his First Epistle (5:13), but Irenaeus and Tertullian—both of the second century—state that Mark was the "interpreter" of Peter. If the early tradition of the church is to be trusted at all, it seems clear that we have in Mark's Gospel Peter's interpretation of the life of Jesus.

There is also good evidence that Mark wrote his Gospel at Rome and for the Romans. Clement of Alexandria (as quoted by Eusebius) says that the Roman hearers of Peter requested John Mark to write down the Gospel preached by Peter, with the result that Mark composed his Gospel.[1]

---

[1] Major, H. D. A., T. W. Manson, and C. J. Wright, *The Mission and Message of Jesus*, (E. P. Dutton, 1938), p. 5.

The recently published *Anti-Marcionite Prologue to Mark* (written A.D. 150-180) says that Mark wrote his Gospel "in the regions of Italy."[2] This tradition is confirmed by the character of the book itself.[3]

The purpose of the Gospel According to Mark is to present Jesus as "the Servant of Jehovah" (cf. Isaiah 52:13), whose sufferings are described in the fifty-third chapter of Isaiah. Jesus is pictured in Mark's Gospel as the Conquering Servant and the Suffering Servant. Like the ox, He stands between the plow and the altar, ready for service or sacrifice, or both. With Jesus it was both—first service, then sacrifice.

The Filial Servant

1. THE TITLE (1:1)

As we found in the case of Matthew, Mark begins his Gospel with a very brief preface, which also constitutes his title for the book, "The beginning of the gospel of Jesus Christ, the Son of God." Thus he introduces his hero and indicates the character of his book. It is the beginning of the good news proclaimed by Jesus.

2. THE MINISTRY OF JOHN (1:2-8)

Having prefixed his title, Mark now begins the Gospel proper with an account of the ministry of John the Baptist. There is an interesting coincidence between this and the words of Peter in Acts 1:21, "Of the men therefore that have companied with us all the time that the Lord Jesus went in and out among us, beginning from the baptism of John." It was natural, then, that the Gospel which records the preaching of Peter should begin with the ministry of John the Baptist.

One of the outstanding characteristics of Mark's Gospel is vividness of description. This coincides well with what we know of Peter. He was a plain, rugged fisherman, who was in the habit of observing carefully what he saw. He was definitely a man of the out of doors, rather than a man of books.

This distinctive trait appears in Mark's account of the ministry of John. He gives us a description of the appearance of the Baptist, "And John was clothed with camel's hair, and

[2] *Ibid.*, p. 4.
[3] See the author's *Story of the New Testament*, pp. 28, 29.

had a leathern girdle about his loins, and did eat locusts and wild honey" (1:6). Doubtless Peter was much impressed with the rough and rugged appearance of this prophet from the jagged hillsides. The wilderness of Judea was a wild, forsaken region of mountains and chasms. It was in this same territory that Jesus fought His duel with the devil.

3. THE BAPTISM OF JESUS (1:9-11)

In keeping with Peter's love for vivid words of description, Mark here uses a different term to describe the opening of the heavens from that used by Matthew and Luke. Their word simply means "opened," while his literally means "splitting apart." We shall find this characteristic of vividness appearing constantly, although it is not always as apparent in the English as in the Greek.

4. THE TEMPTATION OF JESUS (1:12, 13).

Mark does not give us the details of Jesus' threefold temptation by Satan, but his choice of words is again striking. While Matthew and Luke say that Jesus was "led" by the Spirit into the wilderness, Mark says, "And straightway the Spirit driveth him forth into the wilderness." The expression which Mark uses means literally "casts him forth" (historical present). Again Peter's vigorous, vivid preaching is reflected.

Mark also adds another unique note, "And he was with the wild beasts." The wilderness was a dismal place indeed, what with the doleful cries of these uncongenial companions.[4]

The Conquering Servant

We come now to the public ministry of Jesus. We shall find the scenes changing very rapidly in Mark's account. The expression "and straightway" occurs over forty times in the Gospel, giving us a gripping impression of rapid movement. If the student will underline in his Bible the occurrences in the first two chapters of "immediately," "straightway" and "forthwith"—all translations of the same Greek word[5]—it will help him to feel the rapidity of action which is the outstanding characteristic of this Gospel.

[4] Matthew indicates that the ministry of angels, mentioned by Mark, took place after the devil had left Jesus, at the close of the forty days.

[5] This Greek word (Eutheos) occurs only eighty times in the entire New Testament, and one-half of these occurrences are in the short Gospel of Mark.

In view of the multiplicity of brief incidents—there being no less than 107 paragraphs in the Revised Version of Mark's Gospel—it will be impossible for us to make a connected study of all of them. We shall have to content ourselves with noting the distinctive items.

Of the incidents in the rest of the first chapter we shall mention only two. In Mark's account of the calling of the four fishermen he alone refers to the hired servants of Zebedee, who stayed with him when his sons responded to the Master's call (v. 20). This indicates that James and John left a lucrative business to follow Jesus.

In his account of the sunset healing service—recorded in all three Synoptics—Mark gives us Peter's impression of the great crowd, in the words, "All the city was gathered together at the door" (v. 33).

The main distinction between Mark's Gospel and those by Matthew and Luke is that whereas they include large sections of teaching, his consists almost entirely of historical narrative. Out of a total of thirty parables of Jesus, Mark records only four—the sower (4:3-9), the seed growing of itself (4:26-29), the mustard seed (4:30-32), and the wicked husbandmen (12:1-9). In contrast to this Matthew has fifteen of the parables and Luke has nineteen. (John's Gospel does not use the parabolic form.) Mark's Gospel, then, is mainly narrative, whereas the other two are largely didactic.

We might note also that out of a total of thirty-six distinct miracles of Jesus recorded in the four Gospels, Mark has eighteen, Matthew twenty-one, Luke twenty, and John only eight.

In the miracles which he records Mark often gives interesting details which are not noted by the other evangelists. This attention to minute details is another outstanding characteristic of this swiftly moving record of the life of Christ.

1. THE HEALING OF THE PARALYTIC (2:1-12)

If the student will read the account of the healing of the paralytic in Matthew 9:1-8, and then read carefully Mark's account, he will see how much more graphic is the latter. The picture is drawn for us in vivid detail by this interpreter of Peter's preaching.

It is true that Luke (5:17-26) does reproduce more of Mark's details than does Matthew. But there are a number of items mentioned only by Mark. He tells us that the paralytic's couch was borne by four. His description of lowering the man through the roof is more picturesque than that of Luke. Whereas the latter simply says that they "let him down through the tiles," Mark writes, "They uncovered the roof where he was: and when they had broken it up, they let down the bed." This gives us the picture of their removing the covering of dirt and other materials on the roof and then digging up the tiles. They were certainly desperate to get the man to Jesus, and He rewarded "their faith."

2. The Conflict with the Pharisees (2:23—3:6)

Mark records the conflict between the Pharisees and Jesus over the question of Sabbath observance. This is an integral part of his presentation of Jesus as the Conquering Servant. He won in mental combats, as well as in other conflicts.

In his account of the healing of the man with the withered hand on the Sabbath day Mark adds two items of interest. He writes of Jesus, "And when he had looked round about on them with anger, being grieved at the hardening of their hearts" (3:5). He also says that the Pharisees took counsel "with the Herodians" (3:6). Ordinarily there was no love lost between these two antagonistic groups, but they got together in their opposition ot Jesus.

3. Jesus by the Seaside (3:7-12)

Most of the material in this paragraph is found only in Mark's Gospel. He indicates the widespread popularity of Jesus at this time. People flocked to Him in multitudes from Galilee, Judea, Jerusalem, Idumea, Perea, and Phoenicia ("about Tyre and Sidon"). South, east, and north all turned out to see this worker of miracles. So large did the crowd become that Jesus had to get into a boat and push away from the shore. The sick people "pressed upon him" (lit., "fell upon him") until he had to escape.

4. Jesus' Mother and Brethren (3:31-35)

All three Synoptics record the fact that the mother and brethren of Jesus wanted to speak with Him, when He was busy teaching the multitudes. Evidently they felt that they still had special claims upon His attention. Jesus reproved this attitude by telling the multitudes that His true family relations now consisted of those who do the will of God.

Mark, as usual, adds a picturesque detail which the other writers omit. He says, "and looking round on them which sat round about him" (lit., in a circle). This notice of the looks of Jesus is characteristic of Mark's Gospel. We have found it already in connection with the healing of the man with the withered hand, and we shall meet it again.[6] Peter, whose heart was broken by the grieved look of Jesus at the trial (Luke 22:61), evidently noted the changes in his Master's countenance. In his new and fascinating life of Christ, *Behold the Man* (Harpers, 1941), Kagawa has beautifully drawn attention to the looks of Jesus.

5. PARABLE OF THE SEED GROWING OF ITSELF (4:26-29)

The fourth chapter of Mark contains three of the four parables recorded in this Gospel. Of these only one is peculiar to Mark.

This parable of the seed growing secretly fits in with the emphasis of Mark's Gospel, which is upon service. It is an encouragement to all who minister to sow the gospel seed faithfully and then trust God to give the harvest.

6. THE GADARENE DEMONIAC (5:1-20)

Matthew and Luke make very little effort to describe the appearance of the demon-possessed man who met Jesus at Gerasa, a little village near the city of Gadara.[7] Matthew, indeed, mentions two demoniacs, but Mark and Luke deal only with the leading one of the two. Mark tells us what a miserable life this man was living. He had been often bound with chains and fetters, which he quickly broke, "and no man had strength to tame him." Night and day he wandered in the mountains and burial caves of that vicinity, screaming and cutting himself with sharp stones. It is a graphic portrayal of the sinner, living in the place of death and practicing self-destruction. Sin is suicide.

The reaction of the people of the region is surprising. Instead of rejoicing at the healing of the demoniac, they begged Jesus to leave at once. Evidently they preferred to have the demons around, if necessary, rather than to lose any more hogs.

[6] See Mark 8:33; 10:21, 23.
[7] Dr. Thomson discovered a ruin on the shore of the lake, now called Khersa. This is probably the Gerasa mentioned by Mark, although some claim it for Gergesa.

7. THE HEALING OF THE WOMAN WITH AN ISSUE OF BLOOD (5:25-34)

Mark's account of this miracle is much more full and graphic than the records in Matthew and Luke. He tells us that the woman "had suffered many things of many physicians, and had spent all that she had, and was nothing bettered, but rather grew worse." A comparison of these words with Luke's interpretation is very interesting. He says that she "had spent all her living upon physicians, and could not be healed of any."

These two statements are strikingly different, but they are by no means contradictory. Both say that she had spent all her money on doctors. But Luke, the physician, is careful to tell us that she had an incurable malady, for he must needs protect his profession. On the other hand, Mark simply states the bold facts from a layman's point of view. The poor woman had spent all her money for medical treatments. Instead of improving, she had grown steadily worse. And these cruel physicians had subjected her to a great deal of suffering without helping her at all. Naturally, Luke would hardly repeat that critical reflection on his profession.

8. THE DEATH OF JOHN THE BAPTIST (6:14-29)

One's man's conscience was beginning to bother him at this time. Herod Antipas[8] had beheaded John the Baptist in prison. Hearing now of Jesus' miracles he thinks that John has risen. Matthew and Mark take advantage of this opportunity to relate the story of the Baptist's death.

Mark's account is much the fuller and more vivid. He says that Herodias "set herself against him." The Greek suggests the colloquial expression "had it in for him." So she tried to kill him, but "she could not; for Herod feared John, knowing that he was a righteous and holy man, and kept him safe." This fear of John was mingled with fear of the crowd, as noted by Matthew. The two accounts can be reconciled in the light of the character of Herod, who was wicked but vacillating, and subject to the domination of his cruel wife, Herodias. She doubtless put a great deal of pressure on Herod to have

[8] Matthew and Luke call him correctly "Herod the tetrarch." Mark's designation, "Herod the king," reflects the popular Galilean usage, with which Peter would be familiar. Herod's capital, Tiberias, was in Galilee. But according to Josephus the execution of John took place in the palace-fortress at Machaerus, east of the Dead Sea.

John executed. Failing in this, she contrived a clever plot to secure her ends, employing her beautiful young daughter, Salome, as the main instrument. Of course it was highly improper for a princess to play the role of a dancing girl, but Herodias was stopping at nothing in her designs against John's life. And, like many other wicked women of history, she succeeded. One is reminded of the massacre of the Huguenots on St. Bartholomew's Day, at the insistent instigation of Catharine de Medici.

9. The Feeding of the Five Thousand (6:30-44)

It is striking that Mark, who pictures most vividly the strenuous life and tireless activity of Jesus, is also the evangelist who tells us most about the withdrawals of Jesus with His disciples toward the close of His public ministry.[9]

The first retirement appears to have taken place when the twelve apostles returned from their preaching tour. Jesus says to them—as recorded only in Mark—"Come ye yourselves apart into a desert place, and rest awhile." Summer time was coming on and it was very hot around the low-lying Sea of Galilee, so Jesus took His disciples to the mountains across the lake where it would be cooler and where He might give them some private instruction.

How much they needed a vacation is indicated by the explanation which only Mark gives, "For there were many coming and going, and they had no leisure so much as to eat." The disciples needed to get away from the crowds in order to recuperate physically and spiritually.

But vacation plans were cut short. When Jesus stepped out of the boat on the eastern shore of the lake, He found a great crowd waiting for Him. After teaching them the rest of the day, Jesus broke the five loaves and two fishes and had the disciples distribute them to the crowd.

This feeding of the five thousand is the only miracle of Jesus which is recorded by all four Gospels. As usual, Mark's account is the most picturesque. He alone mentions the green grass, and then he says the people reclined "in ranks." The Greek reads, "garden beds, garden beds." Mark has here preserved for us the beautiful picture as seen by Peter's appreciative eyes. The people with their bright oriental gar-

9 See *The Story of the New Testament*, p. 30.

ments of red and yellow reclining in groups on the green grass of the mountain side looking like a magnificent panorama of flower beds. We may thank Peter for capturing the scene and Mark for reproducing it for us.

10. THE QUESTION OF HAND WASHING (7:1-23)

We have already noted the conflict between the Pharisees and Jesus over this matter, in Matthew's account. We want here to call special attention to the interesting additions given by Mark. This happens to be an instance where Mark explains a Jewish custom for his Roman readers. Such an explanation was not at all necessary in Matthew's Gospel, which was written for the Jews. After telling of the complaint which the Pharisees made because the disciples failed to wash their hands properly before eating, Mark explains: "For the Pharisees, and all the Jews, except they wash their hands diligently, eat not, holding the tradition of the elders; and when they come from the marketplace, except they bathe themselves, they eat not; and many other things there are, which they have received to hold, washing of cups, and pots, and brazen vessels" (vs. 3, 4).

The word "diligently," which describes the way they washed their hands, is literally "with the fist." It is not necessarily implied here that the disciples ate with soiled hands. But they failed to fulfill the ceremonial custom of washing their arms up to the elbow vigorously with the fist. This was not an injunction of the Mosaic law, but of the tradition of the elders, which had come to have binding force.

11. THE HEALING OF THE DEAF MUTE (7:31-37)

This miracle, which is recorded only in this Gospel, gives us a good example of Mark's love for minute descriptive details. He tells us that Jesus "took him aside from the multitude privately, and put his fingers into his ears, and he spat, and touched his tongue; and looking up to heaven, he sighed, and saith unto him, Ephphatha, that is, Be opened." The vividness of this narrative precludes necessity for comment.

12. THE FEEDING OF THE FOUR THOUSAND (8:1-9)

Matthew and Mark both report the feeding of the four thousand, as well as the feeding of the five thousand. Critics have often contended that we have here a confusion in the use of two accounts of the same incident.

But against that we should remember that both Gospels record both incidents. And both of them record Jesus' later reference to the two feedings.[10] Furthermore, both writers are consistent in preserving a distinction between the two Greek words for basket. In all six references to the feeding of the five thousand[11] the same Greek word is used for basket, one which signifies a lunch basket. These may have been the twelve lunch baskets of the twelve apostles. In all four references to the feeding of the four thousand[12] a word is used which might be translated "kit," such as that in which a workman might carry his tools.

13. THE HEALING OF THE BLIND MAN AT BETHSAIDA (8:22-26)

This miracle, recorded only by Mark, reminds us of the healing of the deaf mute. The same vividness of detail appears. "And he took hold of the blind man by the hand, and brought him out of the village; and when he had spit on his eyes, and laid his hands upon him, he asked him, Seest thou ought?"

The reason Jesus led the man outside the village and commanded him not to go back into the town was probably that He now wished to avoid publicity during these closing days of His ministry. He wanted time for instructing His disciples.

14. THE HEALING OF THE EPILEPTIC BOY (9:14-29).

After the transfiguration, described in all three Synoptics, Jesus came down from the mountain with Peter, James and John. On the way down He mentioned again His coming sufferings at Jerusalem.

Mark adds a very interesting observation at this point. He says, "And straightway all the multitude, when they saw him, were greatly amazed, and running to him saluted him" (v. 15). Evidently some of the afterglow of the transfiguration still lingered on His face, so noticeable that it caused great excitement on the part of the crowd.

As soon as Jesus drew near, a man fell on his knees before Him and begged Him to heal his son. The boy is described by Matthew as being "epileptic" (Matt. 17:15). Mark's account, as usual, is the fullest of the three. He tells that Jesus

[10] Matthew 16:9, 10; Mark 8:19, 20.
[11] Matthew 14:20; 16:9; Mark 6:43; 8:19; Luke 9:17; John 6:13.
[12] Matthew 15:37; 16:10; Mark 8:8, 20.

questioned how long this condition had existed, and that the father finished his reply by saying, "But if thou canst do anything, have compassion on us, and help us."

The Greek text of Jesus' answer is very striking. He picked up the man's words and threw them back to him as a challenge. Literally, "as to the 'If thou canst,' all things can to the one who believes" (v. 23). The question of ability was on the father's side, not on the side of Jesus.

While He was seeking to teach the man this important lesson of faith, the curious crowd was running up to watch the antics of the boy. Seeing this, Jesus immediately cast the unclean spirit out of the demoniac.

When the disciples asked Jesus why they were unable to help the boy, He told them that their lack of power was due to lack of prayer. Prayer brings the omnipotence of heaven to bear on the problems of earth.

15. THE MISTAKEN ZEAL OF JOHN (9:38-50)

Mark and Luke tell of John's report to Jesus concerning a man that was casting out demons in Christ's name. Because he would not join their company the apostle ordered him to stop his activities. Jesus rebuked this display of a narrow, sectarian spirit, so unlike that of the Master himself. Then he went on to give some further teaching on the point.

One of the favorite contentions of the extreme liberals is that we ought to get back past the theology of Paul and of John to "the simple teachings of Jesus." Some who have thoughtlessly taken up the cry seem to forget that the strongest teaching on hell fire anywhere in the New Testament is to be found in these teachings of Jesus.

Writers have made much of the fact that the Greek word Hades—wrongly translated "hell" in the King James Version—does not necessarily mean a place of punishment. That is so. But Jesus here uses the term "Gehenna" (vs. 44, 46, 47), which was applied to the constantly burning place of refuse outside Jerusalem—the valley of the son of Hinnom mentioned by the prophets of the Old Testament.

The Greek word translated "unquenchable" (v. 44) is *asbestos,* which we have taken over into English for a noninflammable substance.

16. JESUS AND CHILDREN (10:13-16)

Sometimes the impression is given that Jesus was an ascetic, an unsociable sort of person. Just the opposite is indicated by the pictures of Him given in the Gospels. He did what most people fail to do; that is, He preserved a proper balance between the spiritual, intellectual, physical and social phases of life. In this, as in all else, He is our perfect example.

The disciples, in this incident, took an attitude that we have seen expressed by religious leaders in our day. They did not want children around, consuming time that ought to be given to more "important" matters. But Jesus rebuked this attitude. He said that unless we had the humility and simplicity of a child we could not enter the kingdom of God. Then, Mark adds one of his unique touches, when he tells us that Jesus took the children "in his arms" and blessed them.

17. THE BARREN FIG TREE (11:19-25)

Both Matthew and Mark relate the incident of the cursing of the barren fig tree by Jesus, and both indicate that it was intended as a striking object lesson on faith. But Mark adds an important saying of Jesus at the close, "And whensoever ye stand praying, forgive, if ye have aught against any one; that your Father also which is in heaven may forgive you your trespasses." An unforgiving spirit is incompatible with a successful prayer life.

18. THE FIRST COMMANDMENT (12:28-34)

Matthew and Mark tell how Jesus, after being questioned by the Pharisees, Herodians and Sadducees, was asked by a scribe to state what was the first commandment of the law. Jesus answered that love of God and of one's neighbor was the heart of the law.

Mark alone adds the reaction of the scribe, who comprehended the truth that love is a more vital matter than ceremonial sacrifices. Because he saw this truth, which is hinted at by David and various Old Testament prophets, this scribe was close to understanding and accepting the new Christian religion.

19. THE POOR WIDOW'S FARTHING (12:41-44)

Mark and Luke record the incident of the widow's gift in the treasury. Jesus sat down nearby to observe the attitudes of those who gave. He saw the rich, with considerable show, but little feeling, toss gold and silver coins into the box. But a poor widow came along and with devoted sacrifice cast in two mites, all that she had.

Jesus said she gave more than the wealthy, with their munificent gifts. In this He laid down the basic principle that our giving is not measured by how much we give, but by how much we have left after giving.

20. THE OLIVET DISCOURSE (chapter 13)

Tuesday of Passion Week seems to have been one of the busiest days in Jesus' ministry. The Synoptics record more of His doings for this day than for any other.

After a busy morning in the temple Jesus left with His disciples. When they called His attention to the beauty and grandeur of the building, He predicted its destruction. Wending their way down across the Kidron Valley and up the slopes of the Mount of Olives the group came to a resting place opposite the temple. The disciples then asked Him when His prediction was to be fulfilled, and what signs would precede it. In answer to their questions Jesus gave His outstanding prophetic discourse.

Jesus told them first that many false Christs would arise (v. 6). History records their names, ancient and modern. Then He told them that there would be wars and rumors of wars (vs. 7, 8). That description holds good for the entire Christian age. He next said that His followers would be persecuted (vs. 9-13); and that has happened somewhere almost all the time since. Only those who endured to the end would be saved.

Then Jesus proceeded to answer their question definitely. As recorded by Luke, He said, "When ye shall see Jerusalem compassed with armies, then know that the desolation thereof is nigh" (Luke 21:20). This desolation took place in A.D. 70, when Jerusalem was destroyed by the Roman armies under Titus. Eusebius (A.D. 326) tells us in his *Ecclesiastical History* (III, 5) that the Christians in Jerusalem left that city, during its last siege, and fled to Pella in the mountains, east of the Jordan. Thus they escaped the terrible massacre that took place when the Romans entered the city.

Matthew and Mark give another sign, "The abomination of desolation, spoken of by Daniel the prophet," standing in the holy place. Some commentators refer this to the emperor's bust on the standards of the Roman legions. This makes it parallel with Luke's account. Others refer Luke's prediction to the destruction of Jerusalem in A.D. 70, and Matthew's to the end of this age.

Perhaps the matter is best settled by introducing the telescopic feature of prophecy. Many of the predictions of the Old Testament prophets had a near, partial fulfillment and also a distant, complete fulfillment. It is thus with many of the Messianic prophecies. It seems most reasonable to adopt that interpretation here. These predictions of Jesus referred first to A.D. 70, but in their final and full significance they reach forward to the end of this age.

Again Christ predicts the rise of false Christs and false prophets (vs. 21-23), the many isms of ancient and modern times. He then goes on to mention signs in the heavenly bodies (vs. 24, 25) as immediately preceding the coming of the Son of man. He gives the parable of the fig tree putting forth her leaves as a sign that summer is approaching (vs. 28-31), and states that no one knows the hour of His return. The closing admonition is to watch carefully and constantly, even as the porter keeps always ready for his master's return (vs. 33-37).

It seems that the reasonable way to interpret this chapter is to hold that Jesus first answered the question of the disciples as to the destruction of the temple (vs. 5-23), and then went on to answer their second question (Matt. 24:3) as to the signs of the end of the age (vs. 24-37).

The Suffering Servant

The chief priests and scribes had been seeking an opportunity to seize Jesus and kill Him. The occasion presented itself as a result of the offer of Judas to betray his Master. When we come to the scene in the garden we find an interesting incident which is recorded only by Mark.

1. "A CERTAIN YOUNG MAN" (14:51, 52)

The story of the young man who followed Jesus to the Garden of Gethsemane and was almost arrested with Him has caused considerable comment. It seems to us difficult to account for the presence of this brief reference except on the basis that John Mark, the author of this Gospel, was the young man of the story.

If the last supper was eaten in John Mark's home, it would seem plausible that Judas Iscariot would first seek Jesus there. Failing in that, he turned toward the garden where Jesus often prayed. Naturally, young John Mark would hasten to warn Jesus of His danger. But he was almost caught himself, escaping only by leaving his night robe in the hands of his would-be captor.

If this was John Mark, what would be more natural than that he should insert this in his own account of Christ's life? It would be an incident which he alone would treasure in his memory.

2. "AND PETER" (16:7)

In the command of the angel at the sepulcher to the women to go and tell Jesus' disciples that He was risen, Mark says significantly, "his disciples and Peter." This is another interesting corroboration of the ancient tradition that this Gospel records Peter's preaching.

How Peter must have treasured those two words in the women's report! They would give him a sweet anticipation of Jesus' words of forgiveness, and would mitigate the bitterness of his soul for denying his Lord. Peter learned, what every disciple of the Master experiences, that our Christ is "most wondrous kind."

III. THE SON OF MAN

The Gospel of Luke

Introduction

The unanimous tradition of the early church ascribes our Third Gospel to Luke, the companion of Paul. Irenaeus writing at about A.D. 185, says, "And Luke the follower of Paul, put in a book the gospel that was preached by him."[1] This would suggest that Luke's Gospel carries with it some of the authority of the Apostle Paul.

The *Anti-Marcionite Prologue to St. Luke's Gospel* preserves an interesting tradition held by the church between A.D. 150 and 180. It says, "Luke is a Syrian of Antioch, a physician by calling, who has become a disciple of the apostles and afterward, having followed Paul until his martyrdom, and having served the Lord without remission, wifeless and childless, in the eighty-fourth year of his age he, full of the Holy Spirit, fell asleep in Boeotia. This man, when there were already Gospels in existence, namely, that according to Matthew which was recorded in Judea and that according to Mark in Italy, having been moved by the Holy Spirit in the district of Achaia, composed the whole of this Gospel."[2]

This excerpt from the second century mentions several points of interest. It says, first, that Luke was a Gentile living in Antioch. Eusebius and Jerome (fourth century) also state that Luke's home town was Antioch. Certainly Antioch plays an important part in the Book of Acts, which was written by Luke.

Then, again, it tells us that Matthew wrote his Gospel in Judea, Mark in Italy, and Luke in Greece (Achaia). This fits in well with the nature of each of these Gospels. Matthew wrote for the Jews, Mark for the Romans and Luke for the Greeks.

[1] Cartledge, Samuel A., *A Conservative Introduction to the New Testament* (Zondervan, 1938), pp. 71, 72.
[2] Major, Manson, and Wright, *op. cit.*, pp. 252, 253.

Luke is mentioned by name only three times in the New Testament. In Philemon 24 Paul speaks of him as a "fellow worker." In Colossians 4:14 he refers to him as "the beloved physician." In Second Timothy 4:11, his last epistle, he says, "Only Luke is with me." Luke was a companion of Paul in his travels, apparently his attending physician in prison, and his closest associate during Paul's last days on earth. His connection with Paul in the missionary work among the Gentiles will be noted in our study of Acts.

Luke wrote to the Greeks to present Jesus as the Son of Man. He shows Him to be the perfect Man, the compassionate Savior, the Friend of sinners, of the poor, of children. We should lose some of the most beautiful touches in the portrait of Jesus if we were to be deprived of the Gospel According to Luke.

The Preface of Luke's Gospel (1:1-4) tells us how he came to write it. We shall quote it in full: "Forasmuch as many have taken in hand to draw up a narrative concerning those matters which have been fulfilled among us, even as they delivered them unto us, who from the beginning were eyewitnesses and ministers of the word, it seemed good to me also, having traced the course of all things accurately from the first, to write unto thee in order, most excellent Theophilus; that thou mightest know the certainty concerning the things wherein thou wast instructed."

This Preface tells us a number of things. It informs us, first, that "many" lives of Christ had already been written when Luke undertook to write his Gospel. Then it suggests that Luke consulted carefully with eyewitnesses before beginning his work. With the help of these written and oral sources of information he traced the course of Christ's life accurately from its beginning. He further tells us that he desired to write an orderly, as well as an authentic, life of Christ. Finally, he dedicates his book to Theophilus, perhaps his wealthy patron. The title "most excellent" would suggest that Theophilus held an honorable position. Luke also intimates that Theophilus was a catechumen, who had just recently been instructed in the Christian way. It is Luke's purpose to confirm his faith by giving him an authentic historical account of the beginnings of Christianity, in the life and death of Jesus Christ.

The Sending of the Son of Man

Luke begins the body of his Gospel, as he suggested in his Preface, by going back to the very first things connected with the life of Jesus. Since John the Baptist was the forerunner of Christ, Luke records the story of his birth.

It is very obvious that the first two chapters of this Gospel are written from the standpoint of Mary, the mother of Jesus and near-aunt of John the Baptist. The suggestion has been made that Luke probably secured his materials for these infancy narratives while Paul was spending two years in prison at Caesarea (Acts 24:27). It seems reasonable, in the light of his Preface, to suppose that Luke visited the aged mother of Jesus and that he heard first-hand from her lips these facts which were so precious in her memory. Some of them she may never have told any man before. But since Luke was a physician, it would be easier for her to talk freely and frankly to him of the sacred scenes connected with the birth of her son, Jesus. It would be natural, too, for her to tell him about the birth of John. Luke alone gives us any of this information.

1. THE ANNOUNCEMENT OF THE BIRTH OF JOHN (1:5-25)

The lamp of God had become very dim in the temple, as in the days of Samuel, the first prophet. Now, when again "the word of the Lord was precious" (1 Sam. 3:1)—the light of prophecy having been extinguished for some four hundred years—God raised up the last of the prophets to proclaim the actual appearance of the Messiah. A new age had dawned.

In spite of the prevalent hypocrisy in the religion of the Jews at this time, there were some faithful souls in Israel. Zacharias, the priest, and his wife, Elisabeth, were a devout couple. They had evidently been praying for a child. While Zacharias was fulfilling his duties in the temple, an angel announced to him the coming birth of a son, who was to be called John.

2. THE ANNOUNCEMENT OF THE BIRTH OF JESUS (1:26-56)

Six months later the angel Gabriel appeared to Mary, a virgin living in Nazareth and betrothed to Joseph. He told her that she was to be the mother of the Messiah, Israel's King. When she expressed her bewilderment as to how this could come to pass, the angel informed her that it would be by the supernatural conception of the Holy Spirit. Hence her child, Jesus, would be holy and would be called the Son of God. He also told her of the coming birth of John.

Mary thereupon took a trip southward into the hill country of Judea. When she entered the home of Elisabeth, the latter greeted her as "the mother of my Lord." This caused Mary to break out in the strains of the beautiful *Magnificat* (1:46-55), a spontaneous psalm very similar to Hannah's song (1 Sam. 2:1-10).

The *Magnificat*—so-called from the first word in the Latin version of it—is one of five poems in these first two chapters of Luke's Gospel. The *Benedictus* of Zacharias (1:68-79) is similar in length. The *Nunc Dimittis* of Simeon (2:29-32) is much shorter. Added to these are the *Gloria in Excelsis* of the angels (2:14), and what is known as the *Ave Maria* (1:28-33).

The presence of these poems in this Gospel are evidence that Luke was a poet, or at least a great lover of poetry. This man who was a physician, poet, author, historian, lover of children, a chivalrous gentleman and a Christian scholar, was probably one of the most beautiful characters in the primitive church. To this is due the "idyllic charm, domestic tenderness, purity and simplicity, the deeply devotional spirit"[3] of these opening chapters of his Gospel.

3. THE BIRTH OF JOHN THE BAPTIST (1:57-80)

When Elisabeth's son was born, she wanted to call him "John." Since the relatives could not understand the choice, they decided to ask the father. Taking a writing tablet, Zacharias wrote the emphatic words, "His name is John." Immediately his dumbness—due to his previous doubting— was healed, and he broke forth into a psalm of praise to God for visiting His people. It is truly a remarkable poem, both for its use of the Old Testament Scriptures and for its predictions of Christ's ministry.

4. THE BIRTH OF JESUS (2:1-7)

Micah had predicted that Christ should be born in Bethlehem of Judea. But Mary and Joseph were living at Nazareth, in Galilee. How was the Scripture to be fulfilled?

[3] *Mission and Message of Jesus*, p. 256.

The answer is contained in the enrollment, or census-taking, ordered by the emperor. It was stipulated that every man must return to his ancestral home. This was to facilitate the business of making it possible to take the census by families. So we find Joseph and Mary, along with the other descendants of King David, moving southward toward Bethlehem, five miles south of Jerusalem.

Here they found the village already filled to overflowing with travelers. Finally they sought refuge in a stable, and there Jesus was born and laid in a manger.

5. The Visit of the Shepherds (2: 8-20)

None of the great ones of the earth bowed at the manger, nor did any heralds proclaim the birth of the King of kings. But angels bent low over a nearby hillside of Judea to disclose the wondrous fact to humble shepherds. That night in the city of David was born a Savior, Christ the Lord.

The shepherds were the first outsiders to see the Christ child, and they became the first heralds of the good tidings. Humble lay preachers they, but the rabbis and doctors of the law were busied with other matters.

6. The First Visit to the Temple (2: 22-39)

At His circumcision, eight days after His birth, the child was formally named Jesus. When He was forty days old, His parents presented Him in the temple. Like Hannah of old, they presented their child to the Lord.

A devout Israelite named Simeon entered the temple while they were there. Taking the infant Jesus in his arms, the venerable saint blessed God for the opportunity of seeing the Messiah, and predicted that He would be a light to the Gentiles. Then he warned Mary of her coming sorrows. At the same time a widow eighty-four years old, the Prophetess Anna, drew near. She likewise gave thanks to God and was speaking continually (imperfect tense) of Him to those who "were looking for the redemption of Jerusalem." There was a nucleus of devout souls even then, God's faithful remnant in Israel.

7. The Second Visit to the Temple (2: 41-51)

The only information that we have concerning the child Jesus from His first visit at the age of forty days until His second visit at the age of twelve years is contained in the statement, "And the child grew, and waxed strong, filled with wisdom (Greek, becoming full of wisdom): and the grace of God was upon him" (v. 40). Luke, as a physician, would be interested in the growth of the child.

At twelve years of age the Jewish boy became a Son of the Law (Ben-Torah). From thenceforth he was himself responsible for the observance of his religious duties. Jesus had now reached that age and was taken up to the temple for the annual Passover, which every adult male was required to attend.

As soon as the festival ceremonies were ended, Joseph and Mary started back northward to Nazareth. When evening came they began to look for Jesus. After searching all through the caravan and failing to find Him among their relatives and neighbors, they turned sorrowfully back to Jerusalem. On the third day they found Him in the temple, astonishing the lawyers with His keen questions and penetrating answers.

When His mother chided Him with thoughtlessness toward them, He reproved her gently for seeking Him elsewhere and said, "Knew ye not that I must be in my Father's house?"[4] Though they failed to understand, and so to appreciate, the significance of His words, Jesus went obediently home with them and "was subject unto them." He thus became a pattern for all Christian youth.

The closing verse of the chapter states that "Jesus advanced in wisdom and stature, and in favor with God and men." That is, He developed mentally, physically, spiritually and socially. He was an example of a truly normal development of a young person during the period of adolescence.

8. The Preaching of John the Baptist (3:1-20)

A unique feature of Luke's Gospel is his reference to contemporary history. Of all the writers of the New Testament, Luke is pre-eminently the historian. Archaeological research has confirmed his reliability in this field, as we shall find more particularly when we come to the study of Acts.

Luke begins his Gospel by giving us the historical setting "in the days of Herod, king of Judaea" (1:5). He tells us that

---

[4] The Greek reads, "in the things of my Father." The use of this expression in the papyri seems to indicate that it should be translated "house" rather than "business."

the birth of Jesus occurred at the time the census was being taken "when Quirinius was governor of Syria" (2:2). And then he gives a very full historical dating for the beginning of the ministry of John:

"Now in the fifteenth year of the reign of Tiberius Caesar, Pontius Pilate being governor of Judea, and Herod being tetrarch of Galilee, and his brother Philip tetrarch of the region of Iturea and Trachonitis, and Lysanias tetrarch of Abilene, in the high-priesthood of Annas and Caiaphas" (3: 1, 2).

We have already noted that Luke was a Gentile—the only Gentile writer of a book of the New Testament. It is not surprising, then, that he should give more attention than the other evangelists to the Gentile world. We found one such reference in the *Nunc Dimittis* of Simeon. And here, in the quotation from Isaiah, Luke adds what Matthew and Mark omit, "all flesh shall see the salvation of God."

9. THE BAPTISM OF JESUS (3:21, 22)

Luke's account of the baptism of Jesus by John is briefer than that of the other two Synoptics, but he adds one item of interest. He says that Jesus was praying when the dove descended upon Him.

Luke's Gospel is pre-eminently the Gospel of prayer. Altogether it contains some twenty references to prayer. Luke is the only one who mentions that Jesus was praying at His baptism, that He prayed all night before choosing His twelve apostles (6:12), that He prayed at Caesarea Philippi (9:18), that He was praying when He was transfigured (9:29), and that it was His praying which led the disciples to ask Him to teach them to pray (11:1).

Luke alone gives us the age of Jesus at the beginning of His public ministry. He says, "And Jesus himself, when he began to teach, was about thirty years of age" (3:23). This was the age at which the priest and Levites were to begin their service in the sanctuary.

10. THE GENEALOGY OF JESUS (3:23-38)

Whereas Matthew's genealogy of Jesus begins with Abraham and descends through David to Christ, Luke starts with Jesus and ascends to the fountainhead of human history,

"Adam, the son of God." Jesus Christ, "the last Adam" (1 Cor. 15:45), is the head of a new race, the Christians.

The Service of the Son of Man

After His temptation, Jesus "returned in the power of the Spirit into Galilee." This expression, which suggests a new power in His life, occurs only in Luke.

1. THE REJECTION AT NAZARETH (4:16-30)

Luke also gives us an interesting account of the reception accorded Jesus the first time He returned to His home town after His baptism. Taking His accustomed place in the synagogue on the Sabbath day, He offered to read the Scripture lesson. A selection from the Law and one from the Prophets was read each Sabbath. Jesus chose the latter and read the beautiful words at the opening of the sixty-first chapter of Isaiah. In accordance with Jewish custom He stood while He read, out of reverence for the Scriptures, and then sat down to preach.

The gracious language of this passage from Isaiah was matched by "the words of grace" which fell from His lips. Yet, in spite of their wonder at His message, the people began to say, "Is not this Joseph's son?" Sensing their attitude, Jesus reminded them of the old proverb, "No prophet is acceptable in his own country." He then cited the cases of Elijah and Elisha in their ministries to Gentiles. This infuriated His townspeople, so that they attempted to kill Him, but He escaped their hands.

2. THE MIRACULOUS DRAUGHT OF FISHES (5:1-11)

In connection with the call of the four fishermen to leave their vocation and become fishers of men, Luke relates this story of the large catch of fish. Jesus had used Peter's boat for a pulpit, and when He had finished He proceeded to reimburse the owner very handsomely. In spite of the vain effort of the night before, the seines were now filled to overflowing. Peter and Andrew had to call on their partners, James and John, to help them haul in their net.

The effect of this miracle upon Peter was similar to that which often attends a display of divine power. Simon fell on his knees before Jesus, crying out, "Depart from me; for I am a sinful man, O Lord." Christ's presence brings conviction for sin.

3. THE HEALING OF THE LEPER (5:12-16)

This miracle, which is recorded in all three Synoptics, reveals the faith of the leper that Jesus could, if He would, heal him. Jesus assured the man that He was just as willing as He was able.

Mark and Luke both note the popular excitement which resulted from this miracle. But Luke alone tells us that Jesus "withdrew himself into the wilderness, and prayed." We wonder how many unrecorded instances of this kind took place.

4. THE RAISING OF THE WIDOW'S SON AT NAIN (7:11-17)

Nain is a little village lying between Gilboa and Shunem on the hillside overlooking the plain of Esdraelon. There is still only one road leading to it, and this runs past an ancient cemetery, located some distance from the gate of the city.

As Jesus came along this road and drew near to the city gate He met a funeral procession moving out toward the cemetery. Behind the casket walked a heartbroken mother. Her husband had died some time before, and now her one remaining support and comfort, her only son, had been taken from her. Life had suddenly gone black, and blank.

Jesus took in the whole situation at a glance. Immediately He was gripped with compassion (aorist tense). Speaking a word of comfort to the mother, He stepped up to the casket and stopped the procession. Of course it is against the law to stop a funeral procession, but the law of death had met a higher power, the Law of Life. Soon the young man was in the arms of his mother, who was now weeping for joy.

How often must that mother have recounted the wonderful incident to her neighbors and friends. And then, after describing the heartache of the death, the funeral, the last glimpse of her only son, she would add, "But Jesus came along that day, and after that everything was different."

5. JESUS AND THE WOMAN WHO LOVED MUCH (7:36-50)

This incident, which is recorded only by Luke, should not be confused with the anointing by Mary of Bethany, recorded in the other three Gospels, which took place shortly before the crucifixion. The fact that the host bears the same name in both cases argues nothing, for Simon was a very common name at that time in Palestine. Two of Jesus' twelve apostles were named Simon.

As Jesus was reclining at the table in the house of Simon the Pharisee a woman of the street came in and stood weeping at His feet. She was not hindered from entering, for in the East at such times of festivity open house is kept and the people in the street look on freely.

As she wept, the woman washed the feet of Jesus with her tears and wiped them with her own hair. Then she anointed them with a perfumed ointment which she had brought with her. Here was another woman whose heart was broken, but from another cause. Perhaps some recent words of Jesus had convicted her deeply for her sinful life, and now she poured upon Him tears of repentance and love.

Sensing the critical attitude of His host, Jesus told the parable of the two debtors, which taught that those who have been forgiven much love much. Then, turning to the woman He spoke gracious words of forgiveness and bade her go in peace.

6. The Women Who Followed Jesus (8:1-3)

Luke gives more attention than any of the other evangelists to the part played by women in the life of Jesus. He mentions several women—Mary Magdalene, Joanna the wife of Chuza Herod's steward, Susanna, "and many others . . . which ministered unto them of their substance." Jesus and the twelve had women attendants to wait on them and supply them with food, and doubtless to wash and mend their clothes.

7. The Inhospitable Samaritans (9:51-56)

The time for the close of Jesus' public ministry was drawing near. So, "he stedfastly set his face to go to Jerusalem."

The account of this last journey of Jesus from Galilee to Jerusalem appears to cover the next ten chapters of Luke's Gospel (9:51—19:28). This section is sometimes called "the Great Interpolation," because so much of the material is peculiar to Luke. It is also spoken of as the "Perean Ministry," since the incidents recorded took place largely in Perea, east of the Jordan, through which Jesus was passing on His way from Galilee down to Jerusalem.

Jesus first tried to go straight southward through Samaria. He sent ahead some messengers to make provision for lodging the group of disciples. But the Samaritans, who were hostile to the Jews and often refused them passage through their territory, would not receive Him because He was headed for Jerusalem.

Immediately James and John felt the flame of indignation kindle within them. They wanted to call down fire from heaven, as did Elijah of old, and destroy these enemies of Christ. Perhaps this incident won for them the nickname, "Sons of Thunder," which Jesus gave them.

But the spirit they showed was foreign to the spirit of the Savior. He rebuked them and went to another village, a Jewish one this time.[5] Probably John never forgot the lesson he learned here. The Son of Thunder later became the great Apostle of Love.

8. The Mission of the Seventy (10:1-20)

Luke has already recorded, in common with Matthew and Mark, the sending forth of the twelve; now he adds the mission of the seventy. It has been suggested that whereas the twelve symbolized the twelve tribes of Israel, the seventy symbolized the nations of the world. Certain it is that Luke thinks more about Gentile salvation than do the other evangelists.

9. The Parable of the Good Samaritan (10:25-37)

This parable and that of the prodigal son are two outstanding ones which are found only in the Gospel of Luke. They both reflect Luke's interest in the compassion of Jesus and in the salvation of the lost.

We may be grateful to the Jewish lawyer who asked Jesus to define his neighbor, for otherwise we might have missed a most beautiful illustration of Jesus' mission to this world. Like the good Samaritan He came where we were, in His incarnation. The wine of cleansing and the oil of healing are pictures of His redeeming love for humanity, which also leads Him to provide for all our needs.

[5] The Greek word used here for "another" (*heteros*) signifies another of a different kind.

But we should not miss the application which Jesus gave. Anyone who is in need, and whom we can help, is our neighbor.

10. MARTHA AND MARY (10:38-42)

The home of Martha and Mary was a favorite haven of rest for Jesus, where He enjoyed calm and quiet in the fellowship of those who loved and understood Him.

But one day when Jesus stopped there a ripple appeared on the surface. Evidently a number of the disciples were invited to the home for dinner, and Martha was "distracted [Greek] by much serving." She was hurried and worried and flurried, as she hustled and bustled about.

Meanwhile, her sister Mary was so utterly absorbed in listening to the wonderful words of Jesus that she had forgotten entirely about dinner. Martha rather petulantly asked Jesus to command Mary to help her. The Master reproved her gently, reminding her that spiritual things come first.

Too much should not be deduced from this incident, however. Christianity is not a religion of Buddhistic contemplation, nor of Hindu denial of life. It is a life lived in the service of love. If we follow Jesus' example, we shall not go astray.

11. THE PARABLE OF THE IMPORTUNATE FRIEND (11:5-13)

The eleventh and eighteenth chapters of Luke give special attention to Jesus' teaching on prayer. Here we find three parables on prayer not recorded elsewhere.

The eleventh chapter begins by telling us that at the close of one of Jesus' seasons of prayer the disciples said, "Lord, teach us to pray." In response to the request Jesus gave them the so-called Lord's Prayer.

Then He went on to give them this parable of the man who knocked on his neighbor's door at midnight until his friend finally gave him the three loaves of bread. If we do not receive at once what we ask for in prayer, we are to keep on knocking until the answer comes.

12. THE PARABLE OF THE RICH FOOL (12:16-21)

One day a man came to Jesus with the request that He make his brother divide the inheritance with him. As a warning against a greedy grasping after material things, Jesus gave this parable, recorded only by Luke.

Here was a man who was worried because he had so much of this world's wealth that he hardly knew what to do with it. Instead of seeking to benefit the poor, he decided to store for the future.

But he was forgetting his eternal future. He was foolish because he thought his soul could feed forever on wheat and barley. He was foolish because he made no provision for eternity. He planned his future without reference to God, but he found that God had the last word.

13. THE PARABLE OF THE BARREN FIG TREE (13:6-9)

It is evident that this parable had reference to the Jewish nation, as in the case of the barren fig tree which Jesus cursed on Passion Week. The three years may refer to the three years of Jesus' public ministry. A little more time would be extended, but soon the nation would be cut off.

14. HEALINGS ON THE SABBATH DAY (chapters 13, 14)

Luke alone records the healing of the hunchbacked woman (13:10-17) and of the man with the dropsy (14:1-6), both of which occurred on the Sabbath day, one in the synagogue and the other in the home of a Pharisee. In both cases the Pharisees were incensed by his act.

15. THREE PARABLES OF THE LOST (chapter 15)

The fifteenth chapter of Luke is one of the most interesting in this Gospel. Here we find the three parables of the lost sheep, the lost coin and the lost son. The last of these, better known as the prodigal son, is one of the most striking of all the parables told by Jesus. The theme of these three is the salvation of the lost, which was Luke's central interest.

The parable of the lost sheep illustrates Christ's seeking after the lost of humanity. The parable of the lost coin suggests the ministry of the Holy Spirit in this age, diligently searching out every lost sinner. The parable of the prodigal son pictures the Father waiting eagerly for the return of His wandering, wayward child.

These three parables also illustrate the two phases of salvation which we noted in the closely connected miracles of healing the woman with the issue of blood and raising Jairus' daughter. It is true that Christ and the Holy Spirit are seeking constantly to save the lost. But it is also true that every sinner must "come to himself" and return to God.

16. Two Parables About the Rich (chapter 16)

The sixteenth chapter of Luke contains two parables, both of which center around a verse inserted between them, "And the Pharisees, who were lovers of money, heard all these things; and they scoffed at him" (v. 14).

a. *The Parable of the Unjust Steward* (16:1-13). This parable is one of the most difficult to interpret of all those told by Jesus. On the surface it seems beset with almost insuperable ethical problems. To some it has seemed that Jesus is here condoning dishonesty.

In the first place, it should be made clear that the lord referred to in verse eight as commending the action of the steward is not Christ but "his lord" (Revised Version); that is, the steward's master.

In the second place, the point which Jesus is making (in verse eight) is that the sons of this world are more prudent in taking care of their material interests, than are the sons of light in caring for their spiritual interests. In other words, Christians are not as carefully concerned about things relating to their eternal future and their heavenly home as are sinners about the things of this life.

Finally, we should not fail to notice that Jesus concludes this talk by emphasizing the importance of faithfulness in all things. Not only should the Christian invest his money in spiritual securities (v. 9), but he should be faithful in the discharge of his responsibilities both in material and in spiritual matters.

b. *The Parable of the Rich Man and Lazarus* (16:19-31). The story of the rich man and Lazarus reveals Jesus' attitude toward the doctrine of hell. Those who scoff at the idea of hell are forced to the position that Jesus did not know what He was talking about when He spoke of fiery torment. Personally, we would rather heed the words of Jesus and pass warning on to others.

The closing words of Jesus, "If they hear not Moses and the prophets, neither will they be persuaded, if one rise from the dead," find striking confirmation in the case of the other Lazarus, whom Jesus raised from the dead. Instead of believing, the Jewish rulers wanted to put Lazarus to death because he was causing many to accept Jesus (John 12:10, 11).

17. THE TEN LEPERS (17:12-19)

Luke alone tells the story of the ten lepers who were cleansed by Jesus. Only one returned to thank Jesus, "and he was a Samaritan." This Samaritan and the good Samaritan of the parable are characteristic of Luke's interest in the Gentiles.

18. TWO PARABLES ON PRAYER (chapter 18)

a. *The Parable of the Importunate Widow* (18:1-8) This parable, sometimes called that of the unjust judge, was intended to teach the same lesson as the earlier story about the importunate friend at midnight. They both fit in with Luke's emphasis upon prayer.

The unrighteous judge, who cared for neither God nor man, decided to heed the insistent pleas of the importunate widow, "lest she wear me out by her continual coming." How much more, said Jesus, will a righteous God avenge the cause of His own children who cry daily to Him for help.

b. *The Parable of the Pharisee and the Publican* (18:9-14). After telling the first parable to encourage His disciples to pray always, and not faint (v. 1), Jesus went on to give another one especially for the benefit of those who were self-righteous and self-sufficient.

A proud Pharisee took his place in the temple where he could be seen and heard by everyone. He then proceeded to pray "with himself," rather than to God, something like the eminent preacher of whom it was written in the newspaper one Monday morning that he "prayed the most beautiful prayer ever offered to a Boston audience."

After thanking God that he was not like the rest of mankind, and reminding the Lord that He was a very good fellow—really a very religious personage—he swept out in his long robes, feeling that he had doubtless made a very good impression on his contemporaries.

Meanwhile, there stood over in a far corner a publican, upon whom the Pharisee had cast contemptuous eyes. Acknowledging his spiritual bankruptcy, he smote his breast and groaned out, "God, be thou merciful to me a sinner."

The Pharisee had asked for nothing, and he got it. The publican had prayed for the most essential thing in the world, divine forgiveness, and he received it. "Blessed," said Jesus, "are the poor in spirit; for theirs is the kingdom of heaven."

19. ZACCHAEUS AND JESUS (19:1-10)

It happened in Jericho. The chief tax collector of the city, a wealthy man named Zacchaeus, had heard that Jesus was passing through town. Being too short to see over the shoulders of the crowd, he swallowed his pride and climbed a tree.

As Zacchaeus looked down on the parade from his perch in the tree, a strange thing happened. Jesus stopped right underneath the sycomore, looked up at Zacchaeus, and then told him to hurry and come down, as He wanted to go home with him for the night.

But some of the folks did not like Jesus' choice of a lodging. So before letting Jesus into his house, Zacchaeus straightened things out, right there on the street—whereupon Jesus pronounced him saved.

And then Jesus uttered those significant words which may well be taken as the key text of Luke's Gospel, "For the Son of man came to seek and to save that which was lost" (19:10).

20. THE PARABLE OF THE POUNDS (19:11-28)

Jesus and His disciples were now only about seventeen miles from Jerusalem, at Jericho. Some of His followers were rather excitedly looking forward to the prospects of His setting up His kingdom when He arrived at the holy city.

To offset this false hope, Jesus told the parable of a certain nobleman who "went into a far country, to receive for himself a kingdom, and to return." He thus sought to prepare His followers for His ascension, and for the interval of time that must elapse before His return as King.

The main lesson of the parable, of course, is the necessity of making good use of our time in faithful, zealous service for our Master until He returns. Those who are earnestly and eagerly caring for His interests will be rewarded when He sits upon His throne.

Matthew has a similar parable, that of the talents (25:14-30), told at a later time. It does not seem unreasonable that Jesus should have told two nearly alike, for a preacher often retells an illustration in slightly different form.

The Sacrifice of the Son of Man

The story of the beginning of the end commences in Luke with the statement that "Satan entered into Judas who was called Iscariot" (22:3). Whereupon Judas held a consultation with the Jewish rulers and promised to betray Jesus into their hands.

1. JESUS' WARNING TO PETER (22:31-34)

Luke alone records how Jesus gave a personal word of warning to Peter that he was to undergo temptation. It is an interesting disclosure of what happens behind the curtain, and reminds us of the opening scene in the Book of Job.

"Simon, Simon, behold Satan asked to have you, that he might sift you as wheat: but I made supplication for thee, that thy faith fail not; and do thou, when once thou hast turned again, establish thy brethren."

Poor Peter! He felt very sure that he was ready to face prison and death with Jesus. It was necessary that he have a revelation of his own weakness to rid him of his feeling of self-sufficiency.

2. JESUS BEFORE HEROD (23:6-12)

All three Synoptics describe Jesus' trial before Pilate. But Luke alone tells how Pilate made a desperate attempt to rid himself of the responsibility of deciding the case of Jesus, by sending him to Herod Antipas, who happened to be in Jerusalem at that time. His excuse for doing this was that since Jesus was a Galilean He came under Herod's jurisdiction.

Herod was glad for the chance to see Jesus, for he had heard of the wonderful works of this new prophet in Galilee. He hoped that Jesus would work a miracle for his entertainment.

When he found Jesus utterly noncommittal, he mockingly clothed Him with a purple robe and sent Him back to Pilate. That day these two rulers became friends, even as the Pharisees, Sadducees and Herodians had joined together their formerly hostile ranks in a common antagonism to Jesus.

3. PILATE'S TESTIMONY CONCERNING JESUS (23:13-25)

One of the striking things about Jesus' trial before Pilate is the governor's repeated avowals of His innocence. He really absolved Jesus of all guilt. His protest to the Jewish rulers is very definite:

"Ye brought unto me this man, as one that perverted the people: and behold, I, having examined him before you, found no fault in this man touching those things whereof ye accuse him. . . . I will therefore chastise him, and release him" (vs. 14, 16).

But the people clamored for His death. "And Pilate spake unto them again, desiring to release Jesus" (v. 20).

Still they shouted, "Crucify him, crucify him." Pilate said to them the third time, "Why, what evil hath this man done? I have found no cause of death in him: I will therefore chastise him and release him" (v. 22). But they shouted more loudly. "And their voices prevailed." How sad, and yet significant, those words!

4. THE RESURRECTION APPEARANCES (chapter 24)

a. *To the Two Disciples Going to Emmaus* (24:13-32). This is Luke's outstanding contribution to the Gospel accounts of the appearances of Jesus after His resurrection. It is a rather long and full narrative, and is found nowhere else.

In the afternoon of that first Easter day two of Jesus' followers were walking out to Emmaus, a nearby village.[6] They were talking sadly of the events of the week-end. Unexpectedly Jesus drew near and asked the subject of their conversation. They expressed surprise that anyone should be ignorant as to the important news. After indicating their disappointment that the Messianic kingdom had not been set up, they went on to relate their perplexity over the story of the women who had found the sepulcher empty.

Jesus chided them with their ignorance of the Messianic predictions in the Old Testament. What a privilege it would have been to have heard His unfolding of Christ "in all the scriptures"!

It was in the act of breaking bread in their home that Jesus revealed His true identity. Then He disappeared from their sight. They hurried back to Jerusalem to share the good news with the other disciples. There they found a confirmation of what they had seen, for the eleven reported that Jesus had appeared to Peter.

[6] Luke must refer to the ancient Emmaus, situated about four miles from Jerusalem. The modern Emmaus is about twenty miles away, too far for a return walk that evening.

b. *To the Eleven in the Upper Room* (24:36-49). While the two from Emmaus were excitedly relating their experience, Jesus suddenly stood in their midst. This appearance on the evening of His resurrection is recorded by John, who also records another one to the eleven on the next Sunday evening. There seems also to be a clear reference to this first Sunday night in Acts 1:4, 5, when compared with the forty-ninth verse here.

c. *At the Ascension* (24:50-53). Luke gives us two definite descriptions of the ascension of Jesus, one in his Gospel, and the other in Acts (1:9-11). He began his narrative of Christ's life and ministry at an earlier point than the others, and now he carries it right to the end of that life on earth.

IV. THE SON OF GOD

The Gospel of John

Introduction

The Apostle John, to whom tradition ascribes the authorship of the Fourth Gospel, was probably one of the youngest members of the twelve. But he was also the one who lived closest to the heart of his Master. In the account of the last supper we read, "There was at the table reclining in Jesus' bosom one of his disciples, whom Jesus loved" (John 13:23). John is not mentioned by name in this Gospel, but is referred to as the beloved disciple.

Liberal scholars are almost unanimous in rejecting the Johannine authorship of the Fourth Gospel. It is admittedly one of the most difficult questions in the field of New Testament criticism today. But the external evidence for the traditional authorship is very strong. Irenaeus (about A.D. 190) says that John wrote the Gospel while at Ephesus. Clement of Alexandria and Tertullian (both about A.D. 200) make abundant use of this Gospel and attribute it to John. Writers of the third century confirm the universal belief of the early church in the Johannine authorship of the Fourth Gospel. Conservatives, therefore, do not feel that they have sufficient reason for rejecting this view.

John was one of the three apostles who were privileged to be with Jesus at the raising of Jairus' daughter, on the Mount of Transfiguration, and in the Garden of Gethsemane. At the crucifixion he received the charge from Jesus to care for Mary, His mother. Tradition claims that he stayed for some time in Jerusalem and that he then became one of the leaders in the important church at Ephesus. It was during his residence there that he was exiled to Patmos. According to what seems to be trustworthy tradition, the Apostle John lived in Ephesus until the very close of the first century.

The Fourth Gospel is written to present Jesus as the Son of God. It does not appear to have been written to any special group, but to Christians everywhere.

This purpose is stated definitely by the author: "These are written that ye may believe that Jesus is the Christ, the Son of God; and that believing ye may have life in his name" (John 20:31). This master key, by which we may unlock every part of the Gospel, is found hanging right at the back door. The Gospel of John was written to demonstrate the deity of Jesus and to produce faith in Him.

The difference between the Synoptic Gospels and the Gospel of John are very apparent. Where they give us objective history, John gives us spiritual interpretation. In the Synoptics Jesus is talking about the kingdom; in John's Gospel He is talking about Himself. They give Jesus' teaching in parables; John presents His teaching in allegories. Where they record His ministry in Galilee, John tells of His ministry in Jerusalem. The Fourth Gospel supplements the Synoptic historical biographies by giving us an interpretative biography of Jesus, the Christ.

The Prologue

Matthew, as we have seen, begins his Gospel with a genealogy of Jesus, in order to introduce the Subject of his biography. Mark has no introduction except the ministry of John the Baptist. Luke has a literary preface which is unique in the New Testament. But John begins with a theological prologue. We may well assume that John's purpose is theological, as Luke's was historical; and the contents of his Gospel bear out the assumption.

The main theme of John's Prologue is the Divine Logos. Plato and Philo had both used the term, but John gives it a higher meaning than had either of them. Jesus is the Word of God, in that He is the expression or revelation of God to man.

The eternity and deity of the Logos are declared in verse one. A statement could hardly be more unequivocal: "In the beginning was the Logos [Word] and the Logos was with God, and the Logos was God." The declaration is very clear that Jesus was God, eternally pre-existent with the Father. In other words, Jesus is identified by John as the Divine Logos.

Thus does the author state with the utmost definiteness the theme of his Gospel.

The third verse describes the creatorship of the Logos: "All things were made through him." This was due to the fact that "in him was life"; that is, inherent life. Christ is the source of all life—material, intellectual, spiritual. What a privilege to have Him in our hearts!

The fourth verse mentions two characteristically Johannine terms, life and light. John uses a few terms over and over again, until they become deeply impressed upon our thinking. His favorite trilogy is *life, light* and *love*. Other words prominent in this Gospel are *believe, truth, witness*. It is John's purpose to furnish indisputable testimony to the truth of Jesus' deity, in order that men may believe (v. 7).

The result of believing in Christ is stated in verse twelve: "But as many as received him, to them gave he the right to become children of God, even to them that believe on his name."

The Incarnation of the Logos is the theme of verse fourteen: "And the Word became flesh and dwelt among us (and we beheld his glory, glory as of the only begotten from the Father) full of grace and truth." How well does that last clause describe the life and ministry of Jesus!

The eighteenth verse gives the purpose of the Incarnation: "No man hath seen God at any time; the only begotten Son, who is in the bosom of the Father, he hath declared him." Literally, "He has led Him forth," so that we might see the unseen God in Christ. The Incarnation was the unveiling of deity.

The Revelation of the Son of God to the World

It is the purpose of John's Gospel to reveal Jesus as the Son of God. If we miss that revelation we have lost the central truth of this Gospel. Yea, we have lost the foundation upon which Jesus said He would build His Church (Matt. 16:18).

1. JOHN THE BAPTIST AND THE JEWS (1:19-28)

It should be noted that the term "the Jews" as used in this gospel refers regularly to the Jewish rulers at Jerusalem. Its usage is almost parallel to that of "the Pharisees" in the Synoptic Gospels. The latter describe the hostility of the Pharisees as developing gradually during Jesus' ministry, while John's Gospel reveals a strong opposition to Jesus on the part of the Jewish leaders from the very first.

When these rulers at Jerusalem heard of John's baptizing at the Jordan, they sent some priests and Levites to ask him who he was. He made it clear at once that he was not the Messiah. When they asked him why he baptized with water, he intimated that he was preparing the way for a greater One who should soon appear.

2. JOHN THE BAPTIST AND JESUS (1:29-34)

It is interesting to note John's frequent time references. The phrase "on the morrow" occurs three times in this chapter (vs. 29, 35, 43), while the second chapter begins with the events of "the third day."

John the Baptist greeted Jesus with the words, "Behold the Lamb of God, that taketh away the sin of the world." He thus linked Christ with the sin offering of the Jewish ceremonial religion, of which offering He was the antitype and fulfillment.

This designation of Christ as a lamb occurs twice in this chapter. It is also found in Acts 8:32 and 1 Peter 1:19. Aside from these places it is found only in the Book of Revelation, where it is used twenty-eight times; so it is almost a strictly Johannine usage.

John's Gospel does not narrate the baptism of Jesus, but there appears to be a reference to it in the statement of John the Baptist that he had seen the Spirit descending as a dove upon Jesus, and that this had been given him as a sign whereby he should recognize the Messiah. "And I have seen, and have borne witness that this is the Son of God."

3. THE FIRST DISCIPLES (1:35-51)

The next day Jesus appeared again to John, as he was standing with two of his disciples. When John greeted the newcomer as on the previous day, the two disciples left the Baptist to follow the Christ.

The account states that one of the two was Andrew. It seems altogether probable that the other was John, the writer of this Gospel, and it is not at all impossible that after Andrew had "first" found his brother, Simon, John may have likewise brought his brother James. The Synoptics record the later call of these four to leave their fishing business and spend all their time with Jesus.

One of the greatest things Andrew ever did was to bring his brother, Peter, to Jesus. The value of this piece of personal work can be appreciated cnly in the light of the Day of Pentecost. It reminds us of the Sunday school teacher who sought out the shoe clerk in Boston and brought D. L. Moody to Christ, or the preacher who laid his hand on the head of an unpromising boy in a most unlikely environment, but gave "Gipsy" Smith to the world.

An outstanding feature of this last section of the chapter is the definite confession that Jesus was the Messiah, given by Andrew (v. 41), by Philip (v. 45), and by Nathanael (v. 49). Nathanael was so impressed by the supernatural knowledge shown by Jesus that he cried, "Rabbi, thou art the Son of God."

The expression "verily, verily" (v. 51) is peculiar to this Gospel. The Synoptics have the single "verily," but never the double form. Jesus used it to introduce declarations of outstanding importance.

4. THE FIRST MIRACLE IN CANA (2:1-11)

The turning of the water into wine at the marriage feast in Cana of Galilee is the first miracle recorded of Jesus. It indicates, for one thing, that Jesus was not an ascetic. He not only attended a wedding feast, but He also added to the enjoyment of the occasion.

It is evident that this incident was intended to convey to our minds a parable of spiritual truth. When the wine of Judaism had run out, Jesus brought in the better wine of the kingdom. We have already noticed His statement that the new wine of the gospel must be put into the new wineskins of the Christian Church (Matt. 9:17).

Jesus' words to His mother should not be taken as implying any discourtesy. "Woman" was a perfectly proper form of oriental address. Jesus simply wanted His mother to realize from the outset of His public ministry that she was not to direct His miracle-working activities.

The purpose of His first miracle was to induce belief in Jesus as the Son of God. "This beginning of his signs did

Jesus in Cana of Galilee, and manifested his glory; and his disciples believed on him" (v. 11). A similar statement occurs in the latter part of the chapter, to the effect that while He was attending the Passover at Jerusalem "many believed on his name, beholding his signs which he did" (v. 23).

The use of the word "sign" here is very significant. The Synoptists designate miracles as "wonders" and "powers." John calls them signs, wrongly translated "miracles" in the King James Version. They are miracles, to be sure. But what he is emphasizing is their *significance* as proofs of Jesus' divine power. Therefore he refers to them as *signs*.

5. THE FIRST PASSOVER (2:13-25)

Since John's main interest is in the Judean ministry of Jesus, he gives scant attention to His travels in Galilee. Here he simply tells us that Jesus went down to Capernaum with His family and His disciples, but that He stayed there only a short time. The Passover season was at hand and He went up to Jerusalem.

The Synoptists record only one Passover during the public ministry of Jesus, while John records three, and possibly four. From the former we would not be sure that the ministry lasted more than one year, but John implies a period of about three years. It seems evident, however, that the events recorded in the Synoptic Gospels call for more than one year of time.

In connection with this first Passover we have the first cleansing of the temple. It is in keeping with John's emphasis on the early opposition of the Jewish leaders that he should describe the earlier cleansing. It is not surprising that Jesus should have had to cleanse the place again at the close of His ministry.

We also have here Jesus' first intimation of His coming death: "Destroy this temple, and in three days I will raise it up" (v. 19). The disciples did not understand this saying of Jesus until after it had been fulfilled in His resurrection. Then they remembered and believed.

6. JESUS AND NICODEMUS (3:1-21)

Personal interviews and private conversations constitute a very interesting feature of John's Gospel. We shall find Jesus talking with the woman at the well, with the impotent man, with the man born blind, with Martha and with Mary. The crowds are not so conspicuous as in the Synoptics. Rather, we see Jesus dealing with individuals.

Nicodemus was a rabbi, an honored leader of his people. The question of Jesus, "Art thou the teacher of Israel?" (v. 10) would suggest that he was at least one of the most outstanding rabbis of his day.

Nicodemus has been accused of cowardliness in coming to Jesus by night. Perhaps "cautiousness" would be a fairer word. We must remember that a great deal more was involved in the association with Jesus of a prominent Jewish rabbi than would be true in the case of a private individual. Then, too, Nicodemus may have chosen that time simply because he wanted a quiet talk with Jesus after the crowds had left.

However that may be, the incident served as the occasion for one of Jesus' most important discourses—that on the new birth. Jesus said that one must be born anew, or from above —the Greek word has both connotations—before he can see the kingdom of God. He further defined the new birth as meaning "born of the Spirit" (v. 8). It is not an outward conformity to creed or to regulations for conduct, but a new life within, generated by the Holy Spirit. And this life which is eternal—qualitatively as well as quantitatively—is received by believing in Jesus Christ.

The question has sometimes been raised as to whether Jesus' words end at verse fifteen, with verses sixteen to twenty-one giving us the writer's interpretation, or whether the whole section is to be taken as from Jesus' lips. But the problem is certainly not one of any vital importance, except to the editors and publishers of recent New Testaments. What we are concerned about is the Spirit-inspired message, whether it be in the words of Jesus or in the added explanation of the writer.

7. John's Last Testimony to Jesus (3:22-36)

Some of John the Baptist's disciples got into an argument with a Jew about the matter of purifying. It ended by their coming to John and telling him, perhaps complainingly, that people were all flocking now to Jesus.

In response, John uttered those beautiful words of self-abnegation: "He must increase, but I must decrease." He was glad for Jesus to take first place.

8. JESUS AND THE WOMAN AT THE WELL (4:1-42)

As Jesus left Judea for Galilee, He was constrained to go through Samaria, instead of taking the usual longer route up through Perea. There was an individual who needed Him. It was this same inner compulsion that Paul spoke of when he said, "The love of Christ constraineth us" (2 Cor. 5:14).

Jesus sat down by Jacob's Well, near the Samaritan city of Sychar. It was the noon hour, and the disciples had gone into the city to buy food.

As Jesus sat there, weary with the journey, a woman drew near to get water. Something evidently was wrong, for women did not usually come in the heat of the day. Jesus engaged her in conversation by asking for a drink. Beginning with their common interest in water, He led her on to see her need of having the water of life. The incident ended with her believing in Him as the Messiah and bringing her friends to Jesus.

This passage gives one of the best lessons in personal work to be found anywhere. Jesus began very tactfully by speaking of water. When the woman hesitated to give Him a drink, on the grounds that she was a Samaritan, He intimated that He had "living water." When she challenged Him on that, He went on to say that His water of life would quench thirst permanently. When she insisted on keeping to the material plane, Jesus suddenly startled her by telling her to get her husband.

When she tried to avoid His demand, He charged her with having had five husbands and living in sin. She acknowledged that He must be a prophet and proceeded to ask a question as to what was the right place for worship, just as many people in a similar situation today will try to argue with the personal worker about the proper mode of baptism or some other theological question. It seems like an effort to get away from facing her sins.

Finally the woman tried one last resort—the usual one in such cases. "Some time"—when the Messiah comes—but,

"Not now." But Jesus had her cornered. He said, "I am he." And she surrendered, her last weapon gone.

Here we have tact, wisdom, persistence, a steady drive toward the goal. The essential thing was that Jesus landed His catch.

9. THE HEALING OF THE NOBLEMAN'S SON (4:46-54)

This "second sign" performed by Jesus in Galilee (v. 54) is recorded for the same purpose as the others—to demonstrate His deity, and to show the effect on those who witnessed it. We are told of the father of the healed boy that "himself believed, and his whole house."

10. THE HEALING OF THE IMPOTENT MAN (5:1-18)

As we have already noted, John's Gospel is devoted almost entirely to the Judean ministry of Jesus. We are never away from Jerusalem very long. Aside from chapters 2, 4, 6 and 21 the scene is laid almost exclusively in or around the Holy City.

The setting for this miracle is a feast at Jerusalem. Many competent scholars feel that this was the Passover. If so, we have four Passovers recorded in John's Gospel, the other three being plainly indicated in 2:13, 6:4, and 12:1. This would make Jesus' ministry something over three years in length.

John's descriptions of scenes in Jerusalem are such as indicate that the writer was well acquainted with the city and also an eyewitness of the miracles of Jesus. He tells us that there was "in Jerusalem by the sheep gate a pool, which is called in Hebrew Bethesda, having five porches." The description is very clear and definite.

A pool has been found in this location and the rubbish has been cleaned out of it. It consists of two pools together, one fifty-five feet long and the other sixty feet long, while both are twelve and a half feet wide. Around and between the pools are five arched porches. There would be room in these for a considerable crowd of people, as indicated by the "multitude" of verse 3.

Among the sick people who were waiting for some mysterious moving of the water—early church tradition states that the water was muddy and strongly tinged with red—there was a man who had been helpless for thirty-eight years. Like many others, he had waited vainly for some unusual, weird happening, as those of modern times who flock to shrines for healing. But healing of body, as well as healing of soul, comes by simple faith in Christ. Jesus told the man to take up his pallet and walk. When the man tried to move in obedience to Christ's command, he found himself healed. The beautiful simplicity of the healing miracle of Jesus is in striking contrast to the spectacular methods of those who capitalize on people's love of the sensational.

It was on the Sabbath day that this healing took place. The Jewish rulers found fault with the healed man for carrying his cot on the Sabbath. The man did not even know the name of the one who had healed him, but when he had met Jesus in the temple he told the Jews who it was. The result was a fresh persecution of Jesus.

When Jesus referred to God as His Father, the Jews were infuriated, "For this cause therefore the Jews sought the more to kill him, because he not only brake the sabbath, but also called God his own Father, making himself equal with God." Those who say that Jesus himself never claimed deity ought to ponder this passage. Certainly the Jews of His day understood Him to mean nothing short of that.

11. THE DISCOURSE ON JUDGMENT (5:19-29)

Because of the attitude of the Jewish leaders in rejecting Him as the Son of God, Jesus proceeded to warn them of judgment. Furthermore, He declared that the judge appointed by the Father was none other than Himself. They were sitting in judgment on Him now, but one day the situation would be reversed.

The basis of Jesus' right to be the Judge of mankind is that He himself became man (v. 27). He will be merciful and fair at the final judgment, for He has shared in the experience of human life, and so has first-hand knowledge of human nature.

12. THE WITNESS TO CHRIST (5:30-47)

As a part of this discourse which arose out of the healing of the impotent man, Jesus cited several witnesses to His divine Sonship. His claims did not rise out of His own fevered thinking: He had a clear inward consciousness as to who He was and why He came. It was the witness of the Father to His own consciousness that constituted for Jesus the valid proof of His Deity (v. 32).

But the people would demand some external evidence. So Jesus cited four witnesses. *First,* there was John the Baptist, whose testimony they had heard. *Second,* there were His works; His miracles of love demonstrated both His divine power and His divine nature. *Third,* there was the witness of the Father, if they would listen to it. *Fourth,* there was the witness of the Scriptures. Jesus said, "Ye search the scriptures, because ye think that in them ye have eternal life; and these are they which bear witness of me." But the sad thing was, "Ye will not come to me, that ye may have life." If they had understood their scriptures (our Old Testament), they would have recognized Jesus as the Messiah promised to them by the prophets of old.

13. THE FEEDING OF THE FIVE THOUSAND (John 6:1-14)

We have already studied this miracle, which is recorded in all four Gospels. So now we shall give attention only to the distinctive elements in the Johannine account.

We are told here that the Passover was at hand. This would explain the large crowd that had gathered preparatory to the trip to Jerusalem. It also confirms Mark's statement that the grass was green, as it was springtime.

John's account is the only one that gives us the story of the boy's lunch. Andrew had discovered that one foresighted lad had brought his lunch basket along. He mentioned it apologetically to Jesus (v. 9), but with it Jesus fed the whole crowd.

The statement "he himself knew what he would do" is typical of John's presentation of Jesus. There are frequent references in this Gospel to the supernatural knowledge of Christ. It is given as one of the evidences of His deity.

The account closes with the statement, "When therefore the people saw the sign which he did, they said, This is of a truth the prophet that cometh into the world."

14. THE DISCOURSE ON THE BREAD OF LIFE (6:22-59)

The feeding of the five thousand was the object lesson which Jesus used as a basis for His sermon on the text, "I am the bread of life" (v. 35). He who had power to feed such a multitude with one boy's lunch had the right to claim that He was the Bread of Life.

Of course, the purpose of Jesus was to turn the minds of the people away from material things to spiritual realities, but that is an exceedingly hard thing to do. It seems sometimes that mankind is incurably materialistic. As long as a preacher talks in terms of outward forms and ceremonies, his religion is popular, but when he dips into the deeper things of the spiritual realm he finds oftentimes that the people have forsaken him, just as they forsook Jesus.

The main discourse ends with verse 40, but the murmuring of the Jews at Jesus' claim to be the Bread of Life brought from His lips a further elucidation of the subject (vs. 42-51). He ended His second talk with the explanation that the bread which He would give for the life of the world was His flesh.

This statement caused a fresh outburst from the Jews. How could He give His flesh to eat? Ridiculous! But Jesus reiterated the point, adding that they must also drink His blood if they were to have any life in them.

15. THE CHALLENGE TO THE DISCIPLES (6:60-71)

The gross materialism of the Jewish leaders was shared, in large part, by the disciples of Jesus. They felt that the teaching of their Master was becoming hopelessly obscure. So Jesus had to tell them plainly that He was not talking about literal flesh, which "profiteth nothing," but about His teachings—"the words that I have spoken unto you are spirit, and are life." Man's soul food is the Word of God—both the written Word and the divine nature of the living Word, which we receive in spiritual fellowship with Christ.

But still many of Jesus' followers could not understand and so they left Him. He turned to the twelve disciples with the challenging question, "Would ye also go away?" (v. 67). Peter, the impetuous spokesman of the group, answered with emphasis, "Lord, to whom shall we go? thou hast the words of eternal life." And then he added, "And we have believed and know that thou art the Holy One of God." What comfort his faith must have brought to Jesus, as He saw many of His disciples disappearing in the distance!

The thousands of Jews from Galilee were looking for a political Messiah. When Jesus refused to play the part (6:15) and talked of spiritual things, they left Him.

16. THE FEAST OF TABERNACLES (chapter 7)

Not only had many of Jesus' disciples left Him, but His own brothers did not believe in Him (v. 5). They expressed their unbelief in the suggestion that if He were really working miracles He ought to go up to Jerusalem and there put on a demonstration of His power.

However, Jesus was not seeking for publicity, but for the avoidance of it, at this time. After His brothers had gone up to the feast, He went secretly. Meanwhile people were wondering where He was and expressing their opinions about Him.

Finally Jesus appeared in the temple and began to teach the people. He reproved them for trying to kill Him, and they answered angrily, "Thou hast a demon: who seeketh to kill thee?" Things were getting rather tense.

When the crowd began to murmur its wonder as to whether He might be the Messiah, "the chief priests and Pharisees sent officers to take him" (v. 32). These officers were so captivated by His teaching that they returned without Him. Their only alibi was, "Never man so spake" (v. 46).

It was on the last day of the feast, probably the added eighth day (Num. 29:35), that Jesus gave His wonderful teaching on the Holy Spirit: "He that believeth on me, as the scripture hath said, from within him shall flow rivers of living water" (v. 38). This is Jesus' description of the Spirit-filled life.

17. THE LIGHT OF THE WORLD (chapter 8)

In the face of the criticism which confronted Him, Jesus made a new declaration: "I am the light of the world" (v. 12). This is the second great "I am" of this Gospel. In chapter six He had said, "I am the bread of life." He later declared Himself to be the Door of the Sheep and the Good Shepherd (chapter 10); the Resurrection and the Life (chapter 11); the Way, the Truth and the Life (chapter 14); the True Vine (chapter 15). In the light of the revelation of God as "I Am" at the burning bush (Ex. 3:14), these may well be taken as assertions of deity.

In spite of the hatred of the Jewish leaders for Jesus "no man took him; because his hour was not yet come" (v. 20). But they continued to argue with Him. Finally, Jesus had to speak those stern words of condemnation, "Ye are of your father the devil, and the lusts of your father it is your will to do" (v. 44). Then He threw out to them a challenge which only He could give: "Which of you convicteth me of sin?" (v. 46).

The discussion ended with Jesus' making that profound statement of His eternal existence: "Before Abraham was born, I am." In the face of that, who can maintain that Jesus disclaimed deity? The Jews understood well enough what He meant, and they immediately tried to stone Him for blasphemy.

18. THE HEALING OF THE MAN BORN BLIND (chapter 9)

Again Jesus announced His text, "I am the light of the world", (v. 5), and then He healed the man born blind as a demonstration and illustration of it. In chapter 6 He performed the miracle first, and then preached His sermon on the Bread of Life. Here the order is reversed.

This is one of the most interesting chapters in the Gospel. Jesus told the man born blind to wash in the pool of Siloam, with the result that he received his sight. When people were discussing the question as to whether he was the former blind man he volunteered the information that he was. When questioned further, he stated that it was "the man that is called Jesus" who had healed him (v. 11).

When the Pharisees got hold of the case, the first thing that interested them was the fact that the healing had occurred on the Sabbath day. Again Jesus was becoming unmanageably insubordinate!

In answer to the Pharisees' question, the healed man gave a simple testimony. They asked his opinion of Jesus. He replied, "He is a prophet" (v. 17). When they called him a second time and tried to confuse him, he stuck to his statement of fact: "One thing I know, that, whereas I was blind, now I see" (v. 25). When they asked him again to describe the miracle, he became disgusted and asked if they wanted to become Jesus' disciples. Cut to the quick, they reviled him and excommunicated him from the synagogue.

When Jesus heard what had happened to him, He revealed Himself to the man as the Son of God. The man believed, and worshiped Him.

This whole incident is an excellent picture of a man who walked in the light he had until that light led him to accept Jesus as His Lord. Christ was for him first a man, then a prophet, but finally the Son of God.

19. The Discourse on the Good Shepherd (10:1-21)

Jesus revealed Himself as the Door of the Sheep (v. 7) and the Good Shepherd (v. 11). He declared that He was the only way of access to the fold of salvation. As the Good Shepherd, He would lay down His life for the sheep. It is a beautiful oriental figure, one used by an ancient shepherd in our favorite Psalm (23).

20. The Feast of Dedication (10:22-39)

In this section we reach one of the dramatic climaxes of this Gospel. The hostility of the Jews had now come to a head, and they drove steadily forward to compass His death.

The Feast of Dedication was instituted to commemorate the restoration of the services in the temple, three years after it had been profaned by Antiochus Epiphanes in 168 B.C. The festival began on the twenty-fifth of December and lasted eight days. This was the last feast Jesus attended before the final Passover, when He was crucified.

On this occasion the Jewish leaders challenged Jesus to declare definitely whether or not He was the Messiah. Jesus reminded them that He had already told them and ended by making the most unequivocal assertion of His deity: "I and the Father are one" (v. 30). The Jews promptly attempted to stone Him.

But Jesus faced them fearlessly and evidently cowed them, so that they dropped their stones. He asked why they wanted to stone Him, and they said, "For blasphemy." After some discussion, "they sought again to take him" (v. 39).

This incident marks the climax of unbelief on the part of the Jewish rulers. In contrast to this attitude we read in the last verse of the chapter, "Many believed on him there." The writer of this Gospel traces the progress of belief or unbelief, and does it so clearly that it is possible to chart the two lines on a graph. The student who wishes to make a careful study of the Gospel would find that a profitable project.

The same miracles and messages of Jesus resulted in belief on the part of some and unbelief on the part of others. It is the same now, and will be to the end of this age.

21. THE RAISING OF LAZARUS (11:1-44)

In some respects this is the crowning miracle of Jesus' public ministry. John records only seven miracles performed by Jesus before His crucifixion, and this is the last and greatest. The Synoptists give two other instances of raising the dead—the daughter of Jairus and the widow's son at Nain—but this is the climactic one, inasmuch as Lazarus had been in the tomb for four days. He was not only dead, but dead and buried.

This incident gives some very important teaching on two vital subjects, faith and love. We shall take the latter first.

When Lazarus became seriously ill, his two sisters sent an anxious message to Jesus, "Lord, behold he whom thou lovest is sick" (v. 3). Jesus' heart was stirred by the news, for we read, "Now Jesus loved Martha, and her sister, and Lazarus" (v. 5). But instead of hurrying to their assistance, He stayed where He was for two days. How can we explain this seeming contradiction?

The solution lies partly in the use of two different Greek words here for "love." The message of the sisters contained the verb *phileo,* which signifies affectionate love, friendship love. But the statement of the fifth verse uses *agapao,* a word which has in it more of reason and less of emotion than the other. It suggests the ideas of respect and deliberate choice. So, while Jesus' affection for these friends of His would have led Him to go at once, His desire for their greatest good caused Him to tarry. He wanted to teach them a lesson of faith which they could not otherwise have learned.

Finally Jesus arrived at Bethany and was met by the distressed sisters, whose sorrow over the loss of their brother was increased by the fact that Jesus seemed to have ignored their call for help. Did He really love them after all?

When Martha met Him, Jesus tested her faith. He wanted her to realize that He could not only heal the sick but raise the dead. To her He made the declaration, "I am the resurrection and the life" (v. 25).

Mary was so overcome with grief that Jesus did not torment her with any conversation. He moved immediately toward the tomb and called Lazarus forth. His love had not failed them, but it had tested them, and their faith in Him had reached a higher level of complete confidence.

22. THE RESULT OF RAISING LAZARUS (11:47-57)

As usual, many believed on Jesus as the result of this miracle (v. 45), while others disbelieved and reported to the Pharisees (v. 46). The Sanhedrin now took definite action in the effort to put Jesus to death (vs. 47, 53). Because of this Jesus retired to the remote village of Ephraim (v. 54). As the Passover drew near, the Jewish leaders gave orders that they should be told of Jesus' location (v. 57).

23. THE ANOINTING AT BETHANY (12:1-8)

John's account of this incident is more specific in indicating that it was Judas Iscariot who especially complained of the waste of ointment by Mary. And then we are given the added explanation that it was "not because he cared for the poor; but because he was a thief, and having the bag took away what was put therein" (v. 6).

24. THE TRIUMPHAL ENTRY INTO JERUSALEM (12:12-19)

This incident is connected in this Gospel with the raising of Lazarus. The people flocked to meet Jesus as a result of the testimony borne by those who had witnessed the miracle (vs. 17, 18).

The great enthusiasm of the multitudes over the arrival of Jesus drove the Pharisees to distraction. They said one to another, "Behold how ye prevail nothing; lo, the world is gone after him" (v. 19). But the pendulum of popular feeling was soon to swing the other way.

25. LIFE THROUGH DEATH (12:20-50)

Some Greeks were attending the Passover Feast and desired to see Jesus. When Jesus was informed of their request, He uttered that significant truth, "Except a grain of wheat fall into the earth and die, it abideth by itself alone; but if it die, it beareth much fruit."

This had a double application. It referred first, of course, to the fact that Jesus must die on the cross before He could become the Savior of the world. But the truth also applies to human individuals. We, too, must die to ourselves if we would truly live.

The Revelation of the Son of God to the Disciples

1. THE LAST SUPPER (chapter 13)

John's account of this incident begins with the statement of Jesus' awareness that His hour had come. As a last object lesson in humility He washed the disciples' feet. John records this in place of the institution of the Lord's Supper, which is found in the Synoptics.

After Jesus had disclosed the tragic fact that one of His chosen twelve would betray Him, Judas Iscariot left the group and went out into the night. With yearning love Jesus then addressed the eleven disciples as "little children" (v. 33) and revealed the sadness of His heart on leaving them. He gave them His "new commandment," that they should love one another as He had loved them (v. 34). This was to be the badge, or insignia, of their discipleship (v. 35).

2. THE LAST DISCOURSE WITH HIS DISCIPLES (chapters 14-16)

There are perhaps no more comforting words in all the Bible than these chapters about "the Comforter." This is the longest and most important passage of scripture on the subject of the Holy Spirit. As Jesus faced His departure from the disciples His greatest concern for them was that they might receive the Holy Spirit, who would be to them "another Comforter" to take His place.

To attempt to interpret this richest portion of the Gospel would be impossible in a brief space. Jesus promised the Holy Spirit to His disciples (14:1-24) and bequeathed to them His peace (14:25-31). He then gave them the figure of the vine and the branches, to impress their minds with the absolute necessity of abiding in Him (15:1-17). He warned them of coming persecution (15:18—16:4) and assured them that it was profitable for them that He should go away, in order that the new Advocate, the Holy Spirit, might come to their hearts (16:5-33).

3. CHRIST'S HIGH PRIESTLY PRAYER (chapter 17).

Before going to the cross Jesus prayed this beautiful prayer for His own. It is a revelation of His great heart of love. In spite of His coming sufferings, His greatest concern was for the welfare of the disciples.

Jesus prayed first for His own glorification (vs. 1-5). Then He uttered three definite petitions for His disciples. He prayed for their preservation (vs. 6-16), for their sanctification (vs. 17, 18), and for their unification (vs. 19-26). It is interesting to note that He voices the first petition once, the second twice and the third three times. Spiritual unity was something that Jesus rated as of primary importance.

The Revelation of the Son of God to the Ages

Jesus' public ministry to the people had been succeeded by His private ministry to His disciples. This in turn gave way to His sacrificial ministry, in which He revealed Himself to the ages as "Jesus Christ, Son of God, Saviour."

1. THE ARREST OF JESUS (18:1-14)

The Johannine account adds one item of interest in connection with the arrest of Jesus. It states that when the soldiers first confronted Him they fell backward to the ground. The writer desires to make it clear that they could not have seized Jesus if He had not chosen to permit it.

This is the only Gospel, also, which tells us that it was Simon Peter who cut off the ear of Malchus, the high priest's servant. Peter made a desperate effort to carry out his promise to protect Jesus.

2. THE TRIAL BEFORE THE HIGH PRIEST (18:15-27)

The account in this Gospel gives the interesting information that one of Jesus' disciples was known to the high priest and so was permitted to enter the place where Jesus was being tried. There can be little doubt that the "other disciple" was John the Apostle. John sought to do Peter a kindness by making it possible for the latter to come inside also. But it really got him into trouble, for the maid who kept the door challenged him as a follower of Christ. Poor Peter was caught off guard and denied his Lord.

3. THE TRIAL BEFORE PILATE (18:28—19:16)

One of the outstanding notes in this record is Pilate's repeated affirmation of Christ's innocence. Three times he declared, "I find no crime in him" (18:38; 19:4, 6). And the only crime the Jews could find in Him was, "He made himself the Son of God" (19:7). Yet for that crime they crucified Him.

4. THE CRUCIFIXION (19:17-37)

This Gospel records the thoughtfulness of Jesus in committing His sorrowing mother to the care of His beloved disciple, John. In spite of the agony of His suffering He took care of His responsibility to His bereaved parent.

But the suffering was to end. Finally Jesus cried, "It is finished," and dismissed His spirit. His mission on earth was accomplished.

5. THE BURIAL (19:38-42)

The one who told of the visit of Nicodemus to Jesus at night is also the only one who mentions his part in the burying of Christ's body. Nicodemus' love for Jesus is shown in the fact that he brought a hundred pounds of myrrh and aloes to use in the preparation of the body for burial. He knelt beside Joseph of Arimathea as they tenderly wrapped the bruised and bleeding corpse in linen cloths and spices. It was an act of love and forms the greatest memorial to these two men.

6. THE RESURRECTION (chapter 20)

John's story of the resurrection supplements the accounts in the other three Gospels. He tells of the visit of Peter and John to the sepulcher (vs. 1-10); of the appearance of Jesus to Mary Magdalene (vs. 11-18, a story of surpassing beauty); of His sudden presence in the midst of the disciples in the upper room that first evening (vs. 19-23); and of His appearance the next Sunday evening to the group with Thomas present (vs. 26-29). We would have missed some of the most precious scenes in the life of Christ had John not written to supplement the other three evangelists.

The Gospel proper closes with chapter 20. It is characteristic of the entire Gospel and of the purpose of the writer that it should end with an emphasis on believing. Thomas, the doubter, was finally made to believe. A blessing is extended to those who believe without seeing (v. 29).

The author of this Gospel tells us that he has selected only a few of the miracles performed by Jesus. He has been compelled to omit "many other signs." Those he did select were chosen for a definite purpose: "But these are written that ye may believe that Jesus is the Christ, the Son of God; and that ye may have life in his name."

The Epilogue

The twenty-first chapter appears to have been added by John after he had completed the main part of the Gospel. His reason for doing this was that he wished to correct a false rumor that was circulating, to the effect that he would not die, so he tells the incident which gave rise to this idea and makes it clear that Jesus did not make the assertion attributed to Him (v. 23).

But we are thankful that some occasion—even if a false report—called for the writing of this interesting incident in the post-resurrection ministry of Jesus. For here we meet Peter and his Lord again in a touching conversation.

The point of this narrative is partly lost in English because we have only one word for love. Jesus said first to Peter, "*Agapas me?*" Peter replied each time, "*Philo se.*" But the third time Jesus asked, "*Phileis me?*"

Jesus asked Peter if he loved Him with that highest love that God demands of His people (Matt. 22:37). Remembering his recent denials, Peter dared not answer with the same word. He simply said, "Lord, you know that I love you warmly." When Jesus adopted his word and said, in effect, "Peter, are you sure that you really care for me?" it broke Peter's heart. He said, "Lord, you *know* I do."

What a picture of Jesus' tender dealing with His own! What would be our answer, if He should ask us the same question?

V. THE EARLY CHURCH

The Acts

Introduction

The Book of Acts is the first church history. It gives us an account of the Day of Pentecost, the birthday of the Church, and traces the spread of Christianity for the first generation (about 30 to 60 A.D.). It gives to us the historical background for understanding the Epistles of Paul.

There does not seem to be any reason for doubting the tradition of the early church that Luke wrote the Book of Acts. Modern scholarship is unanimously agreed in holding that the Third Gospel and Acts were written by the same man. So the external evidence for one applies to the other.

With regard to internal evidence the most significant point is the occurrence of the "we passages" in Acts. Most of the book is written in the third person, but in the so-called "we" sections the first person plural is adopted.

The use of "we" would indicate that the author participated in the events of the book at that point, and so we learn that the writer of Acts joined the Pauline missionary party at Troas, as it left for Europe (16:10), and traveled with it to Philippi.

When the missionaries left Philippi to go to Thessalonica the author of Acts remained at the former place, as indicated by the change again to the third person. The first person occurs again in the twentieth chapter, where we read, "We sailed away from Philippi" (20:6). It would appear that the writer had stayed at Philippi, as pastor of the church, in the interim between Paul's visit there on his second journey and his return to the city on his third journey. After that he evidently stayed with Paul most of the time until the end of the great apostle's life.

Of the companions of Paul mentioned by him in his epistles only two are not named in Acts. These are Luke and Titus. As between the two we may let the external evidence decide the question in favor of Luke.

Since the Book of Acts does not relate the death of Paul, but leaves him a prisoner in Rome, it seems reasonable to hold that it was written at the end of the apostle's two years' imprisonment there, around A.D. 61. It is also significant that Acts does not refer to the destruction of Jerusalem which occurred in A.D. 70.

The purpose of the Book of Acts is to give us an account of the rise and early spread of Christianity. Together with the Gospels it gives us the historical foundations upon which rests the Christian Church.

Christianity in Jerusalem

1. THE INTRODUCTION (1:1-5)

The writer of Acts begins with a reference to his former treatise, the Gospel of Luke, and addresses the same man, Theophilus. He says that the Gospel recorded all that Jesus "began both to do and to teach." The implication is that Acts is to give us what Jesus continued to do and teach through His apostles.

Luke tells us the length of Jesus' post-resurrection ministry and summarizes for us its nature: "To whom he also showed himself alive after his passion by many proofs, appearing unto them by the space of forty days, and speaking the things concerning the kingdom of God."

The main concern of Jesus at this time was that the disciples should tarry at Jerusalem for "the promise of the Father," the baptism with the Holy Spirit. If they had failed to do so, the Book of Acts would never have been written, for the events it describes would not have occurred.

2. THE ASCENSION (1:6-11)

The last time the disciples saw Jesus they asked Him a question which still plagued their minds: "Lord, dost thou at this time restore the kingdom to Israel?" It is evident that they were still far from understanding the significance of His death and resurrection.

In answer to their question Jesus told them the essential thing was not the knowledge of dispensational data, but the power of the Holy Spirit in their lives. There were some things they were not to know: "But ye shall receive power, when the Holy Spirit is come upon you: and ye shall be my witnesses both in Jerusalem, and in all Judaea and Samaria, and unto the uttermost part of the earth."

This verse, Acts 1:8, is the key to the Book of Acts. The power of the Holy Spirit in the lives of the apostolic Christians is the only adequate explanation for the wonderful achievements recorded in this history of the early church.

Acts 1:8 also suggests the outline of the book, which describes the spread of Christianity: (1) in Jerusalem (chapters 1-7); (2) in Judea and Samaria (chapters 8-12); (3) in the Gentile world (chapters 13-28).

In connection with the ascension of Jesus we have a definite promise of His return. His coming again will be unexpected, visible, bodily: "This Jesus . . . shall so come in like manner as ye beheld him going into heaven."

3. The Upper Room (1:12-14)

After Jesus was gone, the disciples returned obediently to Jerusalem to wait for the coming of the Holy Spirit. They gathered in a large upper room, perhaps the place where the last supper was held. It may have been in the home of John Mark's mother.

Here the eleven gathered to pray, accompanied by the mother of Jesus and the women who had followed Him. It is interesting to find Jesus' brothers here in this prayer meeting. Evidently the crucifixion and resurrection had caused them to believe in Him.

4. The Choice of Matthias (1:15-26)

The group in the upper room swelled to a congregation of about one hundred and twenty. With such a large nucleus, Peter thought it was time to take care of some matters of church organization, so he suggested that they elect someone to take the place of Judas Iscariot.

The entire incident reveals a lack of seeking divine guidance. In the first place, they should have waited for the coming of the Holy Spirit to lead them. In the second place, they did a rank injustice to God by tying His hands to the two horns of a dilemma. Whichever way He (?) caused the lot to go, either Justus or Matthias would be elected. Probably

God's choice, to be revealed in due time, was the great Apostle Paul.

5. PENTECOST (2:1-13)

The first chapter is really introductory to the most important event in the Book of Acts, the coming of the Holy Spirit on the Day of Pentecost. This event marks the birthday of the Christian Church.

The account of this epoch-making occurrence is very brief, but vivid. In four verses the picture is drawn for us—the sudden noise like a hurricane; the flame of fire that divided into tongues of fire on each person; and then the essential fact, "they were all filled with the Holy Spirit."

The phenomenon of speaking in tongues is mentioned only three times in the Book of Acts: here, at the Gentile Pentecost in the house of Cornelius (10:46), and at the Ephesian Pentecost (19:6). It is not referred to in connection with the coming of the Holy Spirit on the believers at Samaria (chapter 8).

It is apparent that the speaking in tongues on the Day of Pentecost was for the specific purpose of witnessing to the many different groups gathered at Jerusalem for the feast. Altogether some fifteen nationalities were represented in the crowd that gathered to hear the apostles. (The "Jews and proselytes" would be two divisions of the entire group.)

6. PETER'S FIRST SERMON (2:14-42)

In his introduction Peter refuted the charge of drunkenness and quoted at length a passage from the prophecy of Joel, which he said was being fulfilled in this pentecostal outpouring of the Spirit. He then preached about Jesus, using as his three main points: I. His crucifixion (vs. 22, 23); II. His resurrection (vs. 24-32); III. His exaltation (vs. 33-36). In conclusion he gave the invitation, and three thousand souls accepted Christ. It was the greatest single day in church history.

7. THE FELLOWSHIP OF THE FIRST BELIEVERS (2:43-47)

Apparently these thousands of newly converted believers stayed at Jerusalem after Pentecost. This necessitated some provisions for their daily needs. In response to this need, a community of goods was inaugurated. This practice seems not to have been employed anywhere else in the early church, and it did not work too smoothly at Jerusalem.

The result of the consecration and fellowship of these first believers was that "the Lord added to them day by day those that were saved" (v. 47)—literally, "those that were being saved," not "such as should be saved" (A.V.). The membership of this early church was composed of those who were truly converted.

8. The Healing of the Lame Man (3:1-10)

Peter and John were going up to the temple together at the time of the evening sacrifice, three o'clock in the afternoon. At the Beautiful Gate they encountered a lame beggar, whom Peter healed "in the name of Jesus of Nazareth." He found that that name still had power to accomplish miracles in people's lives.

9. Peter's Second Sermon (3:11-26)

The healed man held a testimony meeting right there in the temple, expressing his joy and gratitude to God. The spectacle of the lame man walking and leaping created a considerable sensation, and soon a crowd had gathered to witness the sight. Peter immediately took advantage of the opportunity to preach to the people.

In his second sermon Peter told his audience to give God the credit for the miracle. He charged the people again with having crucified their Christ. But God had raised Him from the dead, and the power of His name had been manifested in the healing of the lame man. What they needed to do was to repent and let God save them.

10. The First Persecution (4:1-22)

The teaching of the resurrection of Jesus was not very savory doctrine to the Jewish rulers, so they locked up the preachers, but that did not stop the ministry of the Holy Spirit in the hearts of the hearers, for "many of them that heard the word believed"—so many, in fact, that "the number of the men came to be about five thousand" (v. 4).

In the morning the Sanhedrin gathered in solemn conclave. The three constituent groups—"rulers and elders and scribes"—were all represented. There, too, were Annas and Caiaphas, who had counseled the death of Christ. Into this court Peter and John were brought.

The attitude of Peter before this august assembly is in striking contrast to his behavior on the night of Jesus' trial. For now it was Peter "filled with the Holy Spirit." He boldly charged the members of the Sanhedrin with being responsible for the death of Christ. And he informed them that the only way of salvation was through the One they had crucified. The only thing the rulers dared to do was to forbid the apostles to preach any more in the name of Jesus.

11. A Prayer Meeting (4:23-31)

When Peter and John reported the threatenings of the Sanhedrin, the believers went to prayer about the matter. They did not ask for protection, but for power. It was not their own safety that concerned them, but the salvation of souls, so they prayed for boldness to go on speaking God's message. Their prayer was answered fully, for we read that "when they had prayed, the place was shaken wherein they were gathered together; and they were all filled with the Holy Spirit, and they spake the word of God with boldness" (v. 31).

12. The Unity and Consecration of the Church (4:32-37)

It is a beautiful picture of the early church which is drawn for us in this passage. "The multitude of them that believed were of one heart and soul"—"they had all things common"—"great grace was upon them all."

But this condition was too nearly ideal to last very long here on earth. The portrait drawn in the fourth chapter is somewhat marred by the lines of the fifth and sixth chapters.

13. Ananias and Sapphira (5:1-11)

Barnabas, a Levite from Cyprus, had sold some land—perhaps back at his island home—and had given the proceeds to the church. Ananias and Sapphira thought it would be nice to get credit for doing the same thing. But they kept part of the money themselves.

The sudden fate which befell these two deceivers may seem rather severe, but we gather from Jesus' attitude how much God abhors hypocrisy. At a time when thousands of people were being added to the membership of the church it was necessary to raise a barrier of warning against those who might slip in from ulterior or unworthy motives. The purpose of this judgment was to keep the church pure. It put the fear of God on the people (v. 11).

14. THE SECOND PERSECUTION (5:12-42)

In spite of the result that "of the rest durst no man join himself to them," yet "believers were the more added to the Lord, multitudes both of men and women" (vs. 13, 14). The hypocrites had been dealt with and the church rolled on!

But the Jewish leaders could not stand to see this new "sect of the Nazarenes" (24:5) growing so rapidly. Moved by the same jealousy that had brought about the death of Jesus, they arrested the apostles and put them in jail (v. 18).

The next morning when they had called a meeting of the Sanhedrin they received an unpleasant shock, for the prison was found empty. Soon the report came that the apostles were teaching in the temple, in accordance with the instructions of the angel who had let them out of jail.

When Peter stood once more before the Sanhedrin he boldly took his stand for Jesus. This so infuriated the elders of Israel that they wanted to kill the apostles, but Gamaliel counseled moderation. His advice was to let this movement alone. If it was of God they had better keep their hands off and if not it would die of itself.

Gamaliel was a great rabbi, grandson of the renowned Hillel and later president of the Sanhedrin, and his word prevailed at this time, so they beat the apostles, forbade them to speak in Jesus' name, and let them go. But "every day, in the temple and at home, they ceased not to teach and to preach Jesus as the Christ" (v. 42).

15. THE APPOINTMENT OF THE SEVEN (6:1-7)

The church had grown so large that a serious problem arose, one that was both economic and racial. The Hellenists felt that they were being discriminated against in favor of the Hebrews (the Palestinian Jews). "There arose a murmuring"; the Greek word suggests the buzzing of bees.

The apostles did not wait until the church had been split in two by this trouble. They immediately sought a remedy. Calling a church meeting, they asked the people to choose "seven men of good report, full of the Spirit and of wisdom." The people wisely chose seven good, Spirit-filled, tactful Grecians to wait on the Grecian widows. The apostles solemnly ordained them for their task (v. 6).

The result of this prompt, wise action was that "the word of God increased; and the number of the disciples multiplied in Jerusalem exceedingly."

16. THE ARREST OF STEPHEN (6:8-15)

Stephen was bigger than his job. He not only waited tables, but also preached. When he got into debates—perhaps with young Saul, who was from Cilicia—his wisdom and the spirit always won out.

Like others who lose an argument, his vanquished opponents wreaked vengeance on him by accusing him falsely. Finally Stephen was brought before the Sanhedrin, which was rather busy taking care of these followers of Christ. As false witnesses recited their speeches, God's love welled up in Stephen's heart until his face shone like that of an angel.

17. STEPHEN'S DEFENSE (7:1-53)

Stephen's sermon is a historical resume of God's dealings with His people. Beginning with Abraham, he comes down through Isaac, Jacob, Joseph, Moses, Joshua, David and Solomon.

Three of these characters are singled out for special notice and might be taken as headings for the three main divisions of the sermon: I. Abraham (vs. 2-8); II. Joseph (vs. 9-16); III. Moses (vs. 17-44).

The fact that Stephen, after speaking at length on these three men, gives such brief attention to Joshua, David and Solomon may be due to a growing restlessness on the part of his audience. His sudden change of tone at verse 51—"Ye stiffnecked and uncircumcised in heart and ears, ye do always resist the Holy Spirit"—suggests an evident animosity on the part of his hearers which led him to conclude his sermon abruptly. But before he stopped, he charged these Jewish rulers with having murdered "the Righteous One."

18. STEPHEN'S DEATH (7:54-60)

One of the saddest sights in this book is the picture of those long-bearded, long-faced, long-robed religious leaders of Israel gnashing their teeth on Stephen like a pack of hungry, snarling wolves. The flower of Judaism was getting rather faded.

When Stephen gave testimony to the heavenly vision he saw of Jesus standing up to receive him, these sanctimonious Sadducees and Pharisees stuck their fingers in their ears and yelled, to drown out his voice, and rushed headlong upon their victim. Only when they had vented their insane wrath on his body with stones did they cease their madness. What a contrast to Stephen who died on his knees, praying for the forgiveness of his murderers.

Christianity in Judea and Samaria

1. THE PERSECUTION IN JERUSALEM (8:1-3)

Strange to say, the result of the death of Stephen was that a great persecution broke out against the church at Jerusalem. It began "on that day" (v. 1). The believers in Jerusalem were scattered out over Judea and Samaria.

The fanatical leader in this persecution was young Saul, at whose feet the witnesses had laid their coats while stoning Stephen (7:58). As a member of the Sanhedrin he had consented to his death (8:1).

2. PHILIP IN SAMARIA (8:4-25)

The persecution at Jerusalem only furthered the spread of Christianity. Those who were scattered abroad preached the Word wherever they went (v. 4).

Among these was Philip, one of the seven deacons. Like Stephen he began to preach. His chosen field was Samaria, where he had a great revival. Even Simon Magus joined the band of believers.

When the apostles, who had stayed at Jerusalem (v. 1), heard of the revival at Samaria they sent down Peter and John to see what was going on. These good men prayed for the converts and laid their hands upon them, with the result that "they received the Holy Spirit" (v. 17).

3. PHILIP AND THE ETHIOPIAN EUNUCH (8:26-40)

While Philip was busy with the growing work at Samaria, he was suddenly directed by an angel to leave the city and go to a wilderness road. It seemed a preposterous thing to do, but Philip obeyed promptly. Because he did so, he found his man. If he had stopped to argue with the Lord about it, as is too frequently the custom with us, he might have missed the eunuch altogether.

Philip heard the Ethiopian eunuch reading aloud from the Book of Isaiah as he rode along in his chariot. The traveler was eager for someone to explain to him the meaning of the Messianic passage in Isaiah 53. When Philip preached Christ to him, he at once believed and asked to be baptized. After the baptism Philip's work was done, and he left the eunuch to go on his way rejoicing.

4. SAUL'S CONVERSION (9:1-18)

All this time Saul was moving about like a war horse, "breathing threatening and slaughter against the disciples of the Lord." Fire and brimstone were the very breath of his nostrils.

Having driven the believers out of Jerusalem, he proceeded to Damascus, with the authorization of the high priest. But while the disciples there were waiting anxiously for the ax to fall on them (vs. 13, 14), God intervened. Saul, who would not listen to the quiet voice of the Spirit, was suddenly knocked to the earth by a lightning bolt from heaven. As he lay there, half-stunned, he heard a voice: "Saul, Saul, why persecutest thou me?" For three days Saul went blind and hungry, while he felt the meaning of those words. At the end of that time he emerged a man who would be just as zealous for Christ as he had been against Him.

There has been considerable discussion as to the place of Saul's conversion. It would seem most reasonable to hold that the young Pharisee was converted when he saw Jesus on the road and that he was sanctified when Ananias laid his hands on him that he might be filled with the Holy Spirit" (v. 17).

5. SAUL AT DAMASCUS AND JERUSALEM (9:19-31)

Soon Saul was preaching in Damascus. "Straightway in the synagogues he proclaimed Jesus, that he is the Son of God." The persecutor had turned preacher.

But Saul had to taste his own medicine. It was not long until the Jews plotted against his life. He escaped from Damascus one night by means of a basket let down from one of the houses on the wall.

When Saul arrived back in Jerusalem the believers there were suspicious of him. They thought he was still a wolf, even if now in sheep's clothing. But bighearted Barnabas performed one of his generous acts by vouching for the new convert.

Immediately Saul began to preach boldly in Jerusalem. Soon he created such a furor among the Jews that it was decided to get him out of the city, so they shipped him home to Tarsus.

6. PETER AT LYDDA AND JOPPA (9:32-43)

Peter is the most prominent character in the first twelve chapters of Acts, as Paul is in chapters 13-28. Aside from the story of Stephen (chapters 6, 7), of Philip (chapter 8) and of Saul's conversion (chapter 9), Peter has held central place and he will continue to do so now to the end of chapter 12.

This section records Peter's healing of Aeneas at Lydda and of Dorcas at Joppa. The result was that in both places many believed in Christ (vs. 35, 42).

7. PETER IN THE HOUSE OF CORNELIUS (chapter 10)

Cornelius was evidently an Italian, in charge of a hundred Roman soldiers at Caesarea. He was a proselyte to Judaism and very earnest in his religion. Because of his sincerity God instructed him to get in touch with Peter, that he might learn of the Christian way.

Meanwhile the Lord had been preparing Peter's heart and mind for this new venture among the Gentiles. Peter was still scrupulous about observing the ceremonial requirements of the Old Testament, and it would take nothing less than a vision from heaven to show him that God designed to accept Gentiles also into the kingdom, apart from the Jewish law.

When the messengers from Cornelius arrived Peter was ready to go with them, because of the vision he had seen (vs. 9-16). He went into Cornelius' house and preached to them about Jesus. While he was in the midst of his discourse the Holy Spirit fell on the group.

8. PETER'S DEFENSE AT JERUSALEM (11:1-18)

When Peter arrived back in Jerusalem he faced some sharp criticism from the Judaistic Christians there. It was a heinous crime to eat with Gentiles.

Peter had only one defense. God had revealed to him in a vision that he was not to make any distinction between Jews and Gentiles. Fortunately, he had taken with him six

Jewish brethren who could testify that Peter was not to blame for what happened at Cornelius' house. God had done it, and Peter could not stop it (v. 17).

9. THE CHRISTIANS AT ANTIOCH (11:19-30)

The believers who were driven out of Jerusalem after Stephen's death traveled far northward to Phoenicia and to Antioch in Syria, as well as out to the island of Cyprus, but they preached only to Jews. An exception took place in the case of some Cyprians and Cyrenians, who broke over the boundaries of race and religion and preached to the Greeks also. Thus was founded at Antioch the first Gentile church.

When the apostles at Jerusalem heard of this they sent Barnabas to Antioch. They were fortunate in their choice. A narrow-minded, bigoted Jewish Christian might have made trouble. But generous-spirited Barnabas encouraged the work. Looking for someone to teach in the new church, Barnabas remembered Saul. Hunting him out at Tarsus, he brought him to Antioch. The result of all this was that Antioch became the home base for the great Gentile mission of the first century and Paul became its greatest missionary.

An interesting thing took place at Antioch when the disciples received a new name, Christians. Whether or not this was given in derision we cannot now tell. It may surprise the reader to learn that the term Christian is used only three times in the New Testament: here; by Agrippa (Acts 26:28); and by Peter (1 Peter 4:16). It was evidently given by the pagan Gentiles to distinguish this new religious group from the Jews.

10. PETER'S IMPRISONMENT (12:1-19)

The story of Peter's deliverance from prison is a very fascinating one, but we cannot now take time for it. We simply call attention to the fact that the church prayer meeting in Peter's behalf was held in the home of John Mark's mother. (She was another one of those good Marys.) It is altogether possible that the upper room there had been hallowed by its associations with Jesus (last supper and resurrection evening) and by the descent of the Spirit at Pentecost, so that it was the common meeting place of the early church in Jerusalem.

11. HEROD'S DEATH (12:20-23)

The horrible death of Herod Agrippa I, grandson of Herod the Great, in A.D. 44 is corroborated by Josephus. He was in the zenith of his power and glory, but pride brought him to destruction.

Christianity in the Gentile World

1. THE INAUGURATION OF FOREIGN MISSIONS (13:1-3)

The great foreign missionary enterprise of the Christian Church began in a prayer meeting. One day the spiritual leaders at the church of Antioch were having a season of fasting and prayer. As they waited before the Lord the Holy Spirit spoke very definitely to their hearts, "Separate me Barnabas and Saul for the work whereunto I have called them."

After further fasting and prayer the church ordained them as its missionaries and sent them away (v. 3). But we read in verse 4 that they were "sent forth by the Holy Spirit." Here was the church working in perfect co-operation with the Spirit to carry out Christ's command to evangelize the world. Though the beginnings of this great movement seem humble, yet the start was wholly in line with the divine will and so met with success.

2. PAUL'S FIRST MISSIONARY JOURNEY (13:4—14:28)

Since Barnabas was named first in the Spirit's call and was the older man he naturally took the lead in this new venture. He probably felt a concern for his old home territory, and so they sailed first to Cyprus.

a. *Cyprus* (13:4-12). Landing at Salamis, they preached in the synagogues of the Jews, a method which Paul followed almost everywhere he went. Then they evangelized their way across the island to Paphos. Here they found the proconsul, Sergius Paulus, eager for light. When their talk with him was opposed by Elymas Magus, Paul decreed blindness for him. His name, Bar-Jesus, means "son of Jesus." But Paul renamed him "son of the devil." The result of the miracle was that the proconsul was saved.

Critics of the last century claimed that Luke blundered here in assigning the title "proconsul" to Sergius Paulus. They said it should be propraetor—that Cyprus was an imperial rather than a senatorial province. But archaeology has confirmed Luke's accuracy at this point, for an inscription has been discovered in Cyprus dated "in the proconsulship of Paulus."

b. *Antioch of Pisidia* (13:13-52). A striking change comes in the narrative after the incident at Paphos, in which Paul had taken a leading part. For one thing, he is called Paul from now on, rather than Saul. And further, his name precedes that of Barnabas hereafter, with very few exceptions. In fact, when they left Paphos the expression "Paul and his company" is used. Clearly Paul had become the leader of the party.

This change in leadership may have been one of the main reasons why John Mark abruptly left and returned home to Jerusalem. He may have felt that his relative, Barnabas, was not being treated fairly.

When Paul and Barnabas arrived in Antioch of Pisidia they attended the synagogue on the Sabbath day. When asked to speak, Paul rose and delivered a message. If the student will make a careful comparison of this first recorded sermon by Paul with that of Stephen (chapter 7), he will discover that they are very much alike. Both give a brief historical sketch of God's dealing with Israel. It appears evident that young Saul was deeply impressed with Stephen's sermon on that memorable day and never forgot it.

When the multitudes flocked to hear Paul preach, the Jews became jealous and opposed the missionaries. The apostles then made that significant declaration, "Lo, we turn to the Gentiles." When their popularity continued to increase, the Jews had them driven out of town.

c. *Iconium* (14:1-7). At Iconium a great multitude of both Jews and Greeks believed. But when the Jews here threatened their lives the missionaries fled to Lystra.

d. *Lystra* (14:8-20). At Lystra they healed a man who was badly crippled. The people excitedly declared in their native speech—which the missionaries could not understand—that the gods had come. When Paul and Barnabas perceived that they were going to be worshiped they uttered a vigorous protest.

The disappointed would-be worshipers took up readily with Jews from Antioch and Iconium who had followed Paul's trail to Lystra. Soon the same crowd was stoning Paul, and left him supposedly dead. But the next day he was ready for another trip.

e. *Derbe and return* (14:21-28). The terminal point of this first journey was Derbe. From there they retraced their steps back through Lystra, Iconium and Antioch, appointing elders in each church to carry on the work.

When they arrived back in Antioch of Syria, the home base for all three of Paul's journeys, they reported to the church there. The thing that impressed them most was that God had "opened a door of faith unto the Gentiles" (v. 27).

3. THE COUNCIL AT JERUSALEM (15:1-35)

A very important event took place between Paul's first and second journeys. Some men had come down from Judea to Antioch and cast a gloom of confusion over the Gentile church there by declaring, "Except ye be circumcised after the custom of Moses, ye cannot be saved" (v. 1).

Paul and Barnabas had sacrificed too much to see their work ruined by these intruders, so they opposed them. After there had been some contention, the church decided to send Paul and Barnabas up to Jerusalem to get the judgment of the apostles and elders in the matter.

This first church council was faced, then, with the very vital question as to whether or not Gentile Christians must keep the law of Moses. We may be truly thankful that they decided in favor of Gentile liberty. Had they tried to keep the new movement tied to the apron strings of Judaism it never could have become the great world religion.

After the council had listened to Peter, Barnabas and Paul, James—who was evidently the moderator or chairman—gave the final verdict. It was incorporated in a letter to the Gentile Christians asking them to abstain from things sacrificed to idols, from blood, from things strangled and from fornication (15:29).

4. PAUL'S SECOND MISSIONARY JOURNEY (15:36—18:22)

After some time spent at Antioch, Paul felt a concern to revisit the churches founded on the first journey. Barnabas agreed to go, but wanted to take John Mark with them. When Paul refused, Barnabas set off for Cyprus with Mark, while Paul chose Silas as his companion for the second journey.

a. *Syria and Asia Minor* (15:40—16:10). Paul took the northern route by land, traveling up through Syria and around the bend into Cilicia, his home province. When he came to Lystra he found a young apprentice in Timothy, who was henceforth one of his closest companions.

Moving along across Asia Minor Paul desired to preach here and there, but the Spirit led him on to Troas. At this place, while waiting for further guidance, Paul received the vision of the man saying, "Come over into Macedonia, and help us" (16:9). The Macedonian call meant Europe.

b. *Philippi* (16:11-40). Luke had joined the party at Troas ("we," 16:10), and he now sailed with Paul and his company for Philippi. Here they found no Jewish synagogue. But on the Sabbath day they discovered a women's prayer meeting down by the river. When the missionaries had presented Christ, a woman named Lydia became the first convert in Europe. She opened her house to the missionary party, so that her home became the meeting place of the first Christian Church in Europe.

Paul cast a demon out of a soothsaying girl, who was hindering their work by giving them undesirable publicity. Thereupon her masters dragged Paul and Silas into court, and that night the missionaries were in jail.

But at the jail Paul found his Macedonian man, the jailer himself. His conversion gave a boost to the infant church at Philippi, and Paul left Luke in charge of the work.

c. *Thessalonica* (17:1-9). At Thessalonica they found a Jewish synagogue, and Paul, "as his custom was," went in. For three Sabbaths he "reasoned with them from the scriptures, opening and alleging that it behooved the Christ to suffer, and to rise again from the dead; and that this Jesus, whom, said he, I proclaim unto you, is the Christ." In other words, he must first prove to his Jewish hearers that the Old Testament teaches a suffering and resurrected Messiah before he could present Jesus to them as their Messiah. This is probably a summary of his preaching to Jews.

A large number of the Greek proselytes to Judaism ("devout Greeks," v. 4) accepted the gospel. But the envious Jews stirred up a mob, and the missionaries had to leave the city. Whenever Paul came to town there was pretty sure to be a revival or a riot, or both. At Thessalonica they described him and his party as "these that have turned the world upside down" (v. 6).

d. *Berea* (17:10-15). The Jews at Berea "were more noble than those in Thessalonica, in that they received the word with all readiness of mind, examining the scriptures daily, whether these things were so." As a result, many of them believed, together with some Gentiles. The church at Berea was thus largely Jewish, while that at Thessalonica was almost entirely Gentile.

But the Jews continued to hound Paul's tracks as they had done in Asia Minor. A delegation of them from Thessalonica followed him to Berea, so that he had to leave this city also.

e. *Athens* (17:16-34). Paul was greatly impressed, and distressed, with the prevalent idolatry in this great center of learning. He supplemented his ministry to the Jews in the synagogue by talking daily with Gentiles in the market place, in accordance with the common practice of the philosophers of that day. When some Epicureans and Stoics met him, they brought him before the Court of the Areopagus, which held its meetings adjacent to the market place, and questioned him about this new teaching.[1]

Paul began his speech tactfully by observing that the Athenians were "very religious" (v. 22). This was evidenced by the fact their city was "full of idols" (v. 16). Taking his start from the altar he had observed with the inscription, "TO AN UNKNOWN GOD," Paul told them that this was the Creator and Sustainer of all things. But when he mentioned the resurrection of Jesus, they laughed him out of town.

The results at Athens were exceedingly disappointing. Only a few individuals believed, and no church was founded.

f. *Corinth* (18:1-17). The great commercial metropolis, Corinth, was a very different city from cultured Athens. Since his funds were getting low, Paul worked at his trade of making tents. He found very congenial associates in Aquila and his wife, Priscilla.

When the Jews refused to accept his message that Jesus was the Messiah (v. 5), Paul made an important declaration: "From henceforth I will go unto the Gentiles" (v. 6). His similar statement at Antioch of Pisidia had local application, but this seems to mark the inauguration of a new policy in Paul's missionary work.

[1] The Court of the Areopagus, which took its name from its original meeting place on Mars' Hill, usually met in the Stoa Basilica, which opened on the market place.

The trial before Gallio has often been misunderstood. The truth is that Gallio exhibited a high sense of justice in refusing to try a case which did not come under the jurisdiction of Roman law. He evidently felt that Sosthenes, the synagogue ruler, needed to be beaten, and so did not interfere. This beating seems to have worked out for his salvation, for Paul later mentions Sosthenes as a coworker (1 Corinthians 1:1).

g. *Ephesus and return* (18:18-22). Having spent a year and a half at Corinth, Paul set sail for home. He stopped briefly at Ephesus, telling the Jews there that he would return later. Sailing to Caesarea, "he went up and saluted the church [probably the church at Jerusalem] and went down to Antioch." This marks the close of Paul's second journey.

5. PAUL'S THIRD MISSIONARY JOURNEY (18:23—21:16)

On his third journey Paul evidently went northward by land up into Asia Minor. There he visited once more the churches founded on his first journey, "establishing all the disciples" (18:23).

a. *Ephesus* (chapter 19). Paul stayed in Ephesus three years (20:31), longer than in any other place, and more space is devoted in Acts to his work there than anywhere else. Ephesus was the most important center in Asia Minor—commercially, politically, religiously—and Paul's unusual attention to it is justified by its later illustrious history as one of the great centers of Christianity.

Apollos had preceded Paul at Ephesus (18:24-28). He was an Alexandrian Jew, an eloquent preacher and a great expositor of the Old Testament Scriptures. But he needed further instruction in the Christian way, and Priscilla and Aquila supplied the lack. Apollos then decided to sail across to Corinth.

When Paul arrived in Ephesus, he found a group of disciples of John the Baptist. They had not even heard of Pentecost. Paul "baptized them into the name of the Lord Jesus"; and when he had laid his hands on them, they received the Holy Spirit.

As usual, Paul reasoned with the Jews in their synagogue, but after three months the opposition became so strong that he changed to the school of Tyrannus, where he taught the

Scriptures daily for two years. From this center the gospel spread throughout the province of Asia.[2]

When the seven sons of Sceva tried to practice exorcism, after the manner of Paul, they got into trouble. The result was that many magicians confessed their sins, and their books were burnt in a large public bonfire. It was a sort of gala celebration for these who had gained their independence from slavish superstition and sin.

But Paul could not stay in a city three years without causing a riot. The opposition this time was headed by Demetrius, the silversmith, whose trade was suffering from the progress of Christianity. The persecution here and at Philippi was motivated by commercial considerations. Elsewhere it was for religious reasons.

The description of the mob at Ephesus is very typical—people running together and yelling insanely. Paul wanted to face the crowd, but his friends wisely dissuaded him (v. 30).

b. *Macedonia and Greece* (20:1-5). From Ephesus Paul went to Macedonia—probably overland to Troas, and then across the water to Philippi. Doubtless he visited the Macedonian churches at Thessalonica and Berea, before going down to Corinth, where he stayed three months.

When he was ready to sail from Corinth back home to Antioch, he heard that the Jews were plotting to seize him. So he walked back through Macedonia to Philippi, and sailed from there to Troas.

c. *Troas* (20:6-12). Paul spent a few days at Troas, where he had received the Macedonian vision. On Sunday night he preached till midnight, as he must leave the next day. When a young man went to sleep and fell out of the window, Paul took care of the interruption, and then continued the service till daylight. Presumably the people had been sufficiently aroused by the accident to stay awake after that!

d. *Miletus* (20:13-38). Paul felt he did not have time to go up to Ephesus, so he sent for the elders of the church there to meet him at Miletus.

Paul's farewell meeting with the Ephesian elders is a touching scene. He reminded them of his earnest, faithful ministry among them. He warned them that there would be heresy and

[2] The Term "Asia" in the New Testament never refers to the continent, but rather to the Roman province of that name, in western Asia Minor.

schism in their midst, but pleaded with them to be true and un-selfish. They wept on his neck, as they realized that they would not see their beloved founder again.

e. *Tyre and Caesarea* (21:1-16). Finding disciples at Tyre, Paul stayed there a week. His visit ended with a farewell prayer meeting on the beach, just before he went on board.

At Caesarea Paul and his party stayed in the home of "Philip the evangelist," whom we have already met at Samaria (chapter 8). His family is interesting in that there were four of his daughters who preached.[3] There were women preachers in the early church.

While they were at Caesarea a Judean prophet, named Agabus, predicted that Paul would be bound at Jerusalem, but when his friends besought him not to go there, Paul expressed his determination to enter that city, even if it meant death.

6. PAUL IN JERUSALEM (21:17—23:35)

a. *The Conference with James* (21:17-26). When Paul and his companions visited James and the other leaders in the church at Jerusalem, the latter requested that he undergo a vow in the temple, to demonstrate to the satisfaction of everyone that he was still faithful to the law. Willing to be "everything to all men," Paul acceded to their wishes.

b. *The Seizure of Paul* (21:27-40). This action of his—which we might be tempted to question—led Paul into trouble. Some of the Jews from Asia Minor had been following his trail for years. Now they had caught up with him, and they proceeded to mob him in the very temple at Jerusalem. They would probably have succeeded in their intention of killing him, had not the Roman guard come to his rescue.

Thinking him to be an insurrectionist, the captain of the guard was hurrying Paul into the tower of Antonia, the Roman barracks, when Paul asked for permission to speak to the crowd. This having been granted, he addressed the Jews in their native Aramaic.

c. *Paul's Defense Before the Jews* (22:1-21). This speech by Paul is largely composed of an account of his conversion, with a brief introduction concerning his honorable birth and his training under Gamaliel. In conclusion he told of a vision he had received in the temple, when the Lord had warned him

[3] New Testament "prophesying" seems to have been mainly preaching.

to leave Jerusalem and go "far hence unto the Gentiles" (v. 21).

d. *Paul's Roman Citizenship* (22:22-30). His reference to the Gentiles was like a red flag waved before the eyes of his Jewish hearers. They immediately clamored for his death, so that the guard had to take him inside the barracks.

As they were binding Paul preparatory to scourging him, he called the attention of the soldiers to the fact that he was a Roman citizen. After the rough treatment he had suffered from the cruel mob, he did not particularly relish the excruciating agony of a scourging. As a Roman citizen he could plead immunity from this until he had been duly condemned.

e. *Paul Before the Sanhedrin* (23:1-10). In order to find out what the trouble was all about, the captain of the guard brought Paul before the Jewish council. When the apostle received cruel treatment, he resorted to the clever device of starting an argument between the Pharisees and Sadducees in the Sanhedrin. The quarrel became so violent that again Paul had to be rescued.

f. *The Plot Against Paul's Life* (23:12-35) Paul had a sister living in Jerusalem, and her son learned of a plot to kill Paul. More than forty men had conspired together under oath not to eat till Paul was dead. Paul's nephew warned his uncle of what had happened. When the captain of the guard was told, he decided that he had better get Paul out of Jerulem before he had more trouble on his hands than he could handle, so he sent him by night under very strong guard to Caesarea, the seat of the Roman government in Judea at that time.

7. PAUL IN PRISON AT CAESAREA (chapters 24-26)

a. *Paul Before Felix* (chapter 24). The Jews had hired an orator, Tertullian, to present their case against Paul before the governor. This he proceeded to do, after considerable ill-deserved flattery of Felix. He charged Paul with being a public nuisance, an insurrectionist and "a ringleader of the sect of the Nazarenes" (v. 5). He also accused him of having profaned the temple.

Paul denied emphatically this last charge, as well as the rest. He then pleaded guilty to just one thing—his faith in

Jesus Christ, which made him a heretic in the eyes of the Jews.

Having had previous knowledge of Christianity, Felix filed the case. Soon after that he and his wife requested Paul to tell them more about this new religion. Paul took advantage of the opportunity to preach the truth to this ungodly couple. Conviction became so strong that "Felix was terrified, and answered, Go thy way for this time; and when I have a convenient season, I will call thee unto me" (v. 25). But probably he never felt conviction again.

b. *Paul Before Festus* (25:1-12). Two years had passed by, and again Paul had to face his angry accusers. He still maintained his innocence of any crime against the Jews or the Roman government.

When Festus suggested taking him up to Jerusalem for trial, Paul, knowing that his life would not be safe in that city, appealed to Caesar. As a Roman citizen he had the privilege of appealing to the emperor for trial.

c. *Paul Before Agrippa* (25:23—26:32). When Herod Agrippa II—son of Herod Agrippa I, whose death is recorded in chapter 12—came to visit Festus, the latter told him of Paul's case. The governor was perplexed to know what accusation to send with Paul to the emperor, so Agrippa agreed to hear Paul and make some suggestion.

In Paul's defense before Agrippa he again recounted his conversion. He declared his complete obedience to the heavenly vision he had received on the road to Damascus. He then proceeded to launch out on a sermon about Christ.

But Festus had had enough, and accused Paul of being mad. After answering the governor courteously, Paul turned squarely to King Agrippa and challenged him to admit his belief in the Hebrew prophets.

Agrippa's answer is probably best represented in the Revised Version: "With but little persuasion thou wouldest fain make me a Christian" (26:28). Thus Agrippa threw off, perhaps laughingly, the conviction which Paul had evidently seen in his face.

8. PAUL'S VOYAGE TO ROME (chapters 27, 28)

The Lord had assured Paul that he was to see Rome (23:11), but probably he never expected to go there as a

—119—

Roman prisoner. However, he reached his destination, in spite of mob and shipwreck.

The description of the terrible storm on the Mediterranean, as well as all geographical allusions and nautical terms, reveals the fact that Luke had traveled widely on the water and also that he was a participator in this harrowing experience on the way to Rome.

When the storm struck in all its fury Paul proved to be the greatest man on board. When everyone had given up hope, he encouraged those in the ship to be of good cheer, for an angel of the Lord had assured him that all lives would be saved. However, the ship itself and its cargo would be lost. Paul's faith was equal to the storm—"I believe God" (27:25).

After fourteen days and nights of dark despair, the ship broke on the shores of the Island of Malta. Here the shipwrecked crew and passengers were received hospitably by the natives. The use of the term "barbarians" (28:2) shows Luke to have had a Greek point of view.

Paul had an unexpected opportunity to minister to the bodies of these islanders, and we may well believe that he ministered also to their souls. Thus the Island of Malta had perhaps its first contact with Christianity.

The Book of Acts closes with Paul living two whole years in his own hired dwelling at Rome—though still an imperial prisoner—"preaching the kingdom of God, and teaching the things concerning the Lord Jesus Christ with all boldness, none forbidding him." At last Paul's desire to see Rome had been fulfilled.

VI. THE PIONEER MISSIONARY

The greatest missionary of all time was the Apostle Paul. He introduced Christianity into Asia Minor, Macedonia, and Greece—three great sections of the eastern Mediterranean world. He did more than any other man to make Christianity the great world religion of this age.

Paul founded churches in most of the large cities where he traveled. Since he could not visit these churches frequently, he wrote letters to them. This explains the origin of most of his epistles.

First Thessalonians

Associated with Paul in the writing of this letter are the names of Silas and Timothy, his two leading companions on his second journey. The former had started out with Paul from Antioch, while the latter, a young disciple, had joined the party at Lystra. Paul probably wrote the two Thessalonian letters from Corinth in A.D. 50 and 51, during his eighteen months' stay there on his second missionary journey.

From the very numerous papyrus letters of the period we learn that correspondents always began by giving their own name and then addressing the one, or ones, to whom they were writing. Paul follows this custom in all thirteen of his epistles. The Greek papyrus letters usually have the salutation *charein*, "joy" or "grace." The characteristic Jewish greeting was "peace." Paul combines these two. In all his epistles he salutes his readers with the words "grace and peace." The Christian gospel was to bring joy and peace to all who would accept it.

After the salutation comes the thanksgiving (1:2). Paul begins almost all his letters with thanking or blessing God. With him praise came first, and then petition.

The great shepherd of the Gentile churches assures the Thessalonian Christians that he is mentioning them in his prayers. Whether written or not, Paul's prayer list must have been a very long one.

The picture of the shepherd is suggested further in 2:7—"We were gentle in the midst of you, as when a nurse cherisheth her own children." Paul was not a professional preacher, but a passionate pastor. "Ye were become very dear to us," he writes (2:8).

There is an interesting parallelism of two passages in chapter one. Verses nine and ten explain verse three. Their work of faith was turning to God from idols; their labor of love was serving the true and living God; their patience of hope was waiting for his Son from heaven.

In many respects the Thessalonians were exemplary Christians. Paul writes, "Ye became imitators of us, and of the Lord" (v. 6). As a result, "Ye became an ensample to all that believe in Macedonia and Achaia" (v. 7). Because they were good followers they became good leaders.

One of the purposes for which Paul wrote this epistle was to comfort these young believers in the persecutions which they were suffering. This is suggested in 1:6—"having received the word in much affliction, with joy of the Holy Spirit." Again, in 2:14, he says, "Ye also suffered the same things of your countrymen." This thought becomes the main theme of chapter three.

The Epistles of Paul are jeweled with his prayers. One such sparkling gem will be found in 3:12, 13—"And the Lord make you to increase and abound in love one toward another, and toward all men, even as we also do toward you; to the end he may establish your hearts unblamable in holiness before our God and Father, at the coming of our Lord Jesus with all his saints." Here is the secret of establishment in holiness.

The subject of sanctification holds a prominent place in this epistle. In the fourth chapter we read, "For this is the will of God, even your sanctification" (4:3).

It is evident from these passages that the emphasis in this epistle is on the moral aspect of sanctification rather than on the doctrinal aspect. Sanctification is both an inward experience and an ethic of life. Paul is here giving special attention to the latter truth. The sanctified life of the Christian is at the opposite extreme from the licentious life of the heathen. Any teaching on sanctification which ignores or neglects the moral implications of holiness is ethically unsound and dangerous. The ultimate test of any doctrine is the character and life which it produces.

There is one more outstanding passage on sanctification in this epistle: "And the God of peace himself sanctify you wholly [or, through and through]; and may your spirit and soul and body be preserved entire, without blame at the coming of our Lord Jesus Christ" (5:23). The emphasis here is on the sanctifying of the entire human personality, resulting in its integration and preservation. This "through and through" sanctification meets the requirements of modern psychology as no other experience does.

The last phrase of this verse turns our attention to another important subject discussed in this epistle, the second coming of Christ. One of the most significant passages in the New Testament relating to this topic is First Thessalonians 4:13-18.

It would appear that the believers in Thessalonica had become troubled over the fact that some of their number were passing away before the return of the Lord. They wondered if their departed loved ones would miss that great event. So Paul writes to comfort them with the assurance that those who sleep in Christ will have a part in the rapture of the saints. This is perhaps the most definite description of the return of Christ to be found in the Scriptures.

Second Thessalonians

Paul begins his second letter by commending the Thessalonian Christians for their faith and love, as well as their patience under persecution (1:3, 4). Evidently the persecutions were still continuing in Thessalonica.

The key to this short letter is probably to be found in the phrase, "the revelation of the Lord Jesus" (1:7). Premillenniallists generally divide the second coming of Christ into two phases—the rapture and the revelation. In the former He comes in the air to catch away His bride, as described in the fourth chapter of First Thessalonians. In the latter He comes with His bride to destroy the Antichrist, as described in the second chapter of Second Thessalonians.

This second phase is identified with "the day of the Lord" (2:2), a phrase which is defined in the Old Testament prophets (for example, Joel 2:1-11) as a day of terrible judgment. Paul tells us that this judgment will be especially upon "the man of sin" (2:3), popularly referred to by prophetic students as the Antichrist.

One of the main points which the apostle makes in his discussion of the second coming of Christ in this epistle is that that event will not take place until there has come first an apostasy (from *apostasis*, the Greek word for "falling away" v. 3). It appears that some of the Thessalonian Christians were expecting Christ to return immediately. This belief had been fostered by forged epistles supposed to have been written by Paul, which led these disciples to believe that "the day of the Lord is just at hand" (v. 2). Paul refutes this false notion, and warns the Christians not to be "busybodies," but to work quietly (3:11, 12).

So this Second Epistle is written to correct a false deduction, derived perhaps from the First Epistle, to the effect that Christ was coming back again at once. This had produced an unwholesome fanaticism in the church at Thessalonica. These two advent epistles, as they are commonly called, supplement each other in their teaching on the second coming of Christ.

Paul closes this second letter with an interesting note: "The salutation of me Paul with mine own hand, which is the token in every epistle: so I write" (3:17). This is the apostle's autograph. He tells us here that he himself signed his own name to each of his epistles—most of which were probably written by amanuenses—to attest their genuineness.

First Corinthians

This epistle was written from Ephesus during Paul's stay of three years there on his third missionary journey, probably in A.D. 55. Nearly five years had elapsed since his pastorate of a year and a half at Corinth (A.D. 50 to 51), on his second journey. In the meantime situations had developed in the Corinthian church that demanded attention.

Paul had received information about some of these unfortunate developments from certain Corinthians who had visited him in Ephesus: "For it hath been signified unto me concerning you, my brethren, by them that are of the household of Chloe" (1:11). About some other matters the Corinthians themselves had written to Paul, "Now concerning the things whereof ye wrote" (7:1). This gives us two main divisions of the epistle: I. The things concerning which he had heard, chapters 1-6; II. The things concerning which they had written, chapters 7-16. Under the first heading three problems are discussed, and under the second, six problems. We shall study these problems in order.

1. Things Concerning Which He Had Heard (chapters 1-6)

a. *Divisions* (chapters 1-4). After a brief introduction (1:1-9), Paul immediately attacks the problem of disunity in the Corinthian church. "I beseech you, brethren, . . . that there be no divisions among you" (v. 10). The Greek word for "divisions" is literally "schisms." The church at Corinth was afflicted with a schismatic spirit.

There were four parties in evidence. The first claimed Paul as their leader. He was the founder of the church, and they would always be loyal to him. The second party admired Apollos for his eloquent preaching and striking appearance. A third group contended that Peter was God's chosen leader for the apostolic church. This had been demonstrated at Pentecost and in the days following. To these Judaizers Paul was a dangerous innovator. The fourth group refused all party names, such as Paulinists and Petrinists. They were simply "Christians." They were probably fanatical and intolerant, priding themselves on being "the spiritual ones," and may have caused as much trouble as any of the other parties.

Over against this petty bickering and loveless quarreling Paul lifted high the cross of Christ (1:17). In their selfish absorption with themselves the Corinthians had lost sight of the crucified Jesus. This led Paul to denounce their misplaced confidence in "the wisdom of the world" (v. 20). "We preach Christ crucified," he declared (1:23). This is God's offer of salvation. Humanity can never save itself by its own wisdom. The wisdom of God is to be found in Christ, who is our righteousness, sanctification and redemption. "But of him are ye in Christ Jesus, who was made unto us wisdom from God, both righteousness and sanctification and redemption" (R.V., margin).[1] That is, in Christ we are justified, sanctified and shall ultimately be glorified (complete redemption). This is the New Testament revelation of the wisdom of God, flowing out of His infinite love for mankind.

In the second chapter Paul goes on to enlarge on the contrast between the world's wisdom and God's wisdom. The latter is centered in "Jesus Christ, and him crucified" (v. 2). It is a mystery to the world (v. 7), but is revealed to believers by the Holy Spirit (v. 10).

In the third chapter Paul returns to the main topic of this section, after one of his frequent excursions along a line of truth suggested by the discussion. He indicates that their divisions are evidence of their carnal condition. With all their boasted wisdom they are really only babes in Christ (v. 1). They have turned their eyes from God to human leaders (vs. 4-7).

In the fourth chapter the apostle shows that pride is one of the main causes of division and strife. What the Corinthian Christians needed more than anything else was humility, a recognition that they were nothing and had nothing apart from Christ. "What hast thou that thou didst not receive, but if thou didst receive it, why dost thou glory as. if thou hadst not received it?" (v. 7). There is no room in the Christian life for boasting.

b. *Immorality* (chapter 5). With all their pride of wisdom and spirituality the Corinthians were condoning sin in their midst. One of the members of the church was living in sin with his father's wife, evidently his own stepmother. Paul rebuked this situation sternly and ordered that the offender should be excluded from the fellowship of the church.

c. *Lawsuits* (chapter 6). The lack of unity among the Corinthian believers had resulted in some of them actually going to law against each other. The apostle chided them for such unchristian actions. "What, cannot there be found among you one wise man who shall be able to decide between his brethren, but brother goeth to law with brother, and that before unbelievers?" (vs. 5, 6).

Then Paul scored a brilliant point. "Nay, already it is altogether a loss to you, that ye have lawsuits one with another"

[1] The Greek suggests that the term "wisdom" is defined by the three succeeding terms.

(v. 7, R. V., margin). Even if a member of the church won a lawsuit against another member, he had already sustained a spiritual loss which was far greater than the material gain.

2. THINGS CONCERNING WHICH THEY HAD WRITTEN (chapters 7-16)

a. *Marriage* (chapter 7). Paul seemed to feel that the ideal Christian state was that of celibacy, or the single life (vs. 7, 8, 25-40). But it should be noted that he definitely disclaimed divine authority for some of his own opinions expressed in this chapter (vs. 6, 12, 25). Furthermore, it is altogether likely that the apostle expected Christ to return during the first generation of the church. In that case, it would seem wiser for men to go out unhindered by family ties in the effort to evangelize the world as soon as possible.

But, passing by Paul's pleas for celibacy, we may note some valuable teachings in this chapter. In verse three he says, "Let the husband render unto the wife her due: and likewise also the wife unto the husband." A large part of the troubles in matrimony result from the fact that the order of these two commands is generally reversed. The next step is to forget the first part altogether.

Paul advises married people against separation, even when one of the two is not a Christian. He says that such a union is valid religiously as well as legally. That is the significance of the seemingly difficult statement in verse 14, "For the unbelieving husband is sanctified in the wife, and the unbelieving wife is sanctified in the brother: else were your children unclean; but now are they holy." If the term "unclean" is interpreted "illegitimate" it makes the point clear. Perhaps some Christians had questioned the validity of a marriage in which one of the two had become a believer while the other remained an unbeliever. We must remember that Paul was writing to meet problems that existed in the church of the first century.

b. *Things Offered to Idols* (chapters 8-10). The Corinthians had written to Paul, asking his advice about eating things that had been sacrificed to idols. Before answering their question he warns them against intellectual pride. He makes the significant observation, "Knowledge puffeth up, but love buildeth up" (8:1, lit., Greek). The one is inflation; the other is construction.

Paul's answer to the question is that an idol is nothing, and therefore a thing is not affected by having been sacrificed to it (8:4; 10:19). But it is best to have nothing to do with idols in any way (10:20).

The discussion of this problem furnished Paul with a starting point for a masterly essay on the subject of Christian liberty. Even though we may know that some things are of no vital consequence, we should be careful not to offend someone who has a weak, or unenlightened, conscience (8:7-12). Love should govern all our actions to make them truly Christian. Paul's own magnanimous spirit is revealed in his statement, "Wherefore, if meat causeth my brother to stumble, I will eat no flesh for evermore, that I cause not my brother to stumble" (8:13). That is a reflection of the spirit of Christ himself.

In chapter nine Paul teaches that a Christian minister should receive material compensation for his services (vs. 7-14). But to prevent being charged with a mercenary spirit the great apostle had labored with his own hands to provide his livelihood (vs. 15, 18). His whole attitude in Christian work is summed up in that sweeping statement, "I am become all things to all men, that I may by all means save some" (v. 22).

Even though the Christian is free he must exercise self-control. After many years of walking with God, Paul still declares, "But I buffet my body, and bring it into bondage: lest by any means, after that I have preached to others, I myself should be rejected" (v. 27). If the spirit is to be kept free, the body must be kept in bondage.

In chapter ten Paul sounds a warning against the dangers resulting from the attitude of liberty. It reminds us of the modern adage, "Eternal vigilance is the price of freedom." Paul puts it thus: "Let him that thinketh he standeth take heed lest he fall" (v. 12). But if we are careful we need not fear, for "There hath no temptation taken you but such as men can bear: but God is faithful, who will not suffer you to be tempted above that ye are able; but will with the temptation make also the way of escape, that ye may be able to endure it" (v. 13). What a comforting thought that with every temptation there comes also the way of escape!

The true attitude of Christian liberty is expressed in the words, "Let no man seek his own, but each his neighbor's good" (v. 24). Paul illustrates this in the case of eating things sacrificed to idols. If to eat would offend some weak brother, we should refrain from doing so (v. 28).

c. *Church Conduct* (chapter 11). The instruction that women should wear veils at public worship must be read in the light of the conditions of the times. Paul did not want the Christian women to be taken for prostitutes, who went about shamelessly with unveiled faces. It behooves the followers of Christ to conform to the best proprieties of their own particular generation. To do otherwise in the name of Christian liberty is to bring reproach on the gospel of Christ.

After his discussion of women at worship (11:1-16), Paul takes up the matter of conduct at the Lord's Supper (11:17-34). It rather shocks us to read that in the Corinthian church this sacred memorial of Christ's death had degenerated into a drunken feast (v. 21). Certainly there were conditions at Corinth that clamored for radical reform.

The statement of verse 23 is highly significant. Paul claims divine authority for the sacrament of the Lord's Supper. "I received of the Lord that which also I delivered unto you." He was not dependent upon the tradition of the disciples for his knowledge, but had received a direct revelation from the Lord concerning it.

It is also interesting to note that Paul follows most closely Luke's account of the institution of the Lord's Supper. This fact agrees with the early tradition about Paul's connection with Luke's Gospel, which we have already noted.

d. *Spiritual Gifts* (chapters 12-14). One of the contributing factors in the strife among the Christians at Corinth was the unfortunate overemphasis upon the possession of spiritual gifts. Those who had gifts of the Spirit looked down on those who had none or who had lesser gifts. All of this fostered spiritual pride and became a lamentable cause of division.

In meeting this situation Paul went to the heart of the problem, "Now there are diversities of gifts, but the same Spirit" (12:4). It was because the Corinthian Christians had become absorbed and obsessed with the gifts of the Spirit and so had lost sight of the Spirit himself that strife and division had crept into the church. The secret of true Christian unity is to be found in the communion and fellowship of the Holy Spirit.

The thirteenth chapter of First Corinthians is the great love chapter of the Bible. It describes the more excellent way which Paul said he would show these quarreling Christians (12:31). Many people have failed to see that the apostle is setting the way of love over against the emphasis upon gifts of the Spirit. Yet that is exactly the point of this wonderful chapter.

In the first verse he strikes at the most troublesome point by saying that the gift of tongues without love means only clamor and confusion. In the second verse he deals with those who prided themselves on the exercise of the gifts of prophecy and faith. They could have these, and yet without love they were nothing. They could even go so far as to glory in martyrdom, but it was all entirely profitless without love.

Paul then goes on to enumerate the qualities of love. It is longsuffering, kind, humble, well-behaved, unselfish, happy about good things, believing, hopeful, enduring, unfailing. Prophecies will be done away with and tongues will cease, but love is eternal. The partial will be succeeded by the perfect. Faith deals with the unseen spiritual realities, and hope deals with the unknown future, but love is of the essence of eternity. It would be absurd to say that God is faith or God is hope, but John twice declares that "God is love" (1 John 4:8, 16). Therefore love is the greatest thing in the universe.

In the fourteenth chapter Paul admonishes the Corinthians to "follow after love" (v. 1). It is commendable to desire spiritual gifts, but they should remember that prophecy, not tongues, is the greatest gift (vs. 1-19). It is evident from this chapter that the crux of the problem was the wrong emphasis at Corinth upon the gift of tongues, with consequent disorder, confusion and strife. Paul admonishes these folks to curb their inordinate affection for outward demonstration. Especially he urges the women not to abuse their new-found freedom by talking out loud in church and disturbing the services (vs. 33-36).

In conclusion the apostle lays down the general principle that should govern all Christian worship, "Let all things be done decently and in order" (v. 40). For, "God is not a God of confusion, but of peace" (v. 33).

e. *The Resurrection* (chapter 15). This is the greatest chapter in the New Testament on the subject of the resurrection. It is also the longest chapter in this epistle. The Book of Acts indicates that the resurrection of Jesus was one of the most important topics in apostolic preaching. Paul here combines this subject with that of the resurrection of the believer.

The chapter begins with a summary of the appearances of Jesus after His resurrection. The significant thing here is that Paul lists his own experience along with the other visible appearances of Jesus, some of which are recorded in the four Gospels.

The Sadducees denied the fact of a resurrection. At Athens Paul found that the Greek philosophers treated the idea with derision. There were also some in the Christian Church who took the same position (v. 12). Paul later mentions others who were guilty of that heresy (2 Tim. 2:18).

Here the apostle emphasizes the seriousness of this error, for if there is no resurrection, then Christ has not risen, and if He has not risen, Christianity is not a faith, but a farce (vs. 12-19).

But Paul has already demonstrated the historical validity of the resurrection of Jesus, by citing various witnesses who saw the risen Christ. Accepting the fact of His resurrection, then, Paul goes on to show that it is the ground for the resurrection of believers. Christ was the firstfruits of that great harvest which will be seen in the resurrection morning (vs. 20-23). The final act of history will be the subjection of all beings and things in the universe to God (vs. 24-28).

Having proved the fact of the resurrection Paul now goes on to discuss the manner of this event (vs. 35-49). He illustrates it by the analogy of the seed which is sown in the ground and comes up a plant. Our heavenly bodies will be as different from these earthly ones as the beautiful, fragrant flower is from the little, dry, ugly seed from which it sprang. "It is sown a natural body; it is raised a spiritual body" (v. 44). That statement answers the oftraised question as to the nature of our resurrection bodies. They will be spiritual bodies, fitted for existence in the spiritual realm of eternity, just as these physical bodies fit us for life in this material realm of time.

For those who are alive at the return of Christ there will be an instantaneous change from corruption to incorruption, from mortality to immortality (vs. 50-58). The reign of death will then be ended.

f. *The Collection* (chapter 16). One of Paul's concerns on his missionary journeys was to collect funds for the needy saints at Jerusalem. In connection with this he laid down a most important statement of principle concerning Christian giving. He said, "Upon the first day of the week let each one of you lay by him in store, as he may prosper" (v. 2). Our giving, then, is to be regular, systematic and proportionate to our income. No better method has ever been found for caring for the material needs of God's work.

The personal greetings at the end of this epistle are very interesting, but we cannot take time for them here. We would close our study of this outstanding letter of Paul by quoting his admonition to the Corinthians, "Let all that ye do be done in love" (v. 14).

Second Corinthians

Soon after sending the so-called First Epistle to the Corinthians Paul was compelled to leave Ephesus.[2] He had dispatched Titus to Corinth to ascertain what the reaction was to the former letter and he was waiting anxiously for his return. When Titus reached him with good news of the general loyalty of the Corinthian church, Paul wrote another letter. This Second Epistle to the Corinthians was written from some city in Macedonia, probably in A.D. 56.

This epistle reveals the humanity of the great apostle more than any of his other writings. It may be listed with Philemon, Philippians, and Galatians as one of the most personal of his letters. Nowhere else do we see so clearly the play of Paul's feelings. He was a man of intense emotion and strong feeling. This, combined with his tremendous will power, made him more zealous than his contemporaries, both as a Pharisee and as a Christian.

[2] See the author's *Story of the New Testament*, p. 74.

—132—

The dominant autobiographical nature of this letter is evidenced by the very frequent use of "I." Most of Paul's letters have a definitely personal flavor, but none more strikingly than Second Corinthians.

The divisions of this epistle are clearly marked. In the first seven chapters we have Paul's defense of his apostleship. Chapters eight and nine are rather parenthetical to the main drive of the epistle. They deal with the matter of the collection. In chapters ten to thirteen, inclusive, Paul sets forth a passionate, pleading defense of his personal character.

1. DEFENSE OF HIS MINISTRY (chapters 1-7)

It is interesting to note that Paul begins both of his letters to Corinth by calling himself "an apostle." He did not find it necessary thus to assert his authority in writing to the Thessalonians, nor later to the loyal, loving Philippians. But to the other churches, and especially in the case of Corinth, he addresses the Christians with apostolic authority.

Paul, after his usual thanksgiving (1:3-7), tells the Corinthians of the crushing burden which he had felt for them after writing to them from Ephesus. "For we would not have you ignorant, brethren, concerning our affliction which befell us in Asia, that we were weighed down exceedingly, beyond our power, insomuch that we despaired even of life" (1:8). Paul knew what it was to have his heart broken for his wayward children.

Even when he left Ephesus and went to Troas, the apostle's anxiety would not allow him to settle down to preaching in that needy field. "Now when I came to Troas for the gospel of Christ, and when a door was opened unto me in the Lord, I had no relief for my spirit, because I found not Titus my brother; but taking my leave of them, I went forth into Macedonia" (2:12, 13). Paul was like a man with a gnawing pain which will allow him no rest.

The attitude of Paul as he wrote First Corinthians is described in 2:4—"For out of much affliction and anguish of heart I wrote unto you with many tears." Paul was a great pastor, as well as a great preacher and teacher.

One of the most significant passages in the New Testament relative to growth in the Christian life is that in 3:18— "But we all, with unveiled face beholding as in a mirror the glory of the Lord, are transformed into the same image from glory to glory." The Greek word for "transformed" (changed," A. V.) is the same as that used for the transfiguration of Jesus.[3] It is a most challenging comparison.

Paul makes a revealing statement in 5:9—"We make it our aim . . . to be wellpleasing unto him." The Greek says, "We are ambitious." This was Paul's one consuming ambition, to please his Lord.

One of the great passages on the atonement occurs in 5:19—"God was in Christ reconciling the world unto himself." Apart from the divine-human Christ there can be no reconciliation between God and man. The sinless Jesus became our sin-offering, that we might become partakers of God's righteousness (5:21).

In 6:4-10 Paul gives some of the distinguishing marks of the Christian ministry. They are worthy of consideration by everyone who seeks to minister to the souls of men.

The apostle refers again to his recent burden in the seventh chapter, "For even when we were come into Macedonia our flesh had no relief, but we were afflicted on every side; without were fightings, within were fears. Nevertheless he that comforteth the lowly, even God, comforted us by the coming of Titus" (7:5, 6). The concern which had gripped him so painfully at Ephesus had followed him to Troas and across to Macedonia. Only the appearance of Titus with good news brought relief from the strain of this trial.

In the eighth verse Paul admits that he had gone so far as to regret having written so sternly to the Corinthians. But now that they have repented and have cleansed their church of the sin in its midst, he rejoices at the result (vs. 9-11).

2. THE COLLECTION FOR THE SAINTS (chapters 8, 9)

At this point Paul digresses for a little to urge the Corinthians to make sure they have ready their contribution to the funds being raised for the poor saints at Jerusalem. He incites them by the example of the sacrificial giving of the Macedonians (8:1-15). Lest they should slip up on this matter, Paul is sending Titus with this letter to see that the collection is taken care of promptly (8:16-24). With him he is sending "the brother whose praise in the gospel is spread through all

[3] Matthew 17:2; Mark 9:2. For a fuller discussion of this point, as also of the Greek words for "seal" and "earnest" in 1:22, see the author's book, *The Quest of the Spirit* (1940), pp. 123-130.

the churches; . . . who was also appointed by the churches to travel with us in the matter of this grace" (vs. 18, 19). The reference is probably to Luke. The Book of Acts indicates that the author of Acts traveled with Paul to Jerusalem on this last trip.

The apostle has boasted to the Macedonians that the Corinthians had already subscribed their contribution. Now he urges them to be sure that the money is collected before he arrives, to save any embarrassment (9:1-5). He concludes by exhorting them to be liberal in their giving, for God will supply all their needs (9:6-15).

3. VINDICATION OF HIS CHARACTER (chapters 10-13).

Now we come to the rapids in this epistle, as Paul's soul plunges from one rock of opposition to another. In chapters 10-13 the apostle is answering the cruel, cutting, contemptuous slanders of his enemies at Corinth. Battered and bleeding, he yet emerges from the conflict victorious in the inner consciousness of his own purity of motive and conduct.

One of the meanest stabs at Paul was to hold up to ridicule his personal appearance. This is fighting in the gutter. "His letters, they say, are weighty and strong; but his bodily presence is weak, and his speech of no account" (10:10). These libelous critics had no compunctions against stooping to the basest type of attack.

It would appear that some were ready to insinuate that Paul preached for monetary profit (11:1-15). He reminds the Corinthians that he did not take from them one thing for his support. He lived by the labor of his own hands and the voluntary contributions of the Macedonian churches.

We may be thankful that Paul had to answer the false accusation of these critics, for in doing so he has given us two interesting chapters from his life story. The first is a summary of the hardships which he had suffered for the sake of the gospel (11:16-33).

It would appear that his enemies at Corinth were Judaizers, who had come there to overthrow his authority. "Are they Hebrews? So am I. Are they Israelites? So am I. Are they the seed of Abraham? So am I" (11:22).

But Paul could tell a story of sufferings which none of them could duplicate. Whipped five times; beaten with rods three times; stoned; thrice shipwrecked; often endangered in his travels by swollen rivers, robbers, the Jews, the Gentiles, city mobs, wilderness perils, stormy voyages, false brethren; worn out with heavy labor, frequent nights of prayer, hunger and thirst, and many fastings; cold from insufficient clothing; and on top of all this the crushing load of anxiety for all his churches—this was the life of Paul, the apostle to the Gentiles. We can only hope that the Corinthian critics were completely silenced when the reading of this epistle was finished.

The other story from Paul's life which is recorded only here is that of the vision which he had seen fourteen years before (12:1-4). He had been caught up into the third heaven, where he had heard words which could not be repeated to human ears.

To keep the apostle humble after this trip to heaven there was given to him a thorn in the flesh (12:7). We are not told what this was. It may have been poor eyesight. At any rate, it was evidently a physical affliction. But the essential thing is that the Lord gave him grace to bear this thorny trial, and thus Paul shines still more brightly as an example of the all-sufficient grace of God.

In the closing part of the epistle Paul tells the Corinthians that he is coming to them soon for a third visit (12:14—13:10). He beseeches them to examine themselves, in order that he may find them in a good spiritual state when he comes.

The letter closes with the favorite benediction of the Christian Church, which is at the same time an affirmation of the doctrine of the Trinity: "The grace of the Lord Jesus Christ, and the love of God, and the communion of the Holy Spirit, be with you all."

VII. THE PEERLESS THEOLOGIAN

We have said that Paul is the outstanding Christian missionary of all time. The same statement may be made about his place as a theologian. The Epistles of Paul constitute the greatest single source of our Christian theology. The importance of Paul's contribution to the propagation, organization and indoctrination of the Christian Church can hardly be exaggerated.

There is a considerable amount of doctrine in the Corinthian letters, but the larger part of them is taken up with the discussion of practical and personal problems. The most doctrinal of all of Paul's epistles is that written to the Romans. But since Galatians has the same theme—justification by faith —it will be profitable to consider these two epistles together.

Galatians

The purpose for which Paul wrote the Epistle to the Galatians is obvious. Some Judaizers had been visiting the churches of this region, teaching the Christians that they must conform to the law of Moses in order to be saved. Paul had preached simple faith in Christ as the only means of salvation and this new teaching was causing confusion among the believers. The apostle sought to remedy this situation by writing this letter.

The Epistle to the Galatians falls naturally into three main divisions. The first two chapters are autobiographical. The third and fourth chapters are theological. The fifth and sixth are practical. These three points, with the introduction and conclusion give us an outline of the epistle.

1. SALUTATION (1:1-5)

Paul begins by asserting and defending the divine origin and authority of his apostleship. It was not from a human source ("from men") nor through human agency ("through men"). In other words, his authority as apostle was not derived from any man-made decree, nor was it received by him through ordination by any official of the church. It came to him directly through Jesus Christ as agent and from God the Father as source.

It is probable that the Judaizers in Galatia were denying Paul's apostolic authority on the ground that he had not been chosen and ordained by Jesus, as had Peter. But Paul declares that the risen Christ had given him a divine ordination to the apostleship.

2. PERSONAL HISTORY (1:6—2:21)

It is noticeable that Paul omits his usual thanksgiving at the beginning of this epistle. Instead he begins abruptly by saying, "I marvel that ye are so quickly removing from him that called you in the grace of Christ unto a different gospel; which is not another gospel" (vs. 6, 7). The repetition of the word "another" in the King James Version fails to bring out the distinction in the Greek text. Two distinct terms are used here, the first of which (heteros) signifies another of a different kind. This so-called gospel of the Judaizers was really no gospel at all.

In the first verse Paul had asserted the divine origin and authority of his apostleship. In the eleventh and twelfth verses he declares the divine source of his message. "For I make known to you, brethren, as touching the gospel which was preached by me, that it is not after man. For neither did I receive it from man, nor was I taught it, but it came to me through revelation of Jesus Christ." This is Paul's answer, not only to the Judaizers of his day, but also to the modern liberals who charge him with corrupting the simple gospel of Jesus with his own speculative theological opinions.

The first two chapters of the Epistle to the Galatians add several items to Luke's account of Paul's life. These supplement rather than contradict the story in Acts.

Paul tells us first that after his conversion he did not consult human leaders, but retired into Arabia to meditate on the meaning of this new faith. It has commonly been held that the apostle spent three years in Arabia. But a careful reading of 1:17, 18 will show at once that there is no justification whatever for this view. It is not clear, however, whether the three years begin with his conversion or with his return from Arabia to Damascus. Pauline chronology is a problematical subject.

The apostle mentions his first visit to Jerusalem (1:18; cf. Acts 9:26-30). Then he tells us that he came into "the regions of Syria and Cilicia." This would seem to indicate that during the half dozen or so years between his departure from Jerusalem and his arrival at Antioch—a silent gap in the Book of Acts—Paul was not wasting his time pining away at his home in Tarsus, but was carrying on evangelistic campaigns in the adjacent territories. It is difficult to think of Paul doing otherwise.

In the second chapter (vs. 1-10) the apostle describes another visit to Jerusalem fourteen years later—or, perhaps, fourteen years after his conversion. Scholars are divided on the question as to whether or not this refers to the time of the Jerusalem Council (Acts 15). At any rate, Paul says that he had a definite divine leading to go and that he laid his gospel before the elders of the church in that city.

The main argument which Paul is presenting in this paragraph is that his gospel was approved by the leaders of the Jerusalem church—James, Peter and John (v. 9). They recognized that God had intrusted to him the gospel for the Gentiles, as to Peter the gospel for the Jews.

Paul then delivers a heavy blow to the Judaizers by telling about the time when he had to rebuke Peter publicly for his narrow sectarian attitude at Antioch (2:11-21). Certainly Peter was not then possessed of papal infallibility!

An outstanding declaration concerning Paul's religious experience is to be found in 2:20—"I have been crucified with Christ; and it is no longer I that live, but Christ liveth in me." The Greek is very emphatic. The selfish *ego* (Greek for "I") is dead. In its place Christ is at the controls of life. "Not I, but Christ" sums up Paul's whole attitude.

3. DOCTRINAL POLEMIC (chapters 3, 4)

Having demonstrated the divine origin of his gospel, Paul now faces the Galatians squarely again. "O foolish Galatians, who did bewitch you, before whose eyes Jesus Christ was openly set forth [placarded] crucified?" (3:1). They had seen clearly, as on a placard, the crucified Christ, but they had been bewitched into turning their eyes away from Him to look elsewhere.

Apparently the Judaizers were teaching not only that one must be circumcised in order to be saved, but also that one must observe scrupulously the entire law if he would become perfect. Paul challenges this heresy with the question, "Received ye the Spirit by the works of the law, or by the hearing of faith? Are ye so foolish? having begun in the Spirit, are ye now perfected in the flesh?" In other words, you were not saved by works, but by faith, and you will be made perfect in the same way.

Paul goes on now to cite the case of Abraham. This patriarch was justified by faith, not by works (3:6-14). The covenant which God made with Abraham was one of promise (3:15-18). The law, which came four hundred and thirty years later at Sinai, had no power to annul this covenant of promise.

For what purpose, then, is the law? It was given as a temporary arrangement for the Israelites until Christ should come, the One promised to Abraham as his Seed that should bless all the nations of the earth (3:19).

The function of the law was to act as a "tutor to bring us unto Christ that we might be justified by faith" (3:24). The tutor (Gr., pedagogue) was a slave who was intrusted with the bringing up of his master's child. Some hold that it was simply the duty of the slave to bring the child to the "schoolmaster," which here would be Christ, not the law. But we know that slaves often acted as the educators of Roman children and it is probable that this is the figure used here.

That such is the case seems clear from the next point in Paul's argument (4:1-7). He says that during his minority an heir is under the care of guardians and stewards, "until the day appointed of the father." Then he inherits his rightful privileges as a son. Christ came to give us the adoption of sons, that we might come into our inheritance as heirs of God. "And because ye are sons, God sent forth the Spirit of his Son into our hearts, crying, Abba, Father" (v. 6). The term "Abba" is Aramaic, the familiar tongue of home life in Palestine at this time. It would be equivalent to our use of "Papa." The Spirit of Christ makes our sonship real, so that we are on familiar terms with our heavenly Father.

In 4:12-20 Paul again pleads with the Galatians to return to Christ. They had loved him with such devotion that they would have been willing to pluck out their eyes and give them to him—perhaps because his own eyes were very poor. He cannot now understand why they have turned away from him so quickly.

The allegory of Hagar and Sarah, or Ishmael and Isaac (4:21-31) is a striking case of Old Testament interpretation. The allegorical method needs to be used with great caution, for it lends itself to wild and foolish speculations. But Paul uses it here to illustrate the truth which he is seeking to drive home. The Galatians must cast out the bondwoman of legalistic Judaism if they are to inherit the promise of God through faith. It was a forceful illustration, drawn from the Scriptures of these Jewish opponents.

4. ETHICAL APPLICATION (5:1—6:10)

One of the main emphases of the Epistle to the Galatians is liberty, or freedom. It is not without significance that Luther's study of this epistle was one of the main factors in producing the great Protestant Reformation. It sounded in his soul the clarion call to the freedom of the Spirit. Actually the situation in Galatia was very similar to that which confronted Luther in Germany.

Paul declares that Christ had called these Galatians to freedom (5:1, 13). They must guard against losing their liberty through surrender to the Judaizers, and thus be "severed from Christ" and "fallen away from grace" (5:4). In Christ Jesus external observances avail nothing, "but faith working through love" (v. 6). "Ye were running well; who hindered you that ye should not obey the truth?" (v. 7).

We should not use our Christian liberty as an occasion for license, "but through love be servants one to another. For the whole law is fulfilled in one word, even in this: Thou shalt love thy neighbor as thyself" (5:13, 14). Paul here agrees with Jesus in his emphasis upon love as the central thing in the Christian life.

The law failed to free men from bondage to the lusts of the flesh. There is only one remedy. "Walk by the Spirit, and ye shall not fulfil the lust of the flesh" (5:16). That is the secret of victory in the life of the Christian.

The fifth chapter closes with a striking contrast between "the works of the flesh" (vs. 19-21) and "the fruit of the Spirit" (vs. 22, 23). It is difficult to see how anyone after reading these lists could fail to covet the experience of the Spirit-filled and Spirit-led life.

There seem to be two mutually contradictory statements in chapter six. In verse two Paul writes, "Bear ye one another's burdens, and so fulfil the law of Christ." In verse five he says, "For each man shall bear his own burden." The solution of the problem lies in the fact that two different Greek words are here translated "burden." The first suggests the idea of a crushing weight. The second means something carried. We are to bear one another's heavy, excessive burdens, but every man must "carry his own load." There is plenty of room for helpers, but none for slackers.

One of the most penetrating truths in this epistle is stated in 6:8, "for he that soweth unto his own flesh shall of the flesh reap corruption; but he that soweth unto the Spirit shall of the Spirit reap eternal life." These are the two ways, so often mentioned in Scripture.

5. CONCLUSION (6:11-18).

Paul was in such haste to write this letter to the Galatians that it appears he did not wait for an amanuensis. He sat down and wrote feelingly out of his own heart. "See with how large letters I write unto you with mine own hand" (6:11). The Greek word for letters here is not the one that means an epistle (*epistole*), but is rather the word for characters of the alphabet.

Romans

The Epistle to the Romans is the most theological of Paul's letters. It is not, however, a complete treatise on systematic theology. For the apostle's discussion of eschatology (doctrine of last things) we must turn to the Thessalonian epistles, as we have seen. For his treatment of the important subject of Christology we shall have to wait until our study of the Prison Epistles.

The field of theology which is covered by Paul in this epistle is known as soteriology, or the doctrine of salvation (from *soter*, the Greek word for Savior). More fully, we might say that he discusses here the doctrines of sin and re-demption. This is particularly the realm of experiential, as differentiated from theoretical, theology. It is significant that the apostle devotes his longest epistle to this subject which is of the greatest vital and practical value for human beings. Paul wrote this important summary of doctrine to the church at Rome which he had never visited, to be sure that it was orthodox in its belief.

The first eight chapters of Romans are *doctrinal,* sum-marizing Paul's teaching on sin, justification and sanctifica-tion. Chapters 9-11 are *prophetical,* a sort of parenthesis be-tween the doctrinal and ethical sections. Chapters 12-15 are *practical,* giving the application of the gospel to Christian liv-ing. Chapter 16 is *personal,* containing greetings to and from friends of Paul. We shall follow this outline in our study of the epistle.

1. INTRODUCTION (1:1-17)

It is interesting to note that Paul here calls himself first a servant (bondservant, or slave) of Jesus Christ, and then an apostle. The thought of service now holds the primary place in his thinking.

The humanity and deity of Jesus Christ are set forth re-spectively in verses three and four. He was "born of the seed of David according to the flesh" and "declared to be the Son of God with power . . . by the resurrection from the dead." The resurrection of Jesus is one of the most important proofs of His deity.

The Roman church had already achieved an outstanding reputation: "your faith is proclaimed throughout the whole world" (v. 8). Yet Paul felt he had something further for them. "For I long to see you, that I may impart unto you some spiritual gift to the end ye may be established" (v. 11). It is altogether possible that the Roman Christians needed some definite teaching on the place of the Holy Spirit in the life of the believer. The considerable emphasis on sanctification in this epistle would seem to corroborate this.

The familiar passage in 1:16 might well be taken as the key verse of this epistle. In fact, the theme of Romans could be stated as: "The gospel, the power of God unto salvation to every one that believeth." More briefly, we could say that the theme is: "The Redemption that is in Christ Jesus" (3:24).

2. DOCTRINAL EXPOSITION (1:18—8:39)

A. SIN (1:18—3:20)

a. *The Sin of the Gentile* (1:18-32). This passage contains the most significant statement in all literature as to the origin of the religions of the world. It is taught almost universally today that religion began with crude nature worship, or animism, and that it ascended up through various stages of polytheism (worship of many gods) until finally the Hebrew prophets evolved the high ideal of an ethical monotheism (worship of one God).

But this passage in Romans tells us that man started with an original monotheism and then descended to a gross polytheism. Beginning with a knowledge of God, he was unthankful, vain in his own reasonings, and spiritually darkened (v. 21). From there he dropped down into idolatry. After making images of himself, then of birds and animals, man finally fell to the depths of degradation in the worship of creeping things (v. 23). This reads more like "the descent of man" than the "ascent of man."

The inevitable consequence of idolatry was immorality (vs. 24-32). This is the blackest picture of sin in the Bible. It is a description of paganism at its worst. And it all follows from man's rejection of the true God.

b. *The Sin of the Jew* (chapter 2). We have seen that the two outstanding sins of the Gentile world were idolatry and immorality. The sin of the Jew consisted of insincerity and inconsistency. The attitude of Jesus in His earthly ministry indicates that God hated the Jewish sins of the spirit as much as He abhorred the Gentile sins of the flesh.

The Jew is pictured in chapter two as one who judges others and justifies himself. That Paul is writing this to the Jews is indicated clearly by verse 17, "if thou bearest the name of a Jew." The apostle is trying here to show those of his own race the unreasonableness and wickedness of their pharisaical, self-righteous attitude.

The main topic of this chapter is the judgment of God (vs. 2, 3, 5)), which is righteous in contrast to the unjust judgment of these Jewish critics. Paul states that God's judgment of every man will be "according to truth" (v. 2), "according to his works" (v. 6), and "according to my gospel" (v. 16). It will be impartial (v. 11) and according to the light which each man has (vs. 12-16). Those who dwell in so-called Christian lands will suffer much greater condemnation than the unfortunate peoples who have not heard of Christ. And those who were brought up in spiritual churches but have rejected for themselves the offer of salvation will receive much severer punishment than those who have not been in touch with vital Christianity (cf. Luke 12:47, 48). The greater the light, the greater the responsibility.

c. *The Sin of the World* (3:1-20). Having "before laid to the charge both of Jews and Greeks, that they are all under sin" (v. 9), Paul now emphasizes the fact that the whole world is guilty before God—"that every mouth may be stopped, and all the world may be brought under the judgment of God" (v. 19).

In verses 10-18 we find another description of the sinfulness of the human heart. The student should note carefully that the tenth verse does not have any reference to the Christian. The whole passage is a picture of the condition of the natural, unregenerated heart of man. It is not fair to apply the statements in the tenth and twelfth verses to the believer in Christ, unless one is ready to include also those in the thirteenth, fourteenth and fifteenth verses. As an eminent Bible expositor has well said, "A text without a context is simply a pretext."

B. JUSTIFICATION (3:21—5:21)

a. *The Means of Justification* (3:21-31). After affirming that the law cannot justify anyone in God's sight (v. 20), Paul declares, "But now apart from the law a righteousness of God hath been manifested" (v. 21). This is not the righteousness of God, simply as an attribute of deity, but specifically a righteousness which God has provided for man. This righteousness is further defined for us in the next verse, "even the righteousness of God through faith in Jesus Christ unto all them that believe." Through faith in Jesus Christ we may have God's righteousness imparted to us.

This righteousness cannot be earned by our own efforts to fulfill the law of God. It is an experience of "being justified freely by his grace through the redemption that is in Christ Jesus: whom God set forth to be a propitiation, through faith, in his blood" (vs. 24, 25). The Greek word translated "propitiation" is used for "mercy-seat" in Hebrews 9:5. Christ is our mercy-seat, where His own blood was sprinkled that we might be forgiven and accepted with God.

The great legal and moral problem of the atonement is how God can "be just, and the justifier of him that hath faith in Jesus" (v. 26). The answer is that Jesus died in our place and paid the debt of our sins.

The summary of this section is contained in verse 28, "We reckon therefore that a man is justified by faith apart from the works of the law." This is the foundation of the distinctive Protestant doctrine of justification by faith alone, which Luther put forth in opposition to the Roman Catholic doctrine of justification by faith and works.

b. *An Example of Justification* (chapter 4). In the fourth chapter Paul presents the example of Abraham, who "believed God, and it was reckoned unto him for righteousness" (v. 3). The apostle also shows that David believed in justification by faith, rather than by works (vs. 6-8).

The argument here is similar to that which we found in the third chapter of Galatians. Abraham was justified in the sight of God by faith before he was circumcised and long before the law was given. It is therefore evident that faith, rather than the works of the law, has always been the ground for justification.

The relation of the resurrection of Jesus to our justification is indicated in verse 25, "Who was delivered up for our trespasses, and was raised for our justification." If Christ had not risen, His death for us would have been in vain.

c. *The Results of Justification* (chapter 5). In the first eleven verses of the fifth chapter the apostle enumerates some of the results of justification. They are "peace with God through our Lord Jesus Christ," "access by faith into this grace wherein we stand," rejoicing in hope of the glory of God, and rejoicing in tribulations.

The ability to rejoice in tribulations is based upon our knowledge of the benefits resulting therefrom, and also upon the fact that "the love of God hath been shed abroad in our hearts through the Holy Spirit which was given unto us" (v.

5). It is the presence of the Holy Spirit in our hearts which enables us to rejoice under trial (cf. Acts 13:52).

Another essential result of justification is stated in verse 9; namely, deliverance from the wrath of God. Verse 10 indicates that while our reconciliation is based on the death of Christ for us, our day by day salvation is to be found in His life. That is, we are actually saved from sin by the new life of Christ within us.

The second part of the fifth chapter (vs. 12-21) emphasizes the fact that Christ's obedience makes up for Adam's disobedience. "So then as through one trespass the judgment came unto all men to condemnation; even so through one act of righteousness the free gift came unto all men to justification of life" (v. 18). Adam's sin brought a reign of death; Christ's sacrifice, the reign of life (v. 17).

C. SANCTIFICATION (chapters 6-8)

a. *Sanctification Through Death to Self* (chapter 6). It would seem that some were arguing that the more we sinned the greater was the opportunity for a display of the grace of God (v. 1). Paul refutes this dangerous heresy by saying that true baptism means death to sin and a new life in Christ.

The death of Christ was not only to atone for our sins, but also to give us deliverance from the inward nature of sin. "Knowing this, that our old man was crucified with him, that the body of sin might be done away, that so we should no longer be in bondage to sin" (v. 6).

But this experience of the crucifixion of the old man is not actual in our own heart and life until we make it so by an act of faith. "Even so reckon ye also yourselves to be dead unto sin, but alive unto God in Christ Jesus" (v. 11). Christ died for our sins, but we are not justified until we accept His sacrifice for us. In the same way it is true that while Christ died to deliver us entirely from sin, we do not actually become dead to sin until we identify ourselves, by faith, with Him in His death.

In the second part of the chapter (vs. 15-23) Paul answers another false deduction from his teaching on grace: "Shall we sin, because we are not under law, but under grace?" (v. 15). This question is due to a lack of understanding as to the true nature of salvation. It is not only forgiveness, but deliverance. "Being made free from sin, ye became servants of righteousness" (v. 18). As Christians we should be concerned not with freedom *to* sin, but with freedom *from* sin. "As ye presented your members as servants to uncleanness and to iniquity unto iniquity, even so now present your members as servants to righteousness unto sanctification" (v. 19). Sanctification, rightly understood, is the true goal of the Christian life.

This wonderful truth of freedom from sin is reiterated once more by Paul. "But now being made free from sin and become servants to God, ye have your fruit unto sanctification, and the end eternal life." (v. 22). This is a gospel worth preaching!

b. *Sanctification Through Union with Christ* (7:1-6). One of Paul's concerns in this letter is to make it clear to the Jews that the Christian is freed from the Mosaic law. He tells them that the coming of Christ marked the death of the law, so that they are free to embrace Christianity. "Wherefore, my brethren, ye also were made dead to the law through the body of Christ; that ye should be joined to another, even to him who was raised from the dead, that we might bring forth fruit unto God" (v. 4). This union with Christ enables us to "serve in newness of the spirit, and not in oldness of the letter" (v. 6). Union with Christ in His death and in His life—this is Christian victory.

c. *The Need of Sanctification* (7:7-25). This autobiographical section has caused a great deal of discussion. Without entering into the controversy as to what period of Paul's life is here described, we may note the essential point which he is making here; namely, that the struggle with "the sin which dwelleth in me" (vs. 17, 20) can be won only through Christ (v. 25). It is because of indwelling sin that we need complete deliverance in Christ.

d. *Sanctification Through the Spirit* (chapter 8). Having dealt with the negative side of sanctification—death to sin—Paul now takes up the positive side. "The law of the Spirit of life in Christ Jesus made me free from the law of sin and death" (v. 2). The only way to be delivered from the principle of sin is to have it superseded by the principle of life. This is accomplished by the indwelling presence of the Holy Spirit.

—148—

The secret of victorious living is walking "after the Spirit" (v. 4). "For the mind of the flesh is death; but the mind of the Spirit is life and peace" (v. 6). To be truly and fully a son of God, one must be led by the Spirit of God (v. 14).

Paul's discussion of the privileges of the Christian believer leads him to glance forward to the climax of redemption (vs. 18-25). Full adoption will mean "the redemption of our body" (v. 23), or glorification. The whole creation will share in this great deliverance (v. 21).

This eighth chapter of Romans is the second most important passage on the Holy Spirit in the New Testament, first place being held by the fourteenth and sixteenth chapters of John's Gospel. The Spirit is mentioned about twenty times in this chapter. Certainly we are justified in saying that the Spirit-filled, Spirit-led life is the normal Christian experience, the life which God intended us to live.

The Spirit helps us in our prayer life, "For we know not how to pray as we ought; but the Spirit himself maketh intercession for us with groanings which cannot be uttered" (v. 26). He helps us to pray "according to the will of God" (v. 27). We need the Holy Spirit for every phase of our life.

Paul closes this wonderful chapter with a ringing cry of triumph: "Nay, in all these things we are more than conquerors through him that loved us" (v. 37). There is no need for defeat in the Christian life.

The expression "all things" is one of the key notes of this chapter. "And we know that to them that love God all things work together for good" (v. 28). "He that spared not his own Son, but delivered him up for us all, how shall he not also with him freely give us all things?" (v. 32). These "all things" are available to those who give their "all" to God, to be filled with His Spirit.

3. PROPHETICAL INTERPRETATION (chapters 9-11)

a. *Israel's Remnant Among God's Children* (chapter 9). Paul was one who felt things deeply. "I have great sorrow and unceasing pain in my heart. For I could wish that I myself were anathema from Christ for my brethren's sake, my kinsmen according to the flesh" (9: 2, 3). He was motivated by the same spirit which led Moses to pray his great intercessory prayer (Exodus 32: 32).

The apostle reasserts the doctrine of the remnant of Israel (9:27), which is prominent in Isaiah. God always has His faithful few.

b. *Israel's Rejection of God's Righteousness* (chapter 10). Again, in the tenth chapter, Paul expresses his longings for the salvation of his people. "Brethren, my heart's desire and my supplication to God is for them, that they may be saved" (v. 1). In addition to praying for his converts the apostle prayed earnestly for his own race.

The way of salvation is stated clearly in verses 9 and 10: "If thou shalt confess with thy mouth Jesus as Lord, and shalt believe in thy heart that God raised him from the dead, thou shalt be saved: for with the heart man believeth unto righteousness; and with the mouth confession is made unto salvation." "For, . . . whosoever shall call upon the name of the Lord shall be saved" (v. 13).

c. *Israel's Restoration to God's Favor* (chapter 11). In the eleventh chapter Paul affirms that God has not "cast off his people" (v. 1), for there is a remnant that will be saved (v. 5). But it will have to be by grace (v. 6). In verses 11-24 he addresses the Gentiles (v. 13) and warns them against a false feeling of security. Just because some Israelitish branches were broken off and they were grafted in their place they should not boast of it. "By their unbelief they were broken off, and thou standest by thy faith. Be not high-minded, but fear" (v. 20).

In verses 25-32 Paul says that the "hardening" in Israel is only temporary, "until the fulness of the Gentiles be come in" (v. 25). Then "all Israel shall be saved" (v. 26).

The apostle closes this section of the epistle with one of his spontaneous outbursts of praise and adoration (vs. 33-36). As he looks forward to the ultimate fulfillment of God's plan for His people, he cries, "O the depth of the riches both of the wisdom and the knowledge of God! how unsearchable are his judgments, and his ways past tracing out!" And then he adds the majestic statement, "For of him, and through him, and unto him, are all things. To him be the glory forever. Amen."

4. PRACTICAL APPLICATION (chapters 12-15)

a. *The Religious Life of the Believer* (chapter 12). On the basis of God's gracious plan of salvation and His mercy toward us, Paul pleads with his readers to consecrate themselves fully to God. "I beseech you therefore, brethren, by the mercies of God, to present your bodies a living sacrifice, holy, acceptable to God, which is your spiritual service" (v. 1). This complete dedication of oneself to God is the necessary foundation for holy living and successful service.

But this consecration carries with it some implications regarding our relation to the world. "And be not fashioned according to this world: but be ye transformed [transfigured] by the renewing of your mind, that ye may prove what is the good and acceptable and perfect will of God" (v. 2).

Having thus set forth the Christian's basic attitude toward God and toward the world, Paul now proceeds to discuss the relation of believers to one another. He shows them how they may put into practice "the renewing of your mind."

The first thing necessary is humility (vs. 3-8), with the recognition that each member has his proper place in the body of Christ. Hence our attitude should always be that of sincere love (v. 9). "In love of the brethren be tenderly affectioned one to another; in honor preferring one another" (v. 10). If this verse were practiced by all professing Christians there would never be a church fuss!

The follower of Christ is to be generous and hospitable (v. 13), truly sympathetic (v. 15), reasonable (v. 16), and peaceful (v. 18). He is never to seek vengeance, but leave that to God (v. 19).

Paul closes this chapter with the statement of a very important principle for successful Christian living: "Be not overcome of evil, but overcome evil with good" (v. 21). This is sound psychology. The best and quickest way to get rid of evil thoughts is not to struggle with them, thus fixing our attention more strongly on them, but to turn our mind to something good, something which is pleasant and interesting. Thus our attention is transferred into a different realm of thinking. One of the great secrets of a happy and holy life is to take a positive and aggressive attitude of victory, rather than a negative, defensive one of frequent defeat. We can do this by being filled with the Holy Spirit and then putting into practice the ethical teachings of these closing chapters of Romans.

b. *The Civil Life of the Believer* (13:1-7). Paul admonishes Christians to be in subjection to the civil government (v. 1), to pay their taxes (v. 6), and to give due respect to those that are in authority (v. 7). The fact of human government is ordained of God for man's protection (vs. 1-4).

c. *The Social Life of the Believer* (13:8-14). The Christian should be careful in the payment of his debts (v. 8). He should love his neighbor (vs. 8-10). He should keep in constant readiness to meet God (v. 11), and avoid being ensnared by the sinful pleasures of this world (v. 13).

d. *The Relation of the Strong to the Weak* (14:1—15:13). "But him that is weak in faith receive ye, yet not for decision of scruples" (14:1). A weak, newly converted Christian may be received into the membership of the church, but he should not be placed in a position of responsibility. A good deal of grief has resulted from failure to heed this advice.

As we found in Paul's discussion of Christian liberty in First Corinthians 8, the "weak" person is defined as one whose conscience is unduly concerned with nonessentials. The apostle illustrates this by the case of strict vegetarians (14:2), and those who observe certain days (v. 5).

It is not our place to sit as judges on our fellow Christians: "Let us not therefore judge one another any more: but judge this rather, that no man put a stumbling block in his brother's way, or an occasion of falling" (14:13). As in Corinthians, Paul urges love as the necessary guardian of liberty (v. 15).

Christianity is not a religion of externalities, but one of inward realities. This truth is well expressed in verse 17: "For the kingdom of God is not eating and drinking, but righteousness and peace and joy in the Holy Spirit." It is not a religion of the law and the letter, but of the spirit.

Instead of hurting and hindering those who are weak, we ought to help them. "Now we that are strong ought to bear the infirmities of the weak, and not to please ourselves" (15:1). We have for this the example of Christ, who "pleased not himself" (v. 3).

Another gracious utterance of Paul is found in 15:13—"Now the God of hope fill you with all joy and peace in believing, that ye may abound in hope, in the power of the Holy Spirit." Christianity is the one religion that gives an abundant hope. But the believer experiences this hope only through the indwelling presence of the Holy Spirit.

e. *Paul's Devotion to Christ* (15:14-33). The great apostle is himself an outstanding example, as well as exponent, of the truths which he has been proclaiming in these chapters. He had presented his body as a living sacrifice to God, and had literally "burned out" for Christ.

Paul was essentially a pioneer missionary. "From Jerusalem, and round about unto Illyricum, I have fully preached the gospel of Christ; yea, making it my aim so to preach the gospel, not where Christ was already named, that I might not build upon another man's foundation" (15:19, 20). He had covered the territory from Jerusalem up through Syria and across Asia Minor, then westward across Macedonia and southward into Greece. He had gone as far as Illyricum, which faced Italy across the Adriatic. Now he longed to take the next step westward, to Rome itself (v. 22). He looks forward to going beyond there to Spain (v. 23).

But his present task is to take to the poor saints at Jerusalem a contribution from the churches of Macedonia and Greece (vs. 25, 26). He is fearful lest this offering may not be accepted graciously, because of the opposition of the Judaizers to him (v. 31), and requests the prayer of the Romans concerning this matter.

5. PERSONAL COMMUNICATION (chapter 16)

The last chapter of this epistle is filled with personal greetings to and from Paul's friends and fellow workers. Some thirty-five people are mentioned by name.

a. *Recommendation* (vs. 1, 2). Paul commends Phoebe, a deaconess of the church at Cenchrea, near Corinth, to the church to which he is writing. She has been a loyal worker in her own church and a helper of Paul. It is noticeable that women hold a large and important place in the list of the apostle's friends given in this chapter. This fact should forever silence those who say that Paul was a woman-hater!

b. *Greetings to His Friends* (vs. 3:16). Priscilla and Aquila head the list, with her name given first. She was evidently the more capable and aggressive of the two. They were carrying on church services in their home.

After greeting numerous converts, kinfolk, friends, fellow workers, and fellow prisoners, Paul ends by saying, "All the churches of Christ salute you" (v. 16). Here was true church unity and fellowship.

c. *Warning Against Schismatics* (vs. 17-20). Paul beseeches his readers to avoid those who cause divisions in the church. They themselves had won a reputation for obedience (v. 19), and he did not want to see them ruined by schisms.

d. *Greetings from Fellow Workers* (vs. 21-24). Timothy was with Paul at this time as his faithful helper. So were three of his kinsmen. The amanuensis or scribe for this epistle, Tertius, sends his own greetings. Also, "Erastus the treasurer of the city saluteth you." By this time the church included in its membership some men of prominent position.

VIII. THE PRISONER OF THE LORD

Toward the close of Paul's life he wrote four epistles from prison, probably at Rome. These were Philemon, Colossians, Ephesians and Philippians. In each of these there are two or three definite references to the fact that he is a prisoner in bonds.

Philemon

This brief letter of only twenty-five verses can hardly be referred to as an epistle. It is rather a personal note from Paul to his friend Philemon.

The occasion for writing the letter is clear. A certain slave named Onesimus had run away from his Christian master, Philemon. In Rome he had found Paul and had been converted—"my child, whom I have begotten in my bonds" (v. 10). Now Paul is sending him back to Philemon, though he would like to have retained his services for himself (v. 13). With Onesimus he sends this note, to assure the runaway slave a welcome home.

Paul addresses Philemon as a fellow worker (v. 1). It has been suggested that Apphia may have been Philemon's wife, and Archippus his son. The church at Colossae was meeting in the house of Philemon, who was probably a man of means with a commodious home.

Paul is overflowing in his thanksgiving to God and his commendation of Philemon's love, faith and hospitality (vs. 4-7). It is evident that this man was an outstanding Christian brother.

In the main body of the letter (vs. 8-20) Paul pleads his case for Onesimus. He reminds Philemon that he might assert his apostolic authority, but he prefers to beseech him as a friend (vs. 8-10). The dominant tone of this little letter is that of Christian love.

There is an interesting play on words in verse 11. The name Onesimus, commonly used for slaves, is a Greek word which means "profitable." Using another Greek term, Paul says that while this runaway had formerly been unprofitable he would now live up to his name.

Philemon was to receive his slave back not simply as a servant but as a brother in the Lord (v. 16). This attitude would have put an end to oppressive slavery among Christians.

Now Paul makes two significant propositions, in verses 17 and 18, "If then thou countest me a partner, receive him as myself. But if he hath wronged thee at all, or oweth thee aught, put that to mine account." Here we have a beautiful analogy to the atonement. Christ says to the Father, "Receive these disciples as you would receive me. I will pay in full the debt of their sins."

Paul concludes his letter by asking Philemon to prepare him a lodging, as he hopes to be released from prison (v. 22). He then closes, as usual, with a benediction, "The grace of our Lord Jesus Christ be with your spirit." Paul and Philemon were both Christian gentlemen of a high order.

Colossians

1. INTRODUCTION (1:1-14)

a. *Salutation* (1:1, 2). Paul associates Timothy with himself in writing this epistle, as he does also in the case of the Thessalonian letters, First Corinthians, Philemon and Philippians. He evidently considered Timothy as his junior partner.

b. *Thanksgiving* (1:3-8). The apostle commends the Colossians for their "faith in Christ Jesus" (v. 4), and their "love in the Spirit" (v. 8). It would appear that Epaphras had been the pastor at Colossae, or at least had preached there (vs. 5-7). But he was now in prison with Paul (Philemon 23).

c. *Prayer* (1:9-14). In this passage we have one of Paul's great prayers, which are especially prominent in Ephesians and in this epistle. He prays that the Colossians "may be filled with the knowledge of his will in all spiritual wisdom and understanding"; that as a result they may "walk worthily of the Lord unto all pleasing, bearing fruit in every good work, and increasing in the knowledge of God"; and that they may be "strengthened with all power, according to the might of his glory, unto all patience and longsuffering with joy." And so the prayer goes, on and on. We really cannot tell where it ends, for it merges into the doctrinal section which follows.

2. DOCTRINE OF CHRIST (1:15—3:4)

In order to understand the significance of Paul's doctrinal discussion, it will be necessary for us to glance first at the heresy in Colossae which he is here combating. In 2:4 he writes, "This I say, that no one may delude you with persuasiveness of speech." Again, in 2:8 he warns, "Take heed lest there shall be any one that maketh spoil of you through his philosophy and vain deceit, after the tradition of men, after the rudiments of the world, and not after Christ."

The nature of the heresy, or heresies, is described in 2:16-23. It had certain Judaistic features: "Let no man therefore judge you in meat, or in drink, or in respect of a feast day or a new moon or a sabbath day" (v. 16). The "worshipping of the angels" (v. 18) was probably introduced from degenerate Judaism.

On the other hand, the asceticism—"Handle not, nor taste, nor touch" (v. 21); "will-worship, and humility, and severity to the body" (v. 23)—may have come from an incipient Gnosticism which burst forth into full bloom in the second century as one of the greatest dangers to Christianity.

There were two main errors in Gnosticism (from Greek *gnosis*, knowledge). The first was that all matter is evil; only spirit is good. This led to asceticism on the part of some to combat the evil which was supposed to reside in the physical body, and to licentiousness on the part of others who contended that the spirit could not be defiled by the evil practices of the body.

Since all matter was evil, the Supreme Being could not have any contact with the material universe. So the Gnostics postulated a series of aeons between the Infinite One and man. These aeons were supposed to be emanations from the Absolute or from each other.

We do not know how much of this teaching had permeated Asia Minor in the first century. But there had appeared in the church at Colossae a strange mixture of oriental mysticism, theosophical speculation, and decadent Judaism. The serious thing was that Christ was pushed aside.

Paul had one simple but complete answer for all this—Christ. Christ is all. The apostle meets the dangerous teachings in the Colossian church by setting forth the true doctrine of Christ.

The Epistle to the Colossians is the greatest of the Christological epistles. The outstanding passage is 1:15-19. Here Paul declares that Christ is the "image of the invisible God." That is, He is the visible representation of the invisible Deity. This reminds us of Jesus' words, "He that hath seen me hath seen the Father" (John 14:9), and of the statement in John 1:18.

As in the case of John's prologue, the next statement refers to the creatorship of Christ: "All things have been created through him, and unto him" (v. 16). Then comes a declaration which is tremendous in all its implications: "in him all things consist" (v. 17). As President Wood, of Gordon College, has well said, "No other theory for the cohering principle has ever been offered in the realms of physics or psychology." When we think of all things in the universe *holding together* in Christ, it completely staggers our powers of thought. Yet that is the transcendent truth which Paul here proclaims.

One outstanding term in this first chapter is a little word with a big meaning—"all." The All-sufficiency of Christ is really the theme of this epistle. We do not need angels or aeons, nor elaborate ritual.

Two other clauses in this passage emphasize the same truth, "that in all things he might have the pre-eminence" (v. 18), and "that in him should all the fulness dwell" (v. 19). To these we may add two declarations found in the second chapter: "in whom are all the treasures of wisdom and knowledge hidden" (v. 3); "in him dwelleth all the fulness of the Godhead bodily" (v. 9). Christ is not only the all-wise One, but He is also the all-divine One. It is difficult to see how Paul could have made any stronger declarations of the deity of Jesus Christ.

After developing the doctrine of the person of Christ, Paul makes a brief reference to the work of Christ (1:20-23). It is God's plan and purpose "through him to reconcile all things unto himself, having made peace through the blood of his cross" (v. 20). As a result of this reconciliation effected through His death, Christ will "present you holy and without blemish and unreproveable before him" (v. 22). That is the goal of redemption—"that we may present every man perfect in Christ" (v. 28). This does not come through asceticism, but through faith in Christ.

Paul had not visited the churches in Colossae and Laodicea (2:1), but this epistle and one which he wrote to the latter place (4:16) must have gone far toward making up for that fact.

There is a corollary to this doctrine of the full deity of Jesus Christ. After stating that doctrine in 2:9, Paul adds, "And in him ye are made full" (v. 10). "In Christ"—that is the central philosophy of life and of the universe. But it is more than that. It is a glorious reality in the experience of the believer who dwells fully "in him." The transcendent truth can be echoed in a triumphant testimony!

The closing appeal of this doctrinal section of the epistle might be noticed fittingly at this point. "If then ye were raised together with Christ, seek the things that are above, where Christ is, seated on the right hand of God. Set your mind on the things that are above, not on the things that are upon the earth. For ye died, and your life is hid with Christ in God" (3:1-3). It is the New Testament counterpart of the experience described in the Ninety-first Psalm.

3. PRACTICAL EXHORTATIONS (3:5—4:6)

On the basis of all that Christ has provided for us, the apostle urges us to "put to death therefore your members which are upon the earth" (3:5). But we are not to stop there. Having "put off the old man with his doings" (v. 9), we are to "put on the new man, that is being renewed unto knowledge after the image of him that created him" (v. 10).

He has described "the old man" and his doings in verses 5-9. Now he describes the new man. "Put on therefore, as God's elect, holy and beloved, a heart of compassion, kindness, lowliness, meekness, long-suffering; forbearing one another, and forgiving each other . . . ; even as the Lord forgave you, so also do ye: and above all these things put on love, which is the bond of perfectness" (3:12-14). "Let the peace of Christ rule in your hearts" (v. 15). "Let the word of Christ dwell in you richly" (v. 16). "And whatsoever ye do, in word or in deed, do all in the name of the Lord Jesus, giving thanks to God the Father through him" (v. 17). In other words, Paul exhorts us to appropriate the value of the wonderful Christological teachings by applying them to our daily lives. Head knowledge must become heart experience which flows out in practical living.

Paul directs specific exhortations to wives, husbands, children, fathers, servants, masters (3:18—4:1). The apostle was concerned with the social application of the gospel.

This section closes with an appeal to prayerfulness and to a godly walk and careful conversation. We need to watch and pray, in order that we shall not deny the gospel of Christ in our daily living.

4. Conclusion (4:7-18)

Tychicus is to carry this letter to Colossae, accompanied by Onesimus, who was from that city (vs. 7-9). This indicates clearly that Colossians was written at the same time as Philemon.

It is interesting to note how many of Paul's associates were with him when he wrote this letter. He mentions six, besides the two messengers, as joining him in sending salutations to Colossae.

Epaphras, who had preached in Colossae, Laodicea, and Hierapolis—three cities on the banks of the Lycus River in Asia Minor—was now in prison. But that did not stop his ministry, for he gave himself to intercessory prayer for the churches in those cities (vs. 12, 13).

The church at Laodicea was meeting in the house of Nymphas (v. 15), as that at Colossae was in the home of Philemon. Church buildings would come later.

Ephesians

There is considerable reason for believing that this epistle was not intended for the church at Ephesus alone, but that it was a circular letter written for all the churches of Asia. The words "at Ephesus" (1:1) do not occur in the oldest and best Greek manuscripts. It would seem that our "Ephesians" was taken from the copy of the letter which was sent to the mother church at Ephesus, the capital city of the province of Asia.

As the epistle to the Romans contains a summary of the doctrines of salvation, so the Epistle to the Ephesians gives a summary of Paul's more mature reflection on God's great eternal purposes for the human race. It was written near the close of Paul's four years' imprisonment, when he had had ample time for meditation and prayer. Probably both of these letters were intended for rather general circulation among the Gentile churches.

1. SALUTATION (1:1, 2)

The introduction and conclusion of this epistle are both very brief. We have here what is really more of a treatise than a personal letter. It was written specifically for Gentile readers (2:11; 3:1), and is addressed to "the saints and the faithful in Christ Jesus" (1:1).

2. DOCTRINAL PRESENTATION (1:3—3:21)

a. *The Christian's Worship* (1:3-23). The epistle begins with a paean of praise (1:3-14). It is a hymn in three stanzas. The first stanza (vs. 3-6) sings of the Father; the second (vs. 7-12), of the Son; the third (vs. 13, 14), of the Holy Spirit.

The opening words of this hymn sound the keynote of the epistle. "Blessed be the God and Father of our Lord Jesus Christ, who hath blessed us with every spiritual blessing in the heavenly places in Christ" (v. 3). Paul has given us in this letter a description of life in the heavenlies with Christ.

This epistle looks farther back and farther ahead than any of Paul's other letters. It deals with God's eternal plan and purpose of redemption. The sovereignty of His will is especially prominent: "according to the good pleasure of his will" (v. 5); "making known unto us the mystery of his will, according to his good pleasure which he purposed in him" (v. 9); "having been foreordained according to the purpose of him who worketh all things after the counsel of his will" (v. 11).

It will be profitable to note just what God in His wisdom and good pleasure has foreordained. Several things are mentioned here: "that we should be holy and without blemish before him in love" (v. 4); "unto adoption as sons through Jesus Christ unto himself" (v. 5); "to sum up all things in Christ" (v. 10); "that we should be unto the praise of his glory" (v. 12).

It should be noticed that the emphasis here is not on predestination to individual salvation. It is rather that God has foreordained that those who are His children should be holy and should live to the praise of His glory. Having given our hearts to Christ we should seek, by conformity to the divine will, to see that God's plan and purpose for us is carried out in full.

The hymn of praise is followed by a prayer (1:15-23). As we have already noted, prayer and praise alternated in the apostle's life. Either one seemed spontaneously to induce the other.

This is one of the greatest of Paul's prayers. He prays that God will grant to his readers "a spirit of wisdom and revelation in the knowledge of him" (v. 17), that they may "know what is the hope of his calling, what the riches of the glory of his inheritance in the saints, and what the exceeding greatness of his power to us-ward who believe" (vs. 18, 19). Our greatest need as Christians is more "knowledge of Him."

b. *The Christian's Redemption* (chapter 2). Having given in the first chapter an excellent sample of Christian worship in praise and in prayer, the apostle now discusses in the second chapter the wonderful fact of the Christian's redemption in Christ Jesus.

The first result of redemption is that it brings us from spiritual deadness to spiritual life (2:1-10). Paul emphasizes the fact that men outside of Christ are dead in trespasses and sins. "But God, being rich in mercy, for his great love wherewith he loved us, even when we were dead through our trespasses, made us alive together with Christ . . . and made us sit with him in the heavenly places, in Christ Jesus" (vs. 5, 6). From death in sin to life in Christ—that is redemption.

But the results of redemption are not confined to this life. As wonderful as is fellowship with Christ here below, it is nothing compared with what we shall experience in eternity. Here we learn something of the kindness of Christ and the riches of God's grace. But He purposes "that in the ages to come he might show the exceeding riches of his grace in kindness toward us in Christ Jesus" (v. 7). How kind can God be? It will take all of eternity for us to find out.

In the remainder of the chapter (2:11-22) Paul emphasizes the truth that in Christ there is no longer any distinction between Jews and Gentiles. Both alike have been reconciled to God through His death on the cross (v. 16). And "through him we both have our access in one Spirit unto the Father" (v. 18). It is the work both of Christ and of the Holy Spirit to bring us into the presence of God, and to bring the presence of God into us (v. 22).

c. *The Christian's Inheritance* (chapter 3). The keynote of this chapter is contained in the word "mystery" (vs. 3, 4, 9). This term was used by the mystery religions of that day for that which was disclosed only to those who had been initiated into the mysteries of the cult. Paul uses it for that which is revealed only to those who have been initiated into Jesus Christ and His Church. He himself had received these things "by revelation" (v. 3), and they can be known only "in the Spirit" (v. 5).

But what is this mystery which had been hidden to previous generations? It was "that the Gentiles are fellow-heirs, and fellow-members of the body, and fellow-partakers of the promise in Christ Jesus through the gospel" (v. 6). All this is the wisdom of God, "according to the eternal purpose which he purposed in Christ Jesus our Lord" (v. 11).

In the closing verses (14-19) of this chapter we have another wonderful prayer from the heart of the Apostle Paul. Note the comprehensiveness of it: "That ye may be strengthened with power through his Spirit in the inward man; that Christ may dwell in your hearts through faith; to the end that ye, being rooted and grounded in love, may be strong to apprehend with all the saints what is the breadth and length and height and depth, and to know the love of Christ which passeth knowledge, that ye may be filled unto all the fulness of God." The climax is complete.

Then Paul closes this first half of the epistle with one of his great benedictions: "Now unto him that is able to do exceeding abundantly above all that we ask or think, according to the power that worketh in us, unto him be the glory in the church and in Christ Jesus unto all generations for ever and ever. Amen." Paul has exhausted the resources of human language in the vain effort to express what he felt in his heart.

3. PRACTICAL APPLICATION (4:1—6:20)

a. *The Christian's Walk* (4:1—5:21). Having taken us up into the heavenlies in the airplane of faith and given us a vast panoramic view of God's great "purpose of the ages," Paul now brings us down to earth again, back to the duties and responsibilities of our daily life, and says, "Walk in the light of this vision splendid."

It is the glory of Paul that he could stand with his head in the heights and his heart in the heavenlies, and yet keep his feet on the earth. He never lost his bearings in the dreamy speculations and misty nebulosities of some mystical thinking. The secret was that he kept his eyes on Jesus Christ.

Five times in this section Paul admonishes us to walk. *First,* he says, "Walk worthily of the calling wherewith ye were called" (4:1).

The special point which he emphasizes under this head is the need of preserving unity in the church: "giving diligence to keep the unity of the Spirit in the bond of peace" (v. 3). God has provided for the building up of the church by giving it apostles, prophets, evangelists, pastors and teachers. The result of their ministry should be that "we all attain unto the unity of the faith, and of the knowledge of the Son of God, unto a full grown man, unto the measure of the stature of the fulness of Christ" (v. 13).

Second, Paul says, "No longer walk as the Gentiles also walk" (4:17). We are to put off the old man, and put on the new man (vs. 22-24). "Be ye kind one to another, tenderhearted, forgiving each other, even as God also in Christ forgave you" (v. 32).

Third, Paul says, "Walk in love" (5:2). Because Christ has loved us, we should love one another.

Fourth, he says, "Walk as children of light" (5:8). Sin revels in darkness. But as Christians we should live transparently pure lives. There will be no dark corners in heaven.

Fifth, Paul says, "Look therefore carefully how ye walk, not as unwise, but as wise; redeeming the time, because the days are evil" (5:15, 16). This is a sort of summary statement with regard to the Christian's walk. "Always Be Careful," it says.

This section ends with a description of the Spirit-filled life (5:18-21). Instead of participating in the drunken revelries of those about us, we should find our highest pleasure in being filled with the Spirit of God.

b. *The Christian's Relationships* (5:22—6:9). As in Colossians, Paul here sets forth the need of proper attention to the matter of social relationships. He discusses the same six classes—wives, husbands, children, fathers, servants, masters.

In his discussion of the duties of husbands, Paul bases his plea on the example of Christ in His relation to the Church. In doing so he gives us one of the outstanding passages in the epistle: "Husbands, love your wives, even as Christ also loved the church, and gave himself up for it; that he might sanctify it, having cleansed it by the washing of water with the word, that he might present the church to himself a glorious church, not having spot or wrinkle or any such thing; but that it should be holy and without blemish" (5:25-27).

Then, lest his readers in their absorption with this marvelous truth should forget what he had just said, Paul adds, "Even so ought husbands also to love their own wives as their own bodies" (v. 28). The husband who ignores this is a poor follower of Christ.

c. *The Christian's Warfare* (6:10-20). The Christian life is a race, but it is also a fight. Hence, the Christian needs to "put on the whole armor of God" (v. 11).

This armor which God has provided for us is described in detail. There is the girdle of truth, to protect some of the vital organs; the breastplate of righteousness, to protect the heart; shoes of the gospel, for marching on stony ground; the shield of faith, to ward off the enemy's darts; the helmet of salvation, to protect the head; the sword of the Spirit, for offensive fighting; and the buckle of prayer to hold the entire armor together. The young Christian might well consider each part carefully and "put on the whole armor."

4. Conclusion (6: 21-24)

Paul is sending this epistle by Tychicus, the same messenger who was to carry Colossians and accompany Onesimus back home (Colossians 4: 7, 9). It is clear that Philemon, Colossians and Ephesians were all sent at the same time.

The apostle closes this majestic epistle with his usual benediction, sprinkling the incense of peace, love, faith and grace upon his readers.

Philippians

The Epistle to the Philippians is one of the most spontaneous of Paul's letters. In it he pours out his heart in love and gratitude to these faithful friends at Philippi, who have done so much for him.

1. Introduction (1: 1-11)

a. *Salutation* (1: 1, 2). The distinctive point of interest in this salutation is Paul's reference to the bishops and deacons. It appears that in the first century each church had several bishops (probably synonymous with presbyters, or elders) and several deacons. Early in the second century (in the Letters of Ignatius) we find each church with one bishop, several presbyters, and several deacons. The idea of episcopal authority over a diocese was a still later development.

b. *Thanksgiving* (1: 3-11). The Philippians were loyal and generous friends to Paul, and he always thinks of them with joy. He prays that their "love may abound yet more and more" (v. 9).

2. Paul's Life at Rome (1: 12-29)

The apostle rejoices in the fact that his imprisonment has given an opportunity for Christian witness to the "whole praetorian guard" (v. 13).

Paul has reached the place where he longs to go to be with Christ, yet he is willing to remain in this world for the sake of those whom he can help (vs. 22-26). He says, "For to me to live is Christ, and to die is gain" (v. 21).

3. An Appeal to Unity (chapter 2)

The apostle sets forth the important principle that unity must be based upon humility and love. He exhorts the

Philippians to "be of the same mind, having the same love, being of one accord, of one mind" (v. 2). If they heed his admonition, "in lowliness of mind each counting other better than himself" (v. 3), there will be no place for quarreling. Pride is the cause of strife.

In order to enforce this plea for humility Paul calls attention to the example of Christ. "Have this mind in you, which was also in Christ Jesus: who, existing in the form of God, counted not the being on an equality with God a thing to be grasped, but emptied himself, taking the form of a servant, being made in the likeness of men; and being found in fashion as a man, he humbled himself, becoming obedient even unto death, yea, the death of the cross" (2:5-8).

This scripture is usually referred to as the "Kenosis passage" from the Greek word for "emptied," *ekenosen,* translated in the King James Version, "made himself of no reputation." It is the outstanding Christological passage in Philippians.

There has been considerable discussion as to what it was of which Christ emptied Himself in His incarnation. The teaching of the New Testament seems clear that He did not lay aside His essential attributes of deity, but that He simply divested Himself of the outward manifestation of glory which was His in the heavenly realm.

The result of His voluntary self-humbling is that God has highly exalted Him and that some day every knee shall bow to Him (vs. 9-11). The path to the crown leads by the way of the cross.

Paul now returns to the topic of unity. "Do all things without murmurings and questionings; that ye may become blameless and harmless, children of God without blemish" (vs. 14, 15). Fussing saints are poor representatives of Christianity.

A high tribute is here paid by the apostle to his young associate Timothy: "I have no man like-minded, who will truly care for your state" (v. 20). "As a child serveth a father, so he served with me in furtherance of the gospel" (v. 22). He hopes soon to send Timothy to Philippi, and to go there himself before long (vs. 23, 24). Meanwhile he is sending back Epaphroditus, who had recently brought a donation to Paul from the Philippians (v. 25).

4. A WARNING AGAINST JUDAISM (chapter 3)

It would seem in 3:1 that Paul is about to bring this letter to a close: "Finally, my brethren, rejoice in the Lord." But, instead, he sounds a warning against the Judaizers, "the concision" (v. 2). He relates his own experience as a Pharisee, but declares, "I count all things to be loss for the excellency of the knowledge of Christ Jesus my Lord" (v. 8). He has found that Christ is worth more than all else put together. His great aim in life is "that I may know him" (v. 10).

In verse twelve Paul says that he is not yet perfect. But in verse fifteen he classes himself as perfect. It is clear that he uses this term with more than one significance, and that its meaning in any particular passage must be decided in the light of the context. It is evident here that in the former verse he is referring to resurrection perfection and in the latter to Christian perfection.

Paul was not basking in the sunlight of past blessings. He says, "One thing I do, forgetting the things which are behind, and stretching forward to the things which are before, I press on toward the goal unto the prize of the high calling of God in Christ Jesus" (vs. 13, 14). And then the apostle calls back over his shoulder to the Philippians to follow him: "Brethren, be ye imitators together of me" (v. 17).

5. CONCLUSION (chapter 4)

This letter is filled with thanksgiving to God and commendation of the Philippians. It is in great contrast to the Corinthian Epistles and Galatians. Paul mentions only one thing that needs correction, and that is a misunderstanding between two women in the church (4:2).

The fourth verse of this chapter gives us the keynote of the entire letter: "Rejoice in the Lord always: again I will say, Rejoice." It is all the more striking that this epistle of joy was written from prison at Rome. Paul had learned the lesson of rejoicing always, no matter what the circumstances of life, and wants his readers to learn the same lesson.

One way we can do this is by not being anxious about anything, but praying about everything with thanksgiving (v. 6). The result will be, "The peace of God, which passeth all understanding, shall guard your hearts and your thoughts in Christ Jesus" (v. 7). In verse eight Paul shows how we can help to guard our thoughts by keeping our mind on things that are pure and pleasant.

One of Paul's great utterances, rising out of his four years' experience in prison, is, "I have learned, in whatsoever state I am, therein to be content" (v. 11). That was a great lesson. Another thing he had learned was, "I can do all things in him that strengtheneth me" (v. 13). Paul was finishing his education at Rome in the school of disappointment.

The apostle concludes by thanking the Philippians for their gift which they had sent by Epaphroditus. In return he gives them the promise, "My God shall supply every need of yours according to his riches in glory in Christ Jesus" (v. 19). God will reward them for their care of His servant.

IX. THE GENERAL SUPERINTENDENT

In the thirty years of Paul's ministry he had founded churches in many of the large cities of the eastern Mediterranean world. We need only to mention Antioch, Iconium, Lystra and Derbe in the province of Galatia, Ephesus in Asia, Philippi and Thessalonica in Macedonia, and Corinth in Greece, in order to see the greater importance of the work of this one missionary.

By the close of Paul's life these churches had become large and flourishing and were now the mother churches for Christian groups in various surrounding communities. Especially was this true of Ephesus, which had become the mother church for at least half a dozen other congregations at Colossae, Hierapolis, Laodicea, Philadelphia, Sardis, Smyrna, Thyatira and Pergamum—all in the province of Asia.

Ephesus was not only a great commercial and political metropolis, and now an important center of Christianity, it was also a leading center of pagan worship. The magnificent temple of Diana, one of the seven wonders of the ancient world, was located at Ephesus. It was therefore necessary to place a strong, reliable man as pastor of this great metropolitan church. For this strategic position Paul chose his faithful young colleague, Timothy.

As general superintendent of all the Gentile Christian Church in the Roman provinces of the great Levant area, Paul had a tremendous task upon his hands. He doubtless wrote many letters to the pastors of all the churches, instructing and admonishing them. But only three of them are preserved to us. One was written to Titus, whom Paul had appointed as district superintendent for the Island of Crete. The other two were to Timothy, who perhaps had to serve in much the same capacity for the province of Asia.

These Pastoral Epistles came from the closing years of Paul's life. They were probably written between 61 and 67 A. D.

First Timothy

1. INTRODUCTION (chapter 1)

a. *Salutation* (1:1, 2). In the first of this epistle we meet with a phrase which is prominent in the pastoral group—"God our Saviour." It occurs again in this letter in 2:3. (See also 4:10). It is more frequently used in the letter to Titus.

b. *Introduction* (1:3-20). When Paul went into Macedonia he left Timothy at Ephesus that he might "charge certain men not to teach a different doctrine." It would seem that heterodoxy was creeping into the Ephesian church. For the sake of all the churches of the province it was necessary to curb this danger at once.

It is evident that the false teachers at Ephesus were Judaizers, who sought to overthrow Paul's work everywhere. He speaks of "fables and endless genealogies" (v. 4), and refers to these intruders as those who were "desiring to be teachers of the law" (v. 7).

A great principle is stated in verse five, "The aim of your instruction must be love that springs from a pure heart and from a good conscience and from a sincere faith" (Goodspeed).[1] The highest thing in Christianity is "love out of a pure heart." Any teaching that aims at something else—however "wonderful" it may be—is misleading.

There is not much exposition of doctrine in the Pastoral Epistles. But there is a good deal of emphasis upon doctrine. The phrase "sound doctrine" (v. 10) is the keynote of the Epistle to Titus. So we shall leave our discussion of it until we study that letter.

Paul's usual thanksgiving comes in verses 12-17. He is grateful to God for saving him, the chief of sinners. He is glad "that in me as chief might Jesus Christ show forth all his longsuffering" (v. 16).

The first chapter ends with a charge to Timothy to "war the good warfare" (v. 18). He is admonished to keep his faith and a good conscience.

2. INSTRUCTIONS CONCERNING THE CHURCH (chapters 2, 3)

As general superintendent Paul exhorts the church to pray for all men and especially for rulers (2:1, 2), for God desires

[1] Goodspeed, Edgar J., *The New Testament, an American Translation* (University of Chicago Press, 1923).

that all men should be saved (v. 4), and so He has appointed one mediator between God and men, the man Christ Jesus (v. 5). This one "gave himself a ransom for all" (v. 6).

In connection with his discussion of prayer Paul gives the instruction that Christian women should dress in modest apparel (vs. 8-10). He also exhorts the women to be quiet (vs. 11-15). This passage should be read in the light of Paul's commendation of Priscilla, Phoebe and others who labored faithfully and efficiently in the early church. It would appear that, as at Corinth, some women were seeking to monopolize the public ministry and the time of the worship services. This Paul forbids.

In chapter three the apostle discusses some of the offices in the church. He first sets forth the qualifications of a bishop, or overseer (vs. 1-7), and then those of a deacon (vs. 8-12). He emphasizes the fact that both of these officials must be men of exemplary life. They must not be novices, but men who have proved themselves worthy (vs. 6, 10). They must have demonstrated their ability for leadership by ruling well their own homes.

The keynote of this epistle is well expressed in 3:15— "that thou mayest know how men ought to behave themselves in the house of God." It is a manual on church administration.

The chapter closes with a sort of credal formula (v. 16), which may have been recited in the early church:

> "He who was manifested in the flesh,
> Justified in the spirit, [or, by the Spirit]
> Seen of angels,
> Preached among the nations,
> Believed on in the world,
> Received up into glory."

3. INSTRUCTIONS CONCERNING THE MINISTRY (4:1—6:19)

a. *The Preservation of Doctrine* (chapter 4). The fourth chapter begins with a warning of coming apostasy (vs. 1-5). In the first verse an expression occurs which has a different meaning from the Pauline usage in the earlier epistles. Heretofore Paul has spoken of "faith" as a personal attitude toward God. In the Pastoral Epistles the expression, "the faith," is used for Christianity, or for the system of Christian doctrine. This indicates the development of a doctrinal consciousness on the part of the church and furnishes the introduction to the later period of creed-making.

Two earmarks of this coming heresy are designated, namely, "forbidding to marry, and commanding to abstain from meats." It is difficult to see how, in the light of this warning, any movement calling itself Christian could allow itself to enforce these very regulations. Yet such is the case.

The key to this section of the epistle may be found in a phrase in the sixth verse, "a good minister of Christ Jesus." What this involved is further defined as being "nourished in the words of the faith, and of the good doctrine." Evidently Paul considered orthodoxy as a primary qualification of a good minister. He would hardly agree with the modern disparagement of the importance of doctrine.

Timothy is not only to teach sound doctrine, but he is also to enforce it. "These things command and teach" (v. 11). Every ordained minister is given authority by the church, and there are times when it is his duty to enforce it.

Paul was concerned lest Timothy's youthfulness should prove a handicap in his important position. It must be understood that this does not suggest that Timothy was in his teens or even his twenties. In the Roman world a person was called "young man" until he was forty-five. Then he became a mature individual, capable of taking his place as such in society.

The apostle tells the young preacher how he can command the respect of his elders. "Let no man despise thy youth; but be thou an example to them that believe, in word, in manner of life, in love, in faith, in purity" (v. 12).

The public ministry of the preacher is summed up in these words: "Give heed to reading, to exhortation, to teaching" (v. 13). The minister is to read the Scriptures to his people, exhort them to obey its precepts, and teach them the way of truth.

There is an interesting reference in the fourteenth verse to Timothy's ordination. "Neglect not the gift that is in thee, which was given thee by prophecy, with the laying on of the hands of the presbytery." It is evident that ordination in the early church was by the laying on of hands of the elders, as we do it today.

In the sixteenth verse Paul gives a very important admonition to this young preacher, "Take heed to thyself, and to thy teaching." It is necessary that a minister should not only give careful attention to his preaching, but first of all he must take heed to his own spiritual life and his outward conduct. He must save himself, as well as those who hear him.

b. *The Care of Widows and Elders* (chapter 5). The fifth chapter contains instructions concerning widows in the church. It appears that many of the younger widows were becoming a problem. The apostle lays down the ruling, "Let none be enrolled as a widow under threescore years old, having been the wife of one man, well reported of for good works" (vs. 9, 10). Paul did not want the church to become a charitable institution for the support of a host of unworthy young women who would bring reproach on the cause.

In the latter part of chapter five (vs. 17-25) the apostle gives instructions concerning the care of elders. They are to be recompensed for their labors in the ministry. They are not to be accused lightly. But the apostle also warns against hasty ordination (v. 22).

c. *The Good Fight of Faith* (6:1-19). The sixth chapter begins with a word of instruction for servants (vs. 1, 2). They are to treat their masters with respect, for the sake of the Christian name. Familiarity as brothers in Christ should not lead a servant to take a disrespectful attitude toward his Christian master.

The importance of doctrine in the mind of the apostle is indicated by the third verse, "If any man teacheth a different doctrine, and consenteth not to sound words, even the words of our Lord Jesus Christ, and the doctrine which is according to godliness." In the eyes of Paul a man who was unorthodox in his theology was a serious menace to the church. He also warns against those who preach simply for money (v. 5).

To Timothy the apostle writes, "But thou, O man of God, flee these things; and follow after righteousness, godliness, faith, love, patience, meekness. Fight the good fight of the faith, lay hold on eternal life" (vs. 11, 12).

Two of Paul's benedictions in this epistle (1:17; 6:15, 16) are similar in their emphasis upon the immortality and invisibility of God. The expression in 6:16, "dwelling in light unapproachable," is a striking piece of theology. Paul does not go into elaborate doctrinal exposition and argument in these Pastoral Epistles, but he does give some powerful epigrammatic credal statements.

After this second benediction Paul adds a sort of postscript (vs. 17-19). He instructs Timothy to warn rich people against trusting in their riches and neglecting eternal things.

4. CONCLUSION (6:20, 21)

The apostle's final charge to his son in the faith is in line with the doctrinal emphasis of the epistle, "O Timothy, guard that which is committed unto thee." The Greek puts it more briefly, "Guard the deposit." The minister has received the Christian doctrine as a sacred trust.

The closing benediction is very brief, "Grace be with you." Paul had already given two striking benedictions. Now, as it were, he says, "Good-by" (literally, "God be with ye").

Titus

1. SALUTATION (1:1-4)

Paul addresses Titus with the same words he used of Timothy, "my true child." It is clear that both of these young men were converted under Paul's ministry. While Timothy had a Greek father and a Jewish mother (Acts 16:1), both parents of Titus were Greek (Galatians 2:3). The apostle intrusted these younger associates of his with important tasks, because they had proved faithful.

2. QUALIFICATIONS OF A BISHOP (1:5-9)

Paul had left Titus in Crete, "That thou shouldest set in order the things that were wanting, and appoint elders in every city, as I gave thee charge" (v. 5). Evidently Paul had not had time to organize the work in Crete, and he appointed Titus to see that each church had its elders. This was the basic minimum of organization in the apostolic churches.

The Island of Crete lies southwest of the peninsula of Greece. It is about 160 miles long, and from 6 to 35 miles wide. It had a large number of cities, in many of which Christian churches had been established.

In connection with his instruction to Titus to appoint elders in every church, Paul gives the qualifications of a bishop. It appears perfectly clear in this passage that elders and bishops were synonymous in the Pauline churches.

The negative qualifications enumerated here reflect the pagan environment of Christianity in Crete. The bishop must be "not self-willed, not soon angry, no brawler, no striker, not greedy of filthy lucre" (v. 7). Positively, he must be "given to hospitality, a lover of good, sober-minded, just, holy, self-controlled" (v. 8). His duties were to include both defense of doctrine—"exhort in the sound doctrine"—and discipline of offenders—"convict the gainsayers" (v. 9).

The expression "sound doctrine" is the keynote of the Epistle to Titus. It occurs here and in 2:1. The word sound, or "healthful" (Gr., "hygienic") is found also in 1:13 ("sound in the faith"), and 2:8 ("sound speech"). If the Christian Church is to be in a healthy condition it must be fed "healthful doctrine." Poisonous teaching is not conducive to spiritual health. The suicidal effects of drinking intellectual poison are being demonstrated amply in the Europe of our day.

3. CHARACTER OF THE CRETANS (1:10-16)

Some of the Jews living in Crete—"they of the circumcision" (v. 10)—were upsetting the Christian cause there. The Cretan character was bad enough, according to one of their own poets, who wrote, "The Cretans are always liars, evil beasts, idle gluttons" (v. 12). Paul tells Titus that he will find it necessary to "reprove them sharply" (v. 13). They were being led astray by Judaizers here also (v. 14).

4. INSTRUCTIONS TO VARIOUS CLASSES (chapter 2)

The apostle gives specific directions as to how Titus should instruct the different groups in the church. He deals with the obligations of the aged men (v. 2), the aged women (vs. 4, 5), the young men (vs. 6-8), and servants (vs. 9, 10). These instructions are worthy of study by Christians today.

Paul follows these admonitions with a sort of doctrinal standard (vs. 11-14). The Pastoral Epistles emphasize both doctrine and conduct, as do most of Paul's letters. This passage combines the two. The Christian life begins with "denying ungodliness and worldly lusts." It consists of living "soberly," in relation to others; and "godly," in relation to God. We are to live in constant expectation of the coming of Christ (v. 13), "who gave himself for us, that he might redeem us from all iniquity, and purify unto himself a people for his own possession" (v. 14).

The last phrase calls for some comment. In the King James Version it is translated, "a peculiar people." Perhaps no word in that version has been more abused through lack of understanding of its true meaning. The word in the Greek has absolutely no suggestion of queerness or oddness. It means simply "precious, valuable, select, special." Three hundred years ago, when the King James Version was made, the word "peculiar" meant just that. But now that meaning is obsolete, and the word suggests to our minds the idea of being odd or queer. The writer has heard this expression quoted over and over again as an excuse for some foolishness or fanaticism. If we are determined to be fanatical, let it be a fanaticism for good works—"zealous of good works" (v. 14)!

The second chapter closes with an exhortation to Titus to maintain discipline in his administration of the church. "These things speak and exhort and reprove with all authority. Let no man despise thee." Titus, because of his youth, needed the same admonition as Timothy.

5. Church Discipline and Doctrine (3:1-11)

The third verse of this chapter gives a picture of man apart from God, while the fourth verse gives a picture of God and His love for sinful man. This is the ground of the appeal in the two verses to obedience and meekness.

We find another doctrinal summary in verses 4-7. It gives us the when, why, and how of salvation.

The doctrinal statement is followed, as usual, by an exhortation to "good works" (v. 8). This phrase might be coupled with "sound doctrine" to indicate the twofold emphasis of the entire epistle.

6. Conclusion (3:12-15)

After urging Titus to meet him at Nicopolis—either the city by that name in Macedonia, or the one on the west coast of Greece—Paul closes with another admonition, which every church might well take to itself, "Let our people also learn to maintain good works" (v. 14). A people who are properly indoctrinated and busy doing good works are an asset to Christianity.

Second Timothy

This is Paul's closing epistle. It contains his last words to the church. Because of that fact, we treasure it as his abiding legacy to us.

Everything in this letter is treated as related to the preacher. A good title for the epistle would be "The Militant Ministry."

1. INTRODUCTION (chapter 1)

Paul addresses Timothy here as "my beloved child" (v. 2). He tells his young colleague that he is longing to see him (v. 4). In his first letter he had warned him not to neglect his gift of preaching (4:14). Now he urges him to "stir up [Gr., stir into flame] the gift of God, which is in thee through the laying on of my hands" (v. 6).

The apostle expresses his firm faith in the declaration, "For I know him whom I have believed, and I am persuaded that he is able to guard that which I have committed unto him [Gr., my deposit] against that day" (v. 12).

The importance of sound doctrine is emphasized in this epistle also. Paul writes, "Hold the pattern of sound words which thou hast heard from me" (v. 13), and then he adds, "Guard the good deposit through the Holy Spirit who dwells in us" (v. 14, literal translation). The Holy Spirit is the great conservator of orthodoxy.

A note of sadness enters this epistle as we read, "This thou knowest, that all that are in Asia turned away from me" (v. 15). It must have brought a cloud of sorrow over the apostle's spirit to be treated thus in his last days.

2. RESPONSIBILITY OF THE MINISTRY (2:1-13)

Timothy has not only received a deposit of doctrine from Paul as a sacred trust; it is his duty to pass this deposit on to others unspoiled. "The things which thou hast heard from me among many witnesses, the same commit thou to faithful men, who shall be able to teach others also" (2:2).

Each generation of the church is obligated to the succeeding generations, to pass on the truth of the gospel in as pure a form as it received it. If any denomination or movement is to survive spiritually, it must see that its message is intrusted to faithful, capable teachers, who shall educate its ministry carefully in the truths of its doctrine. This is the solemn responsibility of our church colleges and theological schools. May God help us of this generation not to fail our young people and children!

The apostle likens the minister to a soldier, an athlete and a husbandman (vs. 3-6). He exhorts Timothy to suffer hardship as a good soldier of Jesus Christ (v. 3). The Christian life is a warfare, and demands the spirit of a soldier who is determined to fight his way through to victory.

3. Warning Against Wordy Debates (2:14-26)

Paul sounds another warning against profitless disputes over meaningless words (v. 14). He exhorts young Timothy, "Give diligence to present thyself approved unto God, a workman that needeth not to be ashamed, handling aright the word of truth" (v. 15). That last clause is best translated, "holding a straight course in the word of truth." It is very easy to get on one side of the road or the other and get caught in a rut, if not in the ditch. Along the highway of truth there need to be frequent warning signs, "Danger; look out for soft shoulders." It is the duty of the preacher to stay in the middle of the road.

Paul also warns Timothy against youthful lusts (v. 22). Then he returns to the subject of disputing with others. He says, "The Lord's servant must not strive, but be gentle towards all, apt to teach, forbearing" (v. 24). This command has been broken by the Lord's servants perhaps as often as any injunction in the New Testament.

4. Warning Against Apostasy (chapter 3)

The apostasy of the last days is predicted a number of times in the New Testament (cf. 2 Thess. 2; 2 Peter 2; 1 John 2; Jude). Here Paul gives a very vivid description of the nature of the apostasy. One does not need to read far before recognizing some of the dominant trends of modern life. Certainly the apostasy here predicted has already begun.

In contrast to the characteristics of the apostates (vs. 2-5), Paul mentions his own "teaching, conduct, purpose, faith, longsuffering, love, patience, persecutions, sufferings" (vs. 10, 11). He then admonishes Timothy, "Abide thou in the things which thou hast learned and hast been assured of, knowing of whom thou hast learned them; and that from a babe thou hast known the sacred writings which are able to make thee wise unto salvation through faith which is in Christ Jesus" (vs. 14, 15). It is through the "inspired of God" (lit., God-breathed) Scriptures that the man of God is fitted out, "furnished completely unto every good work" (v. 17).

5. FINAL CHARGE TO TIMOTHY (4:1-8)

Paul's final charge to Timothy is to "preach the word; be urgent in season, out of season; reprove, rebuke, exhort, with all longsuffering and teaching" (v. 2). This suggests something of the work of the ministry.

Not content with these injunctions, Paul continues, "But be thou sober in all things, suffer hardship, do the work of an evangelist, fulfill thy ministry" (v. 5). The word fulfill might well be rendered "fill full." That is a challenge to every minister of the gospel.

In the sixth verse Paul writes, "For I am already being offered, and the time of my departure is come." The word "offered" is literally "poured out as a drink offering." In heathen worship the drink offering was poured out last, just before the fire was lighted. Paul realized that the time of his embarkation had come.

Verse seven gives Paul's "Swan Song"—"I have fought the good fight, I have finished the course, I have kept the faith." In the fury of the battle and the strain of the race-course he had held firmly to the faith. He is challenging Timothy to do the same.

6. CONCLUSION (4:9-22)

Paul again urges Timothy to come to him as soon as possible. Demas, whom he had formerly mentioned as a coworker, has now forsaken him. Others have gone on various missions to distant places. Only Luke is with the apostle in these last days in prison (v. 11). He asks that Mark be brought along. In spite of his age and his approaching death, he asks for his books, especially the valuable parchments (v. 13). He feels the need of his books as much as his coat.

Just before signing his name, with his benediction, the lonely apostle writes once more, "Give diligence to come before winter." Paul was still human, but he was a chosen vessel in God's hands for the great work he had performed.

X. THE FINAL REVELATION

Hebrews

The Epistle to the Hebrews is the most literary of the books of the New Testament. Its language is nearer to the classical Greek than that of any other book, and it is marked by a lofty rhetorical style. While John's style is very simple and Paul's is very broken, that of the Epistle to the Hebrews is polished and smooth.[1]

As its name suggests, this epistle was written to the Hebrews. Its purpose is to warn the Jewish Christians against going back into Judaism. Its theme is the Superiority of Christianity to Judaism, or the Finality of the Christian Revelation.

The key word of the book is "better." Despite the imposing ritual, elaborate ceremonialism, and impressive history of Judaism, Christianity is the better religion.

The book is filled with argument and exhortation. But whereas Paul in his epistles usually presents the doctrine first, and then the practical application last, the Epistle to the Hebrews has an alternating series of exposition and exhortation. This is the most marked feature in the plan of the book.

1. THE BETTER MESSENGER (chapters 1, 2)

The opening lines of this epistle are majestic. They contain one of the greatest declarations ever made to man, "God hath spoken." This is the divine answer to human skepticism. Christianity is the religion of a divine revelation. It is not the record of man's groping after God, but the history of God's self-revelation to man. God has revealed Himself in Christ, through whom He has spoken His final word to man.

Reference is made in the first verse to the various instalments ("divers portions") and the varying methods ("divers manners") by which God spoke to man in the days before

[1] For a discussion of the question of the authorship of Hebrews see the writer's *Story of the New Testament*, pp. 102-105.

Christ. It suggests to us the whole history of God's dealings with His people, as recorded in the Old Testament Scriptures.

Following this most important statement as to the fact of divine revelation (1:1, 2), we have another outstanding Christological passage.[2] After referring to the Son's work as Creator (v. 2), he says of Him, "who being the effulgence of his glory, and the very image of his substance." Christ is the manifestation of God's glory and the exact reproduction of His nature. The Greek word translated "image," found only here in the New Testament, is *character,* of which our English word is simply a transliteration. It means a "stamp," or "impress."

Seven things are declared of Christ in verses 2-4. He is the Heir of all things, and so the end of all history; the Creator of all things, and so the beginning of all history; the Sustainer of all things, and so through all history; the Brightness of God's glory; the express Image of God's person, or the very *character* (Greek word) of God; the Purifier of sins; the Coregent with the Father ("sat down on the right hand of the Majesty on high"). We have a great Christ!

In the fourth verse the Son is declared to be "better than the angels." The word "angel" comes directly from the Greek and means "messenger." Hence, Christ is the better Messenger from God.

The Israelites held that their covenant was given by angels on Mount Sinai. They challenged Christianity to parallel this in its origin. But the writer of Hebrews demonstrates at length that Christ, the Messenger of the new covenant, is better than angels.

The Epistle to the Hebrews is saturated with the Old Testament. This is apparent especially in the typology of the book and in the quotations from the Old Testament. No less than seven such quotations occur in this first chapter. Five of these are from the Psalms, one is from Second Samuel, and one is from the Septuagint version of Deuteronomy.

One fact seems obvious from a study of these quotations: that Christ holds a larger place in the Old Testament Scriptures than has generally been recognized. Some of these passages are from acknowledged Messianic Psalms. But we

[2] See also John 1:1-18 and Colossians 1:15-19.

should probably not have classed Psalm 102 as Messianic except for this quotation. One may well ask whether Christ is not the central figure of the Old Testament as well as the New.

In the second chapter we are warned, "Therefore we ought to give the more earnest heed to the things that were heard, lest haply we drift away from them." Drifting constitutes one of the greatest dangers in the Christian life. One does not have to do anything to drift.

To emphasize more strongly the serious sin of neglect, the writer says, "How shall we escape, if we neglect so great a salvation?" (v. 2). Neglect is not as heinous a sin as rejection, but if continued in it is just as fatal.

The humanity of Jesus is discussed at more length in Hebrews than anywhere else in the New Testament. We are told that in His incarnation He was made for a little while lower than the angels (v. 9), taking on human nature. Then comes that difficult statement that Christ was made "perfect through sufferings." The word "perfect" has essentially the idea of bringing to completion. At least, then, we may say that suffering was a necessary part of completing Christ's work of redemption. That is the minimum meaning.

It is stated clearly in the fourteenth verse that the purpose of Christ's incarnation was that He might through death accomplish the deliverance of humanity. In the seventeenth and eighteenth verses it is further revealed that He partook of our human nature in order that He might sympathize truly with us in our frailties. Because He has experienced the weakness and sufferings of human life He has become "a merciful and faithful high priest"—merciful to forgive quickly, and faithful to watch over us carefully. We have a High Priest who knows just how we feel when tempted. That is wonderful consolation.

2. THE BETTER REST (chapter 3, 4)

In the first two chapters we found that Christ is better than the angels. In chapter three He is declared to be better than Moses, and in chapter four, better than Joshua.

Christ is better than Moses, because while Moses was a faithful servant in God's house, Christ is a Son over that house (3:5). This house is the family of God on earth.

We should never put Jesus on the same plane with merely human teachers or prophets. Peter did that on the Mount of Transfiguration and was rebuked for it. Mohammedanism classes Jesus with Abraham and Moses as one of the prophets of God, and Modernism has hardly done better. One of the emphases of this epistle is on the finality of Jesus Christ—that Jesus stands absolutely unique in human history as alone the Son of God, God manifest in the flesh. No person can be loyal to the New Testament and stop short of this. And if the New Testament be not true, what foundation do we have for our Christian faith?

An interesting expression occurs in the seventh verse of the third chapter, "as the Holy Spirit saith." This is followed by a quotation from the ninety-fifth Psalm. Here is a very definite claim that the Old Testament Scriptures are inspired by the Spirit of God.

One of the key words of Hebrews is "lest." It occurs in the twelfth and thirteenth verses of this third chapter, "Lest haply there shall be in any one of you an evil heart of unbelief in falling away from the living God: . . . lest any one of you be hardened by the deceitfulness of sin." Another warning is found in 4:1, "Lest haply, a promise being left of entering into his rest, any one of you should seem to have come short of it."

It has been well pointed out that these three verses, taken with 2:1, constitute a series of warnings against backsliding. If we drift away from the gospel message we are in danger of falling away from God. The next step is hardening of our hearts by the deceitfulness of sin, and the end is failure to enter into God's rest. The thing to guard against is the drifting.

These warnings are illustrated by the example of the Israelites. Through disobedience and unbelief they were prevented from entering the promised land of rest (3:18, 19). It may be noted that these two verses emphasize the close identity between unbelief and disobedience. They are Siamese twins in human experience.

Another key expression of the Epistle to the Hebrews is "Let us." It occurs four times in the fourth chapter: "let us therefore fear," lest we come short of God's rest (v. 1); "let us therefore give diligence to enter into that rest" (v. 11); "let us hold fast our confession" (v. 14); "let us therefore draw near with boldness unto the throne of grace" (v. 16).

The subject of rest is the main theme of chapters three and four. In the third chapter it is stated that disobedience and unbelief kept the Israelites under Moses from inheriting their rest. In the fourth chapter (v. 3) we read, "For we who have believed do enter into that rest." Faith is the gateway into the land of rest.

Four distinct kinds of rest are spoken of in chapter four. In the fourth verse we read of *creation* rest. Verse nine tells of "*sabbath* rest"; literally, a keeping of Sabbath. Verse eight mentions *Canaan* rest (also 3:11, 18); verses one, three, ten, and eleven speak of *Christian* rest.

The Christian rest is a cessation from our own works (v. 10) and a trust in what God has done for us and is doing in us. The secret of soul rest is complete surrender to the will of God. It means "let go" of yourself, and "let God" have His way.

This section closes, as did the previous one (2:17, 18), with a reference to the High Priest (4:14-16). A very striking expression occurs only here in the New Testament, "Jesus the Son of God." It is the combination of His humanity and deity that makes Christ an efficient and sufficient High Priest.

The Jews prided themselves on the possession of a high priest who could atone for their sins. The writer of Hebrews answers for the Christian, "We have a high priest." He can be touched with the feeling of our infirmities, because of His humanity. But He is unique in that He was tempted "without sin." This can mean both that He did not sin as a result of His temptation and that He had no inward sin as a source of temptation. Either interpretation would be correct.

Because we have such an approachable, yet appropriate, High Priest, we are exhorted to "draw near with boldness unto the throne of grace, that we may receive mercy, and may find grace to help us in time of need" (v. 16).

3. THE BETTER HIGH PRIEST (chapters 5-7)

a. *The Humanity of Christ* (chapter 5). Having twice referred to Jesus as our High Priest, the author of Hebrews now takes up a more careful discussion of the priesthood. This subject really extends through chapters 5-10, but we have broken it up, for convenience of study, according to various phases that are emphasized.

First we are told the qualifications and duties of a human high priest. He is supposed to offer "both gifts and sacrifices for sins" (5:1). He must be one who can feel gently toward the ignorant and erring. He has to offer for his own sins, as well as for the sins of the people. Above all, he must really be called of God, as was Aaron.

A comparison is then drawn between the Jewish high priest and Christ. He also was appointed by God (vs. 5, 6). His humanity is described in striking fashion (vs. 7-10). The earthly life of "prayers and supplications with strong crying and tears" found its climax in Gethsemane, when the Son of God said to His Father, "Not my will, but thine, be done." It was the temptation to reject His Father's will which caused Him the keenest suffering. He was subjected to the excruciating ordeal in order that He might learn obedience by the things which He suffered (v. 8). He must prove His loyalty to His Father's will by His deeds of obedience. When he had experienced the perfection of suffering, He became our Savior.

The writer pauses at this point to bemoan the spiritual dullness of his readers (5:11-14). They ought to be teachers, but actually they have to be fed as babies. How few people are grown up spiritually!

b. *A Warning Against Apostasy* (chapter 6). Because of the conditions of his readers, the writer of Hebrews digresses in chapter six to urge them to advance. The first verse expresses one of the keynotes of the epistle, "Let us press on unto perfection." The best way to guard against the danger of going backward is to press forward.

Hebrews 6:4-6 is one of those passages that have caused considerable discussion among Bible students. We shall quote it in full to get it before us for examination. "For as touching those who were once enlightened and tasted of the heavenly gift, and were made partakers of the Holy Spirit, and tasted the good word of God, and the powers of the age to come, and then fell away, it is impossible to renew them again unto repentance; seeing they crucify to themselves the Son of God afresh, and put him to an open shame."

The first thing we would note is that the clause "if they shall fall away" in the King James Version is definitely an incorrect translation. This is a participial construction, exactly parallel to the preceding expressions. The text is describing those who have had these gracious experiences and then have fallen away.

Having eliminated the "if," we still face another objection made by some of our brethren. They claim that verses four and five do not describe a converted man at all, but only one who has heard the gospel. We leave it to the intelligence of the reader to settle this question for himself, after a careful rereading of those verses.

There remains one other problem, which is more vital to us. Having established the fact that a person can backslide, the problem of verse six is, Can he ever be reclaimed?

The answer to this is that the expression "fell away" probably refers to apostasy rather than mere backsliding. It describes those who have willfully rejected Christianity. The writer is warning Hebrew Christians of the seriousness of forsaking the Christian faith to return to Judaism. Those who do so are rejecting the sacrifice of Christ and are thus without any hope of salvation. No backslider should be discouraged from returning to God because of this scripture.

In the last paragraph of the sixth chapter (vs. 13-20) we are reminded of the firm foundation of the Christian hope. We have both God's word and His oath that He will fulfill His promises. This hope is anchored within the veil of heaven, where Christ has gone as our forerunner, to prepare for our coming.

c. *The Order of Melchizedek* (chapter 7). Chapter seven develops the thought that Christ is a high priest after the order of Melchizedek, not after the order of Aaron. A description is given of Melchizedek, who received only a bare mention in the Old Testament (Genesis 14:18-20), but whose name occurs nine times in Hebrews.

Some think that Melchizedek was a historical character of the time of Abraham. Others, equally devout and learned, hold that he was a theophany; that is, an appearance of God in visible form. The language of verse three, "Without father, without mother, without genealogy, having neither beginning of days nor end of life," should probably not be pressed as an argument for the second view. It may mean only that there is no record of his ancestry or his birth and death.

The writer pauses (vs. 4-10) to show that Melchizedek was greater than Abraham, and so greater than Aaron, because Abraham paid tithes to him. The point of interest for us is that tithing antedates the Mosaic law. It is evidently a principle which was established in the beginning, by which man should recognize and acknowledge God's ownership of himself and his property. Every time we pay our tithes we testify to the fact that we belong to God, together with all we have.

The remainder of the chapter emphasizes the imperfections of the Aaronic priesthood, in contrast to the priesthood of Christ. The latter is a never-ending one in the person of the eternal Son of God (vs. 16, 17). His appointment has been confirmed by God's oath (vs. 20-22). The Levitical priesthood experienced a frequent change of personnel; Christ is High Priest forever (vs. 23, 24). "Wherefore also he is able to save to the uttermost [Gr., *completely*] them that draw near unto God through him, seeing he ever liveth to make intercession for them" (v. 25).

One more point is made in the closing paragraph of the chapter (vs. 26-28). The Levitical high priest had to offer sacrifices daily for his own sins and for the sins of the people. But Christ made a sacrifice "once for all, when he offered up himself." He is the perfect High Priest.

4. THE BETTER COVENANT (chapter 8)

After summing up his discussion of the priesthood of Christ (vs. 1-5), the author goes on to say that our High Priest is "the mediator of a better covenant" (v. 6). The first covenant was unsatisfactory, because it did not provide the power to obey it. So God has made another covenant with mankind through Christ.

The description of this new covenant is quoted at length from Jeremiah (31:31-34). The essence of it is:

"I will put my laws into their mind,
And on their heart also will I write them."

This new covenant is not to be characterized by a code of external laws. Rather, it is to consist of an inward experience, by which the heart of man will be inclined to do the will of God. This covenant finds its fulfillment in those whose hearts are sanctified by the indwelling presence of the Holy Spirit.

5. THE BETTER SACRIFICE (chapters 9, 10)

Chapter nine begins with a description of the ancient tabernacle and its worship (vs. 1-10). The point which is emphasized is that the way into the holy of holies, where the Shekinah of God's presence dwelt, was closed in the tabernacle on earth. None could venture within its sacred precincts except the high priest, and he only once a year, and then "not without blood" (v. 7).

But Christ our High Priest "through his own blood, entered in once for all into the holy place, having obtained eternal redemption" (v. 12). That is, he presented His own blood in the presence of the Father in heaven as the atonement for our sins.

The word "obtained" is literally "found" in the Greek. This suggests the fact that Christ sought for our redemption until at last He found it on the cross. His search included those lonely vigils of prayer, culminating in the agonies of Gethsemane and Calvary. But finally He could cry, *"Eureka!"* ("I have found"). That is the significance of the cry from the cross, "It is finished." The centuries of waiting and the years of service and suffering had ended in the procurement of our redemption.

The writer of Hebrews continues with his argument. If the blood of goats and bulls and the water of purification made with the ashes of a red heifer (Numbers 19) could cleanse the Israelites of old, "how much more shall the blood of Christ, who through the eternal Spirit offered himself without blemish unto God, cleanse your conscience from dead works to serve the living God?" (v. 14). It is a point well made. The sacrifice of Christ is of infinitely more value than all animal sacrifices put together. He is the one and only perfect Sacrifice.

The words "covenant" and "testament" are both translations of the same Greek word. There has been considerable discussion as to which is the preferable rendering. It seems that both ideas are used by the writer of this epistle. The Israelites, as was generally true of ancient peoples, were in the habit of making covenants, or binding agreements. The idea of a testament, or will, was developed especially by the Romans, who were strong on legal procedure.

Whereas the idea of "covenant" seems to fit best in most cases in Hebrews, that of "testament" certainly is more appropriate in 9:16, 17. It took the death of Christ to put His "last will and testament" into effect for His people.

A very important general truth is stated in 9:22, "Apart from shedding of blood there is no remission." A bloodless religion, be it Christian Science "falsely so called" (1 Tim. 6:20) or misnamed modern Christianity, can do nothing to take away the sins of humanity.

The sufficiency of Christ's one sacrifice for sin is stated again in 9:26—"but now once at the end of the ages hath he been manifested to put away sin by the sacrifice of himself." The ages of innocence, promise and law culminated in the sacrifice of the Son of God, which atoned for the sins of all time and introduced the age of Christianity.

In chapter ten the writer returns to his point that the blood of animals could never take away sins (v. 4). The fact that these sacrifices were made again each day shows that they had no final value (v. 11). But Christ, "when he had offered one sacrifice for sins forever, sat down on the right hand of God" (v. 12). He had made a sacrifice which was sufficient for all time.

A most important result of Christ's death is that the way has been opened for us into the very presence of God. "Having therefore, brethren, boldness to enter into the holy place by the blood of Jesus, by the way which he dedicated for us, a new and living way, through the veil, that is to say, his flesh" (10:19, 20). In the death of the Son of God the inner veil before the sanctuary was torn apart, and the way has been opened through Christ for our entrance into the holy of holies where God dwells.

On the basis of this glorious truth, the author makes three exhortations, each based on the key expression, "Let us." He says, "Let us draw near with a true heart," having been cleansed from sin; "let us hold fast the confession of our hope that it waver not," for God is faithful to His promise; "and let us consider one another to provoke unto love and good works" (10:22-24).

Drawing near will help us to hold fast. And the consciousness of God's near presence will help us to "provoke unto love," instead of provoking to anger.

We have in this tenth chapter another passage of grave warning against turning away from Christ (10:26-31). The one who willfully rejects the blood of Christ and repudiates its sacred efficacy (v. 29) will find that he had no other sacrifice for his sins (v. 26). The Jews who returned to Judaism were spurning their only hope of salvation. In spite of persecution (vs. 32-39) the Hebrew Christians must remain true to Christ.

6. THE BETTER COUNTRY (chapter 11)

The eleventh chapter of Hebrews is the great Faith Chapter of the Bible. To attempt even a brief exposition of its contents would require more space than we can spare in our present study. So we shall only skim the surface.

Faith operates with regard to the unknown future and the unseen present. It is an "assurance of things hoped for, a conviction of things not seen" (v. 1). It is the basis of our knowledge of the origin of the universe (v. 3). Apart from God's written revelation, which we accept by faith, we have absolutely no certain knowledge on this subject.

The writer illustrates the value and effectiveness of faith in the lives of Abel (v. 4), Enoch (vs. 5, 6), Noah (v. 7), Abraham and Sarah (vs. 8-19), Isaac (v. 20), Jacob (v. 21), Joseph (v. 22), Moses (vs. 23-28), the Israelites (vs. 29, 30), and Rahab (v. 31).

It would seem that at this point the author of Hebrews was in the same predicament as this poor scribe. The subject was growing on his hands so that he was forced to stop short and summarize the rest of the Old Testament record of faith (vs. 32-40).

7. THE BETTER LIFE (chapters 12, 13)

Chapter twelve begins with a twofold exhortation, "Let us . . . lay aside every weight," and "let us run with patience the race that is set before us." The Christian life is a long race. We need to strip ourselves for a good start and then keep on running with perseverance.

The writer points out the value of God's chastening. It is for our profit, "that we may be partakers of his holiness" (v. 10).

The better life includes obedience to the command, "Follow after peace with all men, and the sanctification without which no man shall see the Lord" (v. 14). This command is followed by a threefold warning, "Looking carefully *lest* there be any man that falleth short of the grace of God; *lest* any root of bitterness springing up trouble you, and thereby the many be defiled; *lest* there be any fornicator, or profane person, as Esau" (vs. 15. 16). This is another striking warning against gradual backsliding.

The remainder of chapter twelve contrasts Mount Sinai with the heavenly Mount Zion. The better life is the heavenly life of fellowship with the living Jesus (cf. also 11:16).

Chapter thirteen gives a series of disconnected exhortations to love the brethren (vs. 1-30), to keep morally pure (v. 4), to be free from the love of money (vs. 5, 6), to be obedient, orthodox, faithful members of the Christian Church (vs. 7-17).

We close with the writer's plea to his readers to go outside the camp of Judaism and ally themselves definitely with Christ, "Wherefore Jesus also, that he might sanctify the people through his own blood, suffered without the gate. Let us therefore go forth unto him without the camp, bearing his reproach" (13:12, 13). It is God's call to us to end all compromise and take our place fully with Christ by letting Him sanctify us with His blood. Thus only can we enter with Him into the holy of holies, here or hereafter. "Blessed are the pure in heart, for they shall see God."

XI. THE HOLY CHURCH

The seven letters which are found in our English New Testaments between the Epistle to the Hebrews and the Book of Revelation are called the General, or Catholic, Epistles. The term Catholic, of course, means universal, as in the Apostle's Creed, "I believe in the holy catholic church."

The earliest form of this creed, dating from the middle of the second century, has simply "the holy church." It is from this fact that we have drawn our title for this chapter.

It will be noticed that instead of being named after the recipients of the letters, as in the case of the Pauline Epistles, the General Epistles are named after the writers.

James

1. SALUTATION (1:1)

Tradition attributes this book—it is more of a treatise or sermon than a letter—to James the brother of Jesus, the one who was for a long time the acknowledged leader of the church at Jerusalem.

James addresses his letter "to the twelve tribes which are of the Dispersion." The general nature of the book confirms this claim that it was written to Jews. It is very much like the Hebrew wisdom literature, of which Proverbs and Ecclesiastes are samples. It also resembles the Sermon on the Mount in its ethical, rather than doctrinal, emphasis.

2. THE VALUE OF TEMPTATION (1:2-18)

The writer gives a difficult assignment when he says, "Count it all joy, my brethren, when ye fall into manifold temptations" (v. 2). The only way one can do that is by remembering that "the proving of your faith worketh patience" (v. 3).

After exhortations to pray in faith (vs. 5-8) and not to trust in riches (vs. 9-11), the author returns to his original subject (vs. 12-18). "Blessed is the man that endureth temptation: for when he hath been approved, he shall receive the crown of life, which the Lord hath promised to them that love him" (v. 12). Life on earth is a period of probation, and it is necessary that we be tried and found faithful before we are eligible for the crown of life. The crown is for the victors in the conflict.

James sounds a warning against accusing God of tempting us. He says that the source of temptation is lust, which leads to sin and culminates in death. God is not the source of evil, but of good. "Every good gift and every perfect gift is from above, coming down from the Father of lights, with whom can be no variation, neither shadow that is cast by turning" (v. 17).

3. HEARERS AND DOERS OF GOD'S WORD (1:19-27)

A characteristic admonition of James occurs in verse 19, "Let every man be swift to hear, slow to speak, slow to wrath." We are to put wickedness out of our lives and listen to the Word of God.

But we are to be doers, as well as hearers, of the Word. Otherwise we are like a man who looks in the mirror, but forgets to wash his face and comb his hair. Jesus finished the Sermon on the Mount by illustrating the same truth.

The first chapter ends with a definition of true religion, "Pure religion and undefiled before our God and Father is this, to visit the fatherless and widows in their affliction, and to keep oneself unspotted from the world" (v. 27). Christianity demands love for our neighbor; but it also enjoins purity of character.

4. WARNING AGAINST PARTIALITY (2:1-13)

Christians are warned against showing respect of persons. The poor are to be treated as courteously as the rich. James points out the fact that the rich are the ones who oppress others (v. 6). They are also apt to be irreligious (v. 7). We should take the attitude which Jesus did.

5. FAITH AND WORKS (2:14-26)

This is one of the most interesting parts of the epistle. James declares that faith must be supported by works, if it is to save one (v. 14). Faith apart from works is dead (v. 17). Works are a demonstration of our faith, "Show me thy faith apart from thy works, and I by my works will show thee my faith" (v. 18). The one whose faith is only a mental belief in God has no more than the faith of a demon.

The twenty-fourth verse proved a difficult one for Martin Luther. "Ye see that by works a man is justified, and not only by faith." The point which James is making is that a faith which does not produce good works is a false one. He was opposing the antinomianism of the early church. Martin Luther found that his Protestant doctrine of justification by faith alone was abused by the antinomianists of his day.

6. THE UNRULY TONGUE (chapter 3).

James declares that the tongue is one of the main sources of trouble among human beings. Doubtless he had plenty of reason for thinking so. Certainly he speaks in very strong terms concerning the matter, "Behold, how much wood is kindled by how small a fire! And the tongue is a fire: the world of iniquity among our members is the tongue, which defileth the whole body, and setteth on fire the wheel of nature, and is set on fire by hell" (vs. 5, 6). Later on he adds, "But the tongue can no man tame; it is a restless evil, it is full of deadly poison" (v. 8).

The chapter closes with a contrast between the boasted wisdom of those who fuss and criticize, and the wisdom which is truly Christian. One of the beautiful passages of the book is to be found in 3:17, 18, "But the wisdom that is from above is first pure, then peaceable, gentle, easy to be entreated, full of mercy and good fruits, without variance, without hypocrisy. And the fruit of righteousness is sown in peace for them that make peace." It does not take much reflection to realize how little of the so-called wisdom of this world exhibits the above characteristics. But the question for us is how much our lives measure up to these standards.

7. WARNINGS AGAINST PLEASURE AND PRIDE (chapter 4)

The Christian will be led astray if he makes pleasure his goal (vs. 1-3). Hence, he should avoid friendship with the world, which is enmity against God (vs. 4, 5). God pushes away the proud, but draws near the humble (vs. 6-10). Pride leads one to judge his brethren, and so is a serious sin (vs. 11, 12).

The chapter closes with a warning against planning the future without reference to God (vs. 13-17). In all our proposals we should say, "If the Lord will."

8. Closing Injunctions (chapter 5)

In the opening paragraph of this chapter (vs. 1-6) James sounds another trumpet blast against the rich who oppress the poor. In this he breathes the spirit of the Old Testament prophets, such as Isaiah and Amos. Doubtless he had meditated deeply in their writings.

The next paragraph (vs. 7-11) enjoins patience under suffering, "Be patient therefore, brethren, until the coming of the Lord" (v. 7). While we wait we are not to murmur impatiently against one another (v. 9).

James gives careful direction for prayers for the sick (vs. 14-16). If we would pray effectually, we must be willing to confess our faults (v. 16). The book closes with an injunction to help restore those who have erred from the way (vs. 19, 20).

First Peter

1. Salutation (1:1, 2)

The author of this epistle is stated to be Peter, the apostle. It is written to the Christian Jews of the Dispersion in Asia Minor.

2. The Blessings of the Christian (1:3—2:10)

The opening part of the epistle gives us its keynote—*hope* (v. 3). The Christians were being persecuted at this time by Nero. Peter encourages them to hold steady and hope in God.

The resurrection of Jesus Christ has given us a living hope of our incorruptible inheritance in heaven. Verse four speaks of the Reserved Inheritance; verse five, of the Preserved Inheritor. The same God who is protecting our inheritance in heaven can guard us down here on earth. This is the Christian's hope.

There is a purpose in the trials which the readers are undergoing, "That the proof [or, proving] of your faith, being more precious than gold that perisheth though it is proved by fire, may be found unto praise and glory and honor at the revelation of Jesus Christ: whom not having seen ye love, on whom, though now ye see him not, yet believing, ye rejoice greatly with joy unspeakable and full of glory" (vs. 7, 8). Here are faith, hope and love. But love is shown as the foundation of all. Because we love Him, we trust Him and rejoice in hope for the future.

The attitude of the Christian in view of his hope is set forth in verse thirteen, "Wherefore girding up the loins of your mind, be sober and set your hope perfectly on the grace that is to be brought unto you at the revelation of Jesus Christ." The second coming of Christ is the Christian's blessed hope, which enables him to endure hardship and suffering.

A second keynote of this epistle is *holiness*. "As he who called you is holy, be ye yourselves also holy in all manner of living; because it is written, Ye shall be holy; for I am holy" (vs. 15, 16). It is primarily holiness of conduct which Peter is emphasizing here. But one cannot live a holy life unless he has a holy heart. We need the inward sanctifying experience to purify the springs of our motives and desires, our thoughts and our actions. Man's method is to begin with outward conduct; that is, by reformation. God's way is to begin with inward desire; that is, by transformation. The first fails to achieve even its external goal. The second changes both the inner spirit and the outer life.

The call to holiness is based not only upon the character of God, but also upon the redemption in Christ (vs. 18, 19). Because He bought us back out of sin, we ought to live as redeemed individuals. Because He was willing to shed His "precious blood," we ought to let Him rule our lives, which now belong to Him by right of redemption, as well as by right of creation.

It is an interesting coincidence that Peter, whose name means "a stone," emphasizes the idea that all Christians are stones. He writes, "Ye also, as living stones, are built up a spiritual house, to be a holy priesthood, to offer up spiritual sacrifices, acceptable to God through Jesus Christ" (2:5).

The latter part of this passage is reflected again in the ninth verse, "Ye are an elect race, a royal priesthood, a holy nation, a people for God's own possession." Peter emphasized the Protestant doctrine of the universal priesthood of believers. In God's sight there is no distinct order of priesthood. Every Christian is a priest.

3. THE DUTIES OF THE CHRISTIAN (2:11—4:11)

Another figure that Peter uses for the Christian life is that of a pilgrimage. "Beloved, I beseech you as sojourners and pilgrims, to abstain from fleshly lusts, which war against the soul" (v. 11). It is necessary for his highest spiritual good that the Christian should feel a detachment from this world. Above all, he must keep the spirit supreme over the body.

The duties of a Christian include obedience to civil laws and rulers (vs. 13-17). By manifesting a right attitude toward the government the believer brings honor rather than reproach to the cause of Christ.

Servants are to be in subjection to their masters (vs. 18-25). Even if punished wrongly they should remember the example of Christ, "Who did no sin, neither was guile found in his mouth; who, when he was reviled, reviled not again; when he suffered, threatened not; but committed himself to him that judgeth righteously" (vs. 22, 23).

There is not very much doctrinal emphasis in the Epistle of Peter. But verse 24 gives a definite statement on the atonement, "Who his own self bare our sins in his own body upon the tree, that we, having died unto sin, might live unto righteousness; by whose stripes ye were healed." That is a clear declaration that Christ's sufferings on the cross were vicarious. He suffered for us, not for Himself.

An interesting expression occurs in the closing verse of the second chapter. Christ is called "the Shepherd and Bishop of your souls." He alone is the Bishop over the whole church. It is significant that none of the New Testament apostles claimed this title.

The third chapter continues the list of duties of various classes in the Christian community. The first set of injunctions is to wives (3:1-6). They are to exhibit a meek and quiet spirit, rather than be taken up with outward adornment.

Next comes the duty of husbands (v. 7). They are to treat their wives with honor and with gentleness. A husband who invokes the Scriptures to make his wife obey him should take care to see that he is also fulfilling his scriptural duties. If both take the right attitude there will be no fussing about who is to be "boss."

The apostle has a word for all of us. He writes, "Finally, be ye all likeminded, compassionate, loving as brethren, tenderhearted, humble-minded" (v. 8). If all Christians would exhibit this spirit it would be the most valuable and effective advertising that Christianity could have.

The last paragraph of chapter three (vs. 13-22) discusses the duties of a Christian under persecution. He is not to be afraid (v. 14). Believers are to "sanctify in your hearts Christ as Lord" (v. 15), and be ready to explain to their persecutors the reason for their faith. When asked to say "Lord Caesar," they were to say "Lord Christ," even if it meant death.

The fourth chapter begins with a discussion of the attitude of the Christian toward suffering, "Forasmuch then as Christ suffered in the flesh, arm ye yourselves also with the same mind" (v. 1). The example He set of patience and forgiveness toward His tormentors is at once a challenge and an inspiration to the persecuted Christians. The sufferings they endured would tend to separate them still more from the world (vs. 1, 2).

At best, these sufferings will not last long. "But the end of all things is at hand: be ye therefore of sound mind, and be sober unto prayer: above all things being fervent in your love among yourselves" (vs. 7, 8). The most important thing in the Christian life is love. It is the highest Christian duty.

4. THE TRIALS OF THE CHRISTIAN (4:12—5:11)

"Beloved, think it not strange concerning the fiery trial among you, which cometh upon you to prove you, as though a strange thing happened unto you: but insomuch as ye are partakers of Christ's sufferings, rejoice" (vs. 12, 13).

The churches of northern Asia Minor, to which Peter was writing, were undergoing a baptism of fiery persecution. But Peter encourages them to rejoice in the sense of God's presence with them (v. 14). The greater the suffering, the greater the glory.

In chapter five Peter admonishes the elders to "tend the flock of God" (v. 2), not for money, "neither as lording it over the charge allotted to you, but making yourselves ensamples to the flock" (v. 3). That is sound advice to all church leaders.

Then he exhorts the younger ones to be in subjection to their elders, and adds, "Yea, all of you gird yourselves with humility, to serve one another" (v. 5). There follow exhortations to humility (v. 6), trust (v. 7), and watchfulness (v. 8). "And the God of all grace, who called you unto his eternal glory in Christ, after that ye have suffered a little while, shall himself perfect, establish, strengthen you" (v. 10).

5. CONCLUSION (5:12-14)

Silvanus, or Silas, was evidently the scribe who wrote this epistle at Peter's dictation (v. 12). The apostle was writing from "Babylon" (v. 13), which is probably figurative for Rome, although many scholars take it as referring to the city of Mesopotamia. Mark, who was Peter's interpreter, includes his greetings. The epistle closes with a benediction of peace.

Second Peter

1. SALUTATION (1:1, 2)

The writer of this epistle calls himself "Simon Peter, a servant and an apostle of Jesus Christ." The epistle is addressed to "them that have obtained a like precious faith with us." The term "precious" was used frequently in the First Epistle.

2. GROWTH IN GRACE (1:3-11)

Through the promises of God we are made "partakers of the divine nature" (v. 4). But we are to give diligent attention to our growth in grace. The secret of this growth is the adding constantly of other Christian virtues—faith, virtue, knowledge, self-control, patience, godliness, brotherly kindness, love (vs. 5-7). He who does this will "never stumble" (v. 10). Here is a sure prevention against backsliding. And it assures us of an abundant entrance into heaven (v. 11).

3. THE CERTAINTY OF THE CHRISTIAN REVELATION (1:12-21)

The apostle knows that "the putting off of my tabernacle cometh swiftly" (v. 14). So he is more urgent in his efforts to establish the church firmly on its foundations.

Therefore he calls attention to these foundations. "We did not follow cunningly devised fables, when we made known unto you the power and coming of our Lord Jesus Christ, but we were eyewitnesses of his majesty" (v. 16). Christianity rests upon solid historical foundations. We have the testimony of reliable witnesses who saw and heard Jesus.

Peter refers to the time that he, together with James and John, was with Christ on the Mount of Transfiguration (vs. 17, 18). But he declares, "We have the word of prophecy made more sure" (v. 19). The New Testament record, fulfilling as it does the predictions of the Old Testament, bears the seal of divine inspiration. As in the case of the former Scriptures, "men spake from God, being moved by the Holy Spirit" (v. 21).

4. FALSE TEACHERS (chapter 2)

The apostle predicts that there will arise in the church "false teachers, who shall privily bring in destructive heresies, denying even the Master that bought them" (v. 1). Christ-rejection is the foremost heresy of the Christian Church. The proportion of ministers today who deny the deity of Jesus Christ is an alarming revelation of the true condition of the Church.

To emphasize the doom of these false teachers, the writer cites the cases of the fallen angels, the people of Noah's day who perished in the flood and the cities of Sodom and Gomorrah (vs. 4-8). He gives a lurid picture of the nature of these false teachers in the Church (vs. 10-22). Language could hardly be more graphic in its condemnation of those who seek to corrupt the gospel of Christ.

5. THE LAST DAYS (3:1-13)

Apostasy and unbelief are to mark the last days. "In the last days mockers shall come with mockery, walking after their own lusts, and saying, where is the promise of his coming? for, from the day that the fathers fell asleep, all things continue as they were from the beginning of the creation" (vs. 3, 4). The writer says that they willfully forget about the flood. This earth, which has been washed with water, must yet undergo a baptism of fire before it will be clean (vs. 5-7).

To those who object that the promises are slow in being fulfilled, the writer answers, "One day is with the Lord as a thousand years, and a thousand years as one day" (v. 8). So we should not become impatient.

The reason God has waited is that He is merciful and does not want to destroy men (v. 9). "But the day of the Lord will come as a thief" (v. 10). The time is uncertain, but the fact is sure. The day of the Lord will be a time of great destruction (v. 10). In view of what is to happen to this earth, "what manner of persons ought ye to be in all holy living and godliness?" (v. 11). These prophecies of the day of the Lord are an incentive to holiness.

The picture of the day of the Lord does not end with destruction. It changes to "new heavens and a new earth, wherein dwelleth righteousness" (v. 13). This is the purpose of the destruction of the old world of sin and wickedness.

6. CONCLUSION (3:14-18)

The writer makes his closing exhortation against the background of this scene. "Wherefore, beloved, seeing that ye look for these things, give diligence that ye may be found in peace, without spot and blameless in his sight" (v. 14). Those who would be inhabitants of the new heavens and new earth must become fit to dwell there.

Jude

Most scholars today hold that Jude was written before Second Peter. Since it has so much in common with that letter it seems best to treat it at this point, before our study of the Johannine Epistles.

1. THE SALUTATION (vs. 1, 2)

The writer identifies himself as Jude, a brother of James. It is generally held that this James is the writer of the epistle by that name, and so Jude would be a brother of Jesus.

The letter is addressed to "them that are called"; that is, to the church in general.

2. THE DEFENSE OF THE FAITH (vs. 3, 4)

Jude declares that his purpose in writing is to exhort his readers to "contend earnestly for the faith which was once for all delivered unto the saints." Already there were heretics in the church, "denying our only Master and Lord, Jesus Christ." It was needful to defend the orthodox teachings of the Christian faith then, as now.

3. THE DOOM OF THE UNGODLY (vs. 5-16)

The main section of the epistle is taken up with an account of God's past judgments on the disobedient. The writer cites the cases of the Israelites in the wilderness, the fallen angels,

Sodom and Gomorrah. The close connection in thought with Second Peter is obvious.

The expressions applied to false teachers in the church are even more striking than Second Peter—"clouds without water"; "autumn trees without fruit"; "wild waves of the sea"; "wandering stars" (vs. 12, 13).

4. THE BUILDING UP IN THE FAITH (vs. 17-23)

It is not only necessary to defend the faith; it is still more essential to build oneself up in the faith. Jude writes, "But ye, beloved, building up yourselves on your most holy faith, praying in the Holy Spirit, keep yourselves in the love of God, looking for the mercy of our Lord Jesus Christ unto eternal life" (vs. 20, 21).

5. BENEDICTION (vs. 24, 25)

This is one of the greatest benedictions to be found in the New Testament. We prefer to let the reader retain it in his memory in the familiar language of the King James Version, so we shall not quote.

First John

1. INTRODUCTION (1:1-4)

The beginning of John's First Epistle bears a striking resemblance to the opening words of the Prologue to his Gospel. These are the only two places in the New Testament where the term *Logos* is applied to Christ. Elsewhere it occurs only as a common noun.

In the first chapter of this epistle we encounter two characteristically Johannine terms, *life* and *light*. Later on we shall find *love* used frequently, as well as *believe, know, witness, truth* and *abide*. There is little room for question as to the unity of authorship of the Gospel and First Epistle.

2. WALKING IN THE LIGHT (1:5—2:17)

The closing part of the first chapter of this epistle (vs. 5-10) is an exceedingly important passage. It tells us that if we walk in the light the blood of Jesus, God's Son, "cleanseth us from all sin." Some Christian objects that he has no sin from which to be cleansed. John answers that if we say we have no sin we deceive ourselves, for the converted man still has sin in his heart. Then he turns to the sinner and says that if we confess our sins God will forgive us and will "cleanse us from all unrighteousness." The one who says that he has never sinned makes God a liar.

In chapter two the apostle says, "My little children, these things write I unto you that ye may not sin" (v. 1). But if any Christian does sin he has an Advocate with the Father, a lawyer to plead his case in the court of heaven. The Greek word for "Advocate" is Paraclete, which is translated "Comforter" in the fourteenth, fifteenth, and sixteenth chapters of John's Gospel. The Holy Spirit is our Helper on earth, while at the same time Jesus Christ is our Helper in heaven. With both of them on our side we can surely make it through, if we do our part.

Two doctrines are especially prominent in the First Epistle of John. They are the two main emphases of the Wesleyan movement—assurance of salvation and perfect love. Both are referred to in this first paragraph of chapter two.

The keynote of John's Gospel is *believing* in Christ, that we may be saved. The keynote of the First Epistle is *knowing* that we are saved. "Hereby we know that we know him, if we keep his commandments" (v. 3).

The result of keeping God's commands is perfect love, "Whoso keepeth his word, in him verily hath the love of God been perfected" (v. 5). It is possible to have a heart which is perfect in love toward God.

The next paragraph (2:7-11) discusses the nature of walking in the light. The essential thing is loving our brethren (v. 10), for this is Christ's great commandment to His followers (v. 7, cf. John 15:12). No matter how careful a Christian is about other things, if he fails in this he is not walking in the light.

In the next paragraph (2:12-17) John addresses three groups in the church, the new converts ("little children") fathers and young men. The first have had their sins forgiven (v. 12). The second have known the Father (v. 13). The third are strong and have overcome (v. 14). He warns all of these not to love the world (v. 15).

3. THE ANTICHRIST (2:18-29)

John declares that already many antichrists have appeared (v. 18). He defines the antichrist as one who denies the deity of Jesus (v. 22). The antidote for the influence of the spirit of antichrist is holding fast to the original doctrines of the Christian faith. "If that which ye heard from the beginning abide in you, ye also shall abide in the Son, and in the Father" (v. 24).

Another antidote for wrong doctrine is the anointing of the Holy Spirit upon our minds and hearts. "The anointing which ye received of him abideth in you, and ye need not that any one teach you; but as his anointing teacheth you all things, and is true" (v. 27). We all need the guidance of the Holy Spirit in our thinking, to keep us from the pitfalls of error.

4. SINLESS CHRISTIANITY (3:1-12)

The first great privilege of the believer is that of being a child of God. When Christ comes, we as children of God will be like the Son of God himself (v. 2). "And every one that hath this hope set on him purifieth himself, even as he is pure" (v. 3). If we expect to see Christ, we are eager to be prepared to meet Him, and that means we must be pure.

Another great doctrine of this epistle is that of sin. John not only discusses assurance of salvation and perfect love, but also sin and error. In the fourth verse he gives us a definition of sin, "sin is lawlessness." Christ was manifested to take away sins (v. 5).

Those who raise their hands in holy horror at the very mention of the idea of sinless perfection have a hard nut to crack in verses six and nine. These declare flatly, "Whosoever abideth in him sinneth not," and "Whosoever is begotten of God doeth no sin." It is the Christian's privilege to live without sinning.

5. EVIDENCES OF OUR CHRISTIAN STATE (3:13-24)

It is the duty of the Christian to love his fellow believers (vs. 13-24). The fact that we do love God's people is one of the signs that we belong to His family. "We know that we have passed out of death unto life, because we love the brethren" (v. 14).

Another test is given in this same paragraph. "Hereby shall we know that we are of the truth, and shall assure our heart before him: because if our heart condemn us, God is greater than our heart, and knoweth all things. Beloved, if our heart condemn us not, we have boldness toward God" (vs. 19-21). Freedom from condemnation is a good sign that our hearts are right.

Still a third test is given in the last verse of the chapter. "And hereby we know that he abideth in us, by the Spirit which he gave us." If we are conscious of the presence of the Holy Spirit in our lives we know that we belong to God.

6. THE SPIRIT OF TRUTH AND THE SPIRIT OF ERROR (4:1-6)

This double expression, which occurs in the sixth verse, fits in with John's doctrine of the antichrist. He warns us to "prove the spirits, whether they are of God" (v. 1). And then he tells us how we may test them. "Every spirit that confesseth that Jesus Christ is come in the flesh is of God: and every spirit that confesseth not Jesus is not of God: and this is the spirit of the antichrist" (vs. 3, 4). That is, every one who denies the true humanity of Jesus Christ is antichrist, as well as those who deny His deity.

In making this point John was probably opposing the teachings of the Docetic Gnostics, who taught that Christ only seemed to have a human body. His body was a sort of phantom appearance. This teaching undermined the atoning value of His death, for in this case Christ, the Son of God, did not die at all.

7. PERFECT LOVE (4:7-21)

This was John Wesley's favorite name for the experience of entire sanctification. He said that he preferred not to use the expression "sinless perfection" because it was generally misunderstood. He declared that the doctrine of sanctification which he taught was nothing more nor less than loving God with all the heart and loving one's neighbor as oneself.

It might be pointed out here that while the Protestant Reformation found the source of its doctrines mainly in the Epistles of Paul, the Wesleyan Reformation was rooted in the writings of John. Luther emphasized faith; Wesley emphasized love.

"Beloved, let us love one another: for love is of God" (v. 7). That is a typically Johannine exhortation.

The love of God was manifested in sending His Son into the world for our salvation (v. 9). Then John adds, "Beloved, if God so loved us, we also ought to love one another" (v. 11). "If we love one another, God abideth in us, and his love is perfected in us" (v. 12).

The true Christian is one who confesses that "Jesus is the Son of God" (v. 15). It is hard to see how those who deny the deity of Christ have any scriptural or historical justification for calling themselves Christians.

Twice in this paragraph we find that striking statement, "God is love" (vs. 8, 16). The doctrine of perfect love is elaborated further in verses 17-19. It is indicated clearly that perfect love is an experience which is attainable in this life.

8. THE WITNESS OF THE SPIRIT (5:1-12)

"It is the Spirit that beareth witness" (v. 7). He that believeth on the Son of God hath the witness in him" (v. 10). The Spirit witnesses to us that Jesus is the Christ, the Son of God; and He also witnesses to God's presence in our hearts.

9. CONCLUSION (5:13-21)

John tells us clearly the purpose for which he wrote this epistle, "These things have I written unto you, that ye may know that ye have eternal life" (v. 13). Comparing this with John 20:31 we see that the Gospel was written that we might *believe* in Jesus as the Son of God, and so have life through Him, while the epistle is written that we might *know* that we have eternal life. One is faith for salvation; the other is assurance of salvation.

Three times in the last paragraph (vs. 18-21) John says, "We know." That is the keynote of this epistle. It deals with the great certainties of the Christian faith.

Second John

This very brief letter is written by "the elder" to "the elect lady." We cannot be certain of either identity. But the language is that of the First Epistle. One needs only to read the main body of the letter (vs. 4-11) to see how closely the thoughts and expressions agree with First John. For that reason this epistle is assigned to John.

Third John

This letter is written by "the elder" to "Gaius the beloved." We do not know who he was, either.

Third John is not so completely Johannine in thought and language as is Second John. But it appears to have been written by the same person.

The occasion of it seems to have been the ambitious pretenses of one Diotrephes, who wanted to rule and ruin the church. The writer of this epistle says he will take care of him when he arrives (v. 10).

XII. THE CONSUMMATION OF HISTORY

We come now in our study to the last book of the New Testament, the Revelation of John. It forms a fitting climax to the Christian Revelation as a whole. It looks forward to the consummation of history in the new heavens and new earth.

There are three main divisions of the Book of Revelation, as indicated by the command in 1:19. The first is "the things which thou sawest," or the vision of Christ described in chapter one. The second is "the things which are," or the description of the condition at that time of the seven churches of Asia, as recorded in chapters two and three. The third is "the things which shall come to pass hereafter," the vision of the future as given in chapters 4-22.

The Past

1. INTRODUCTION (1:1-8)

The Book of Revelation, like the entire New Testament, is primarily "the revelation of Jesus Christ" (v. 1). It is declared to be a record of "the things which must shortly come to pass." That word "must" should be emphasized. In spite of all opposition God will work out inevitably His plans and purposes.

Another word in the first verse is of utmost importance for an intelligent study of this book. We are told that He "signified" it to His servant John. Walter Malone, the sainted founder of Cleveland Bible College, used to pronounce it "sign-ified." That suggests to us the fundamental fact that Revelation is a book of signs and symbols, and must be interpreted as such.

The third verse pronounces a blessing on those that read and hear and keep the words of this prophecy. It is possible to read the Bible without hearing its message. It is also possible to hear the truth of God's Word and yet not heed it.

After the brief prefatory paragraph (vs. 1-3), we have the salutation of "John to the seven churches that are in Asia" (vs. 4-7). Asia, as we have seen, means the Roman province of that name in western Asia Minor.

The salutation closes with a prediction of the return of Christ (v. 7). This is introductory to the entire Book of Revelation.

In the eighth verse the Lord calls Himself "the Alpha and the Omega." These are the first and last letters of the Greek alphabet and suggest that He is the beginning and end of history. He also refers to Himself as the One "who is and who was and who is to come." He alone fills the present, the past and the future. He is the Eternal, Almighty One. And He is our God.

The setting of the vision is given in verses 9-11. John was in lonely exile on the little rocky Isle of Patmos, in the Mediterranean, where he had been banished for his Christian testimony. This was probably during the persecution under Domitian.

But he was also "in the Spirit on the Lord's day." Although far away from Christian fellowship, John was observing the Christian day of worship by being in a spiritual frame of mind. Thereby he was conditioned to receive the vision which now came to him.

Before he saw the vision of Christ and the later visions of the future, John was instructed, "What thou seest, write in a book and send it to the seven churches" (v. 11). This explains the origin of the Book of Revelation. It was written in obedience to a divine command.

2. THE VISION OF JESUS CHRIST (1:12-20)

The first thing that John saw was seven golden candlesticks. These are interpreted (v. 20) as symbolizing the seven churches. Then he saw "in the midst of the candlesticks one like unto a son of man" (v. 13). The vision was of Jesus in the midst of His Church. At a time when the Christian Church was being subjected to the fires of persecution, John saw Jesus, the all-powerful Christ, standing in the midst of the church. What comfort it must have brought to the heart of the aged apostle! The persecutions were only temporary; the presence of Christ was eternal.

We cannot here enlarge on the description of the appearance of "the Living one" (v. 18). But we would call attention to one statement, "He had in his right hand seven stars"

(v. 16). These stars are interpreted (v. 20) as symbolizing "the angels of the seven churches." We have already noted that the word "angel" means "messenger." So the reference is obviously to the pastors of the seven churches. To know that he is held in the strong right hand of the Son of God should be a great consolation to every pastor.

The Present

The second and third chapters of Revelation contain the seven letters written to the seven churches of Asia. These describe the conditions existing in those churches at that time. They seem to give us an outline view of the various periods of church history. But it should also be kept in mind that all the conditions described here can be found in every period of the history of the Christian Church.

1. EPHESUS (2:1-7)

The church at Ephesus had been founded by the Apostle Paul and pastored by him for its first three years. Later Timothy had been its pastor. During the last quarter of the first century it appears that the Apostle John resided there, probably as a sort of superintendent of the churches in Asia. The fact that he writes to the seven churches there would seem to indicate that they were his special care.

Since it had been blessed with such splendid pastoral oversight, we are not surprised to learn that the church at Ephesus was a model of zeal, steadfastness and orthodoxy. But it had one thing wrong with it: It had left its first love (v. 4). It was sound and strong in head and hands; but it was beginning to suffer with heart trouble. The Great Physician prescribed the cure, "Repent and do the first works" (v. 5).

2. SMYRNA (2:8-11)

The description of the church at Smyrna suggests the period of persecution (second and third centuries), as that of the church at Ephesus suggested the apostolic age (first century). Christ introduces Himself as the One "who was dead, and lived again." He had been put to death, and so could sympathize (literally, *suffer with*) the early Christian martyrs.

The persecution came first from the Jews (v. 9) and later from the Romans. But Jesus said, "Fear not the things which thou art about to suffer" (v. 10). They might receive the martyr's crown down here, but the One who wore the crown of thorns said, "Be thou faithful unto death, and I will give thee the crown of life" (v. 10). They might be put to death by their persecutors; but, "He that overcometh shall not be hurt of the second death" (v. 11).

It might be noted in passing that the introductions and conclusions of these letters have a significant relationship to the descriptions found in the main body of the letters. A study of this feature will prove interesting to the reader.

3. PERGAMUM (2:12-17)

The church at Pergamum was afflicted with false teachers. There were some who held the doctrine of Balaam, or professionalism in the ministry. Others held the doctrine of the Nicolaitans. This is interpreted by some as referring to the elevation of the clergy above the laity. Historically it appears that the Nicolaitans were a sect marked especially by immoral, licentious living. They are so described by the fathers of the second century.

These errors, and many other, appeared in the church when persecution ceased by the order of the emperor Constantine, at about A.D. 313. Political favor proved to be more of a curse than a blessing, as worldliness invaded the church.

4. THYATIRA (2:18-29)

The main trouble with the church at Thyatira was the presence of the wicked prophetess Jezebel. Some of the Greek manuscripts read, "thy wife Jezebel," which probably reflects an early tradition that Jezebel was the pastor's wife at Thyatira.

This condition of affairs is generally referred to the period of the growth of the papacy, or about A.D. 600 to 1100. It was a time when the leadership of the church sank to the lowest moral depths and the "Holy City" of Rome became a center of abominable iniquity.

But then, as always, there was a true remnant of the godly. These were urged to hold fast to what they had (v. 25).

5. SARDIS (3:1-6)

Sardis is sometimes referred to the period before the Reformation, when only a few were true to God (v. 4). Christ said of this church that it was "dead" (v. 1). It seemed alive outwardly, with its elaborate organization. But there was no living organism within.

6. PHILADELPHIA (3:7-13)

Some hold that the description here refers to the Reformation period, which began in 1517. Others apply it to the great modern missionary movement, which began in 1792. This is on the basis of the "open door" of verse 8. The description of this church could well fit the whole modern period since the Reformation.

7. LAODICEA (7:14-22)

The Laodicean church boasted of its riches. But Jesus said it was poor and wretched and blind. The description is that of a church marked by worldly prosperity and spiritual poverty. Certainly there is much of that condition today. The beautiful stone buildings with their tall spires are in striking contrast to the "church in thy house" (Philemon 2) of the first century. But there is almost as great a contrast between the power of the apostolic church and the weakness of much of modern Christendom.

The Future

1. THE VISION OF HEAVEN (chapters 4, 5)

After John had received the messages for the seven churches, he saw "a door opened in heaven (4:1). The scene now shifts from earth to heaven. That this section of revelation fits in with the third division of 1:19 is settled definitely by the words of the verse here, "Come up hither, and I will show thee the things which must come to pass hereafter."

The futuristic school of interpretation holds that with the beginning of the fourth chapter the rest of the Book of Revelation refers to events that will take place in connection with and following the second coming of Christ.

The fourth and fifth chapters describe the vision of heaven which John saw. The first sight that greeted his eyes was that of a throne, with God seated upon it and the rainbow of promise around it. Four and twenty elders were seated upon thrones, with white garments and gold crowns. There were also four living creatures who cried, "Holy, holy, holy" (v. 8).

John next saw a book in the hands of the one sitting on the throne. It was sealed tightly with seven seals. For some time it appeared that no one would be found who was worthy to break the seals and open the book. But at last the One who was both Lion and Lamb (vs. 5, 6), our Lord Jesus Christ, appeared on the scene and was acclaimed worthy. Heaven was thereupon filled with praise and adoration to the Son of God (vs. 9:14).

The sealed book seems to refer to the redemption of humanity. Only Christ could solve the problem of human salvation, by His death on the cross.

2. THE SEVEN SEALS (chapters 6, 7)

The sixth chapter describes the first six seals. The first seal (vs. 1, 2) disclosed a white horse, whose rider went forth "conquering and to conquer." This rider appears to be Jesus Christ.

The second seal (vs. 3, 4) revealed a red horse. The description indicates clearly that this symbolized the wars of the tribulation period at the close of this age. It would seem now in 1942 that the god of war is riding his red horse furiously all over the earth. His "great sword" of modern war machinery is causing the most devastating destruction of life and property in the whole history of human warfare.

The third seal (vs. 5, 6) revealed a black horse, which symbolized the famine conditions that will prevail at the close of this age. As we noted in our study of the Olivet discourse, all these situations have existed throughout this gospel age, but they will increase in intensity at the close.

The fourth seal (vs. 7, 8) disclosed a pale horse. We are told definitely that the rider was named Death. It is indicated that one-fourth of the population of the earth will be killed by various means.

The fifth seal (vs. 9-11) revealed the souls of those who had been martyred for their loyalty to Christ.

The sixth seal (vs. 12-17) was marked by great disturbances in nature—earthquakes, sun and moon blackened, falling stars and other phenomena. So terrible will this manifestation of God's wrath be that sinners will cry to the rocks and mountains, "Fall on us, and hide us from the face of him that sitteth on the throne, and from the wrath of the Lamb" (v. 16).

The seventh chapter records the sealing of the 144,000. This was done before the terrors of the seventh seal were poured out on the earth.

The identity of these 144,000 is one of the disputed points of interpretation in the Book of Revelation. It is not our purpose to enter into controversial discussion in our present study. We shall content ourselves with presenting the facts here given.

It is stated that 12,000 were sealed out of each tribe. Joseph and Joseph's son, Manasseh are listed, while Dan is left out. Evidently these sealed ones were to be protected from the judgments that were to befall mankind.

After these things John saw a great multitude clothed in white robes, with palms of victory in their hands. He was told, "These are they that come out of the great tribulation, and they washed their robes, and make them white in the blood of the Lamb" (v. 14). It would appear that many people will be saved during the period designated as "the great tribulation."

3. THE SEVEN TRUMPETS (chapters 8-11)

The opening of the seventh seal (8:1) was followed by a period of silence in heaven. It was the sudden calm before the storm. The breaking of the furies of judgment upon the earth was announced by seven angels with seven trumpets.

The first angel sounded his trumpet (v. 7), and a third part of the green vegetation of the earth was destroyed by fire and hail. The second angel sounded (vs. 8, 9) and a third part of the sea became blood, so that a third part of marine life was destroyed, together with a third of the ships on the water. The third angel sounded (vs. 10, 11), and a third part of the rivers and fountains became wormwood. The fourth angel sounded (v. 12), and a third part of the sun, moon and stars was darkened. Then an angel cried, "Woe, woe, woe," for those who must suffer the three remaining judgments.

The ninth chapter records at more length the effect of the sounding of the fifth and sixth trumpets. The fifth trumpet (vs. 1-11) called forth from the abyss a host of locustlike creatures, with the sting of scorpions in their tails. Tormented by these locusts, men would seek vainly for death (v. 6). The king of these locusts was Apollyon, which means "Destroyer."

The sounding of the sixth trumpet (vs. 13-21) was the signal for the loosing of four angels, who were commissioned to kill the third part of humanity. This was accomplished by the plagues of fire, smoke and brimstone.

The saddest part of this description is that which records the effect of these judgments on those who remained alive, "And the rest of mankind, who were not killed with these plagues, repented not of the works of their hands" (v. 20). Neither the love nor the judgment of God induced repentance in them.

The tenth chapter tells of the angel with the little book. When he cried with a great voice, seven thunders uttered their messages. But John was forbidden to write what they said (v. 4).

The angel with the book declared that there would be no further delay in the execution of God's judgments (v. 6). John was then commanded to take the book from the angel and eat it. The Prophet Ezekiel had the same experience (Ezekiel 3:1-3). The book is there described as filled with woes and lamentations. Doubtless this book was of the same nature. In both cases it was the message of judgment which was to be proclaimed.

Chapter eleven records first the measuring of the temple of God. It is then stated (v. 2) that the Gentiles will oppress "the holy city," Jerusalem, for forty-two months, or three and one-half years. This is generally taken as referring to the Great Tribulation, or the second half of the seventieth week of Daniel's vision (Daniel 9:27).

The same period is spoken of as lasting 1,260 days, or forty-two months of thirty days each (v. 3). During this time "my two witnesses" will prophesy. These are sometimes interpreted as being Moses and Elijah, because of the nature of the plagues (v. 6). Others think that Enoch and Elijah are intended, because they are the only two men recorded in the Bible who have not died, and these witnesses are put to death (v. 7). As in the case of most of the problems of interpretation in Revelation, it is certainly the part of both wisdom and humility to refuse to dogmatize in such matters. Frankly, we cannot understand the attitude and spirit of those who are positive that they are right in their particular interpretation of a given passage, when other students equally devout and learned hold an entirely different view. It is the author's feeling that a man's wisdom in this exceedingly controversial field is in inverse proportion to his dogmatism. No other book of the Bible has called forth so much sheer speculation, of the type which the Scriptures themselves condemn as "private interpretations" (2 Peter 1:20).

The latter part of chapter eleven (vs. 15-19) describes the seventh trumpet. The angel announced, "The kingdom of the world is become the kingdom of our Lord, and of his Christ: and he shall reign for ever and ever" (v. 15).

The last phrase is literally "unto the ages of the ages," which might be taken as one of the key phrases in the Book of Revelation. It occurs eleven times in all (1:6, 18; 4:9; 5:13; 7:12; 10:6; 11:15; 15:7; 19:3; 20:10; 22:5). These passages would make a profitable study.

4. THE WOMAN AND THE DRAGON (chapter 12)

"And a great sign was seen in heaven." With these words we are introduced to the vision of the woman and her male child. "And there was seen another sign in heaven" (v. 3), that of the dragon who waited to devour the child. The use of the term "sign" is one of the common features of John's Gospel and Revelation.

The interpretation of this vision is very difficult. The child is Christ. That much is clear. It is commonly held that the woman is Israel, the nation that gave birth to the Messiah. The 1,260 days would naturally be taken here as referring to the Great Tribulation, in accordance with the rest of revelation. That would seem to necessitate a gap between the fifth and sixth verses, to allow for this gospel age.

Seiss interprets the woman as referring to the Church of both the Old and New Testament periods. The visible church, symbolized by the woman, brings forth the invisible, or true church, typified by the man-child. This interpretation resolves the historical problem here.

There is no question as to the identity of the dragon. He is called "the Devil and Satan, the deceiver of the whole world" (v. 9). With his angels he is cast down to the earth.

5. THE TWO BEASTS (chapter 13)

This chapter records the visions of two beasts, one that came up out of the sea (vs. 1-10), and the other that came up out of the earth (vs. 11-18). The first beast was given authority by Satan (v. 2) to rule for "forty and two months" (v. 5). The many references to this period of three and one-half years cannot be without significance. A large section of Revelation (chapters 4-19) appears to refer to the Great Tribulation, as it is called.

We are told that this beast will blaspheme God (v. 6) and make war on the saints (v. 7). All those whose names are not written in the book of life will worship him (v. 8).

The second beast is evidently the one who is called "the false prophet" (20:10). He will cause people to worship the beast (v. 12) and will support his authority with miracles (v. 13), here called "signs" as in John's Gospel. Everyone will be compelled to receive the mark of the beast (v. 16).

6. THE HOUR OF JUDGMENT (chapter 14)

The fourteenth chapter records a series of visions seen by John. The first was that of "the Lamb standing on the Mount Zion, and with him a hundred and forty and four thousand" (vs. 1-5). The description given here of the 144,000 might well fit the saints of this age.

Next, John saw an angel "flying in mid heaven" and proclaiming that the hour of God's judgment had come (vs. 6, 7). A second angel followed, announcing the fall of Babylon (v. 8). A third angel gave solemn warning against receiving the mark of the beast (vs. 9-13).

The chapter closes with the vision of Christ, who appeared with the sickle of judgment (vs. 14-20). The clusters of humanity were fully ripened in wickedness (v. 18). Christ was commanded to reap the harvest of earth for punishment (v. 15).

7. THE SEVEN PLAGUES (chapters 15, 16)

The judgments of God are increasing in their intensity. John writes, "I saw another sign in heaven, great and marvelous, seven angels having seven plagues, which are the last, for in them is finished the wrath of God" (15:1).

This expression, "the wrath of God," occurs frequently in the description of the terrors of the Great Tribulation. It will be found again in this chapter (v. 7). It appears twice in the previous chapter (14:10, 19). How sad that men will insist on rejecting the love of God until that love, dammed up, becomes the wrath of God.

The seven angels were given "seven golden bowls full of the wrath of God" (v. 7). "And the temple was filled with smoke from the glory of God and from his power; and none was able to enter into the temple, till the seven plagues of the seven angels should be finished" (v. 8). When men, through their unbelief and disobedience, shut off the manifestations of God's power and glory in salvation, then they will see His power and glory manifested in judgment. That is one of the great lessons of the Bible and of history.

Chapter sixteen describes the actual pouring out of the seven plagues, after the setting for the scene has been given in chapter fifteen. The first plague was that of "a noisome and grievous sore upon the men that had the mark of the beast" (v. 2). The second angel turned the sea into blood (v. 3). The third turned the rivers and fountains into blood (vs. 4-7). The fourth caused the sun to scorch men with fire (vs. 8, 9). The fifth plague struck the throne of the beast, so that his kingdom was darkened (vs. 10, 11). The sixth angel dried up the River Euphrates, to prepare the way for the kings of the east to come to the battle of Armageddon (vs. 12-16). In this connection we have mention of the trinity of evil with which Satan meets the triune God—the dragon, the beast, and the false prophet (v. 13). The dragon, Satan, seeks to displace God. The beast is the Antichrist. The false prophet tries to imitate the work of the Holy Spirit.

8. The Fall of Babylon (chapters 17, 18)

Chapter seventeen describes the vision which John saw of the scarlet woman seated upon a scarlet beast. The woman's name was "Babylon the Great" (v. 5). She was identified by the angel as being "the great city, which reigneth over the kings of the earth" (v. 18).

Doubtless the Christians of John's day took this description as referring to the city of Rome, which they called Babylon. Prophetic students of our day speak of a revived Roman empire. It seems clear that the reference here is to the supreme political power.

Chapter eighteen gives further indication that Babylon means the wicked world-system which will dominate mankind in the time of the end. It appears that it will be a political and economic control of power. It is significant to note that in the list of merchandise given here (vs. 12, 13) the "souls of men" are placed last, as though of least value. The description of conditions at the close of the age reflects the growing domination of materialism in the minds of men.

9. THE TRIUMPH OF CHRIST (chapter 19)

There are two main events recorded in this chapter, "the marriage supper of the Lamb" (v. 9), and "the great supper of God" (v. 17). The first covers verses 1-10, the second, verses 11-21.

The marriage supper of the Lamb takes place after the fall of Babylon. Blessed, or happy, are those who are privileged to attend this greatest festival of all time. The significant statement for us now is, "his wife hath made herself ready" (v. 7).

The second half of the chapter pictures Christ, called "Faithful and True," riding forth on a white horse. The name on His armor is "King of kings, and Lord of lords" (v. 16). The armies of the beast are destroyed and the dead bodies of his soldiers become a prey for the birds of the air. What a tremendous contrast between the two suppers!

This scene is generally referred to as the battle of Armageddon, coming at the close of the Great Tribulation. We are told that the beast and the false prophet are taken and cast into "the lake of fire that burneth with brimstone" (v. 20).

10. THE FINAL JUDGMENT (chapter 20).

The twentieth chapter records first the binding of Satan for a thousand years in the abyss (vs. 1-3). During that time he will have no power to deceive and tempt mankind.

Next comes a reference to the Millennium (vs. 4-6). Those who were true to God "lived, and reigned with Christ a thousand years" (v. 4). The wicked dead were not resurrected until after the thousand year period. "Blessed and holy is he that hath part in the first resurrection" (v. 6), which comes before the Millennium.

Many reject the idea of a Millennium. But that term is simply the Latin for a thousand years. And one must face the fact that the expression "thousand years" occurs no less than six times in the first seven verses of this chapter. We can hardly ignore it.

The third paragraph of the chapter (vs. 7-10) describes the battle of Gog and Magog, which will take place at the close of the Millennium. Satan will be loosed and will gather his hosts against the saints. But his armies will be destroyed, and he will be cast into "the lake of fire and brimstone, where are also the beast and the false prophet" (v. 10). That will put an end to the evil work of Satan and his colleagues.

The last paragraph (vs. 11-15) gives a vivid description of the Judgment of the Great White Throne. It appears that this will be the final judgment. All the dead will be judged "according to their works" (v. 12). Death and Hades will be cast into the lake of fire, which is the second death (v. 14). "And if any was not found written in the book of life, he was cast into the lake of fire" (v. 15).

11. THE NEW HEAVEN AND THE NEW EARTH (chapters 21, 22)

After all the terrible judgments described in this Book of Revelation, ending in the overthrow of Satan and his banishment to the lake of fire together with his followers, there is a complete change of scene. With the banishment of sin from God's universe, the new heaven and new earth can be ushered in.

The most glorious feature of this new regime will be the presence of God. "Behold the tabernacle of God is with men, and he shall dwell with them, and they shall be his peoples, and God himself shall be with them, and be their God" (21:3). There will be no more death, pain, nor sorrow (v. 4). "And he that sitteth on the throne said, Behold, I make all things new" (v. 5). This is the New Order for which we long have waited!

The larger part of these two chapters (21:9—22:5) is taken up with a description of the New Jerusalem, "the bride, the wife of the Lamb." It is a thing of beauty and of transparent purity, lighted by the presence of God himself (v. 23). The city will forever be kept holy, for "there shall in no wise enter into it anything unclean, or he that maketh an abomination and a lie: but only they that are written in the Lamb's book of life" (v. 27).

From the throne there proceeds the "river of water of life," with the "tree of life" growing on both its banks (22:1, 2). There shall be no more curse, but God's people shall reign forever and ever (vs. 3-5).

Again, in the closing part of this book, we are told that these things *"must* shortly come to pass." This ought to cause us to lift up our eyes toward heaven with a fresh hope for the return of our Lord and the consummation of history.

"Behold, I come quickly" (v. 12). That is the last promise of the Bible, repeated with emphasis, "Yea: I come quickly" (v. 20). It is the personal promise of Jesus to us, His followers. Let us all join in the closing petition, "Amen: *come,* Lord Jesus."

K1